EQUALITY
AND
PUBLIC POLICY

Nelson-Hall Series in Political Science

Consulting Editor: Samuel C. Patterson
The Ohio State University

EQUALITY
AND
PUBLIC POLICY

VERNON VAN DYKE
University of Iowa

Nelson-Hall Publishers
Chicago

Acknowledgments
John Brigham of the University of Massachusetts read the manuscript of this book, and Richard Meade served as editor. I wish to thank them both for their numerous helpful suggestions.

Project Editor: Richard Meade
Manufacturer: Edwards Brothers

Library of Congress Cataloging-in-Publication Data

Van Dyke, Vernon, 1912-
  Equality and public policy / VernonVan Dyke.
    p. cm. —(Nelson-Hall series in political science)
  Includes bibliographical references.
  ISBN 0-8304-1208-5
  1. Equality. 2. Equality before the law. I. Title. II. Series.
JC575.V36 1990
323.42—dc20
                                                                909-5674
                                                                CIP

Manufactured in the United States of America

10 9 8 7 6 5 4 3 2 1

 TM The paper used in this book meets the minimum requirements of American National Standard for Information Sciences—Permanence of Paper for Printed Library Materials, ANSI Z39.48-1984.

Contents

1 Introduction

In the constitution of the United States the fourteenth amendment says that no state shall deny to any person of the equal protection of the laws, and according to the courts the federal government is under a like restriction because of the due process clause of the fifth amendment. A number of statutes also prohibit discrimination and call for equal treatment.

The question is what the rule of equal and nondiscriminatory treatment means. To be equal, must treatment be the same? In that case a government that required one person to attend school would have to require everyone else to attend too, which would obviously be absurd. But if equal does not mean the same, what does it mean? And if the requirement of equal and nondiscriminatory treatment is so vague that we have a range of options, then what standards should guide our choices? On the basis of what arguments?

The constitution does not speak of equality of opportunity, but a number of laws endorse it as an official goal, and almost everyone says that he favors it. But the idea of equality of opportunity is as vague as the idea of the equal protection of the laws. Without stretching too many points, we can assume that children in the same family have equality of opportunity, but how about children in different families? How about the prince and the pauper?

This book attacks the above questions, especially the question of equal and nondiscriminatory treatment. It does not take up the question of equality in the broader sense of equality of condition or result. More specifically, it does not ask to what extent public policy is or should be aimed at closing the gap between the rich and the poor.

The chapters are grouped into five Parts.

Those in Part I take up theoretical and conceptual issues. What general meaning is it sensible to give to the idea of equal and nondiscriminatory treatment? Who count as "persons" entitled to such treatment, and why? (A fetus? An anencephalic infant? A brain dead body?) What meaning is it sensible to give to the idea of equality of opportunity?

Parts II, III, and IV all deal with practical problems, and Part V includes one short concluding chapter.

The practical problems of Part II are those that government faces in its own activities and programs. They relate to elections, education, personnel policies, public services, welfare programs, the administration of justice, and taxing and spending.

The principal problem with elections is that the system employed may "dilute" or "debase" the black vote. Whites have been attempting this on a fairly widespread basis. A related problem is whether and in what ways it is legitimate to take race explicitly into account in elections. And problems arise out of the fact that a sizeable proportion of the American people speak a language other than English.

Problems in the field of education are more varied, though again race plays an important role. Battles are still being fought over segregation and integration at the elementary and secondary levels, but perhaps the more interesting problems are those relating to higher education. For example, must a traditionally black state college follow policies designed to bring its identifiability as a black college to an end?

Issues about sex discrimination arise in education too. For example, if an outstanding girl basketball player wants to try out for the boys' team, does the rule of equal treatment require that she be permitted to do so? Why or why not? And problems about financing the schools arise. For example, if one school district spends twice as much per pupil as another, are taxpayers denied equal protection in one district and school children in the other?

Serious and neglected problems exist concerning the personnel policies of government. In addition to the obvious ones about the employment of women in civilian capacities, does the army deny equal protection to either men or women when it sends men, but not women, into combat? Is the army free to refuse to accept homosexual persons into its ranks and to discharge any homosexual person who gets in?

In connection with welfare services, may government pay the medical expenses of an indigent woman who carries her baby to term and refuse to do the same for another indigent woman who has an abortion? May it pay the medical expenses of a person over 65 while refusing to do the same for a person below 15?

In the administration of justice, what happens and what should happen if the lawyer for a defendant uses peremptory challenges so as to exclude blacks from the jury? What happens, and what should happen, if the courts within a state impose the death penalty much more frequently on blacks than on whites who have been convicted of murder? If you know only Spanish and want to sue your employer, what does equal treatment require concerning the language in which the proceedings occur?

The taxing and spending measures of government inevitably affect people differently. Why are the differences so rarely treated as discriminatory? What limits does the rule of equal treatment impose where taxing and spending are concerned?

Part III focuses on governmental regulation of the nongovernmental. That sounds simple, but what are your criteria for deciding what is governmental and what is not? For example, if a city allows an activity to occur in a public park, is its involvement sufficient to make the activity governmental? For example, may it permit the use of a ball diamond in the park by a team that excludes blacks?

And another kind of problem comes up. Even if an activity is purely private, with no governmental involvement, is it nevertheless of sufficient public concern to justify regulation? You don't want to regulate the activities of every bridge or poker club, and you don't want to prosecute a housewife for refusing to invite an other-race person as a dinner guest, but how about restaurants, hotels, stores, and other "places of public accommodation?" Should the owner of a business be free to say that she will serve only white persons? Should a large service club, like Rotary, be free to restrict its membership to men only? Should a landlord be free to refuse to rent an apartment to a homosexual person? In the name of promoting and maintaining racial integration, should a housing project be free to follow a quota system, reserving, say, 65 per cent of the dwelling units for whites and 35 per cent for minority persons?

Comparable sorts of issues arise in connection with employment and pay in private businesses. Suppose that an employer engages in ratio-hiring, choosing by race among qualified applicants so as to make sure that whites and blacks are on his pay role in the same proportion as in the labor pool from which he draws. Can a white who is passed over claim rightfully that he is a victim of reverse discrimination, contrary to law? Since women live longer than men, is it permissible either to require them to pay more into pension funds or to receive less per month once they retire? Should an employer who is willing to hire women be free to refuse to hire women with young children, or is this sex discrimination? Since the law permits a woman to marry a man, may it refuse to permit a man to do the same? Many gays want to marry each other, and so do many lesbians.

Part IV focuses on what I call special problems—problems that don't fit neatly or exclusively into the earlier categories. Questions about affirmative action come up at several points in the book, but are treated most coherently in Part IV. The chapter on equality and inequality relates mainly to the fact that, although we go to great lengths to uphold the principle of one person one vote, we turn around and subvert that principle by allowing money to be used in elections in such a way as to create gross inequalities in influence, raising the question whether the equal protection of the laws is after all denied. And the chapter on equality and collective entities concerns the point that, although the right to equal treatment belongs to individual persons, you sometimes can protect individuals only by protecting the class or community to which they belong.

The concluding chapter gives a summary sketch of the principles that the Supreme Court has developed in interpreting the rule of equal and nondiscriminatory treatment, offers a criticism, and makes a suggestion.

The theme running through the book goes as follows: The commitment to equal and nondiscriminatory treatment implies a presumption that, in the public realm, the treatment of different people should be the same. But the presumption is rebuttable. It runs into the fact that differential treatment is desirable and even unavoidable in many of the activities in which government and private persons engage. So in effect the function of the commitment to equal treatment is to require that differentiation shall occur only for good reasons. It must be justifiable.

The good reasons derive from our concern for rationality, fairness, and various other public values. We want to interpret the requirements of equal treatment so as to avoid the arbitrary and so as to avoid subverting other values that are also precious. The list of other values keeps changing and so does their meaning, but it obviously includes liberty (freedom), the promotion of the general welfare, and national security.

We define the different values so as to make them as compatible as possible with each other, but conflicts arise nevertheless; and when that happens we balance the values off against each other, deciding what relative emphasis to give them in the situation that we confront. The fact that we require ten-year-olds to go to school but impose no similar requirement on thirty-year-olds illustrates the point. Many of the judgments, like this one, seem intuitively reasonable, and are so much a matter of convention or custom that we are scarcely aware of making them. But many others are difficult, leading to disagreement about what is required if treatment is to be nondiscriminatory. One judgment may prevail at one time or with one group of people, and a different judgment may prevail at another time or with a different group of people. As some issues are definitively resolved, or seem to be, others can be expected to appear. And so the process of choosing among values and balancing them off against each other can be expected to go on indefinitely. Equal treatment takes on additional meanings as new problems arise and as people challenge old practices.

EQUALITY: ITS MEANING AND RATIONALE

2 Equal Treatment: Its Meaning

If you say that two plus two equals four, you are saying that two plus two is the same as four. The idea of equality automatically suggests the idea of sameness. But this idea obviously creates problems where the equal treatment of persons is concerned. In requiring attendance at school, must government treat everyone in the same way? In raising armed forces, must it draft either everyone or no one? The answers have to be in the negative, but how do you justify differentiation in the face of the requirement of equal treatment? And what does equal treatment therefore mean?

The object in this chapter is to work the answer out. The focus is on equal treatment as a rule of public policy.

The Customary Answer

The customary answer traces back to Aristotle's statement that "injustice arises when equals are treated unequally, and also when unequals are treated equally" (Ginsberg 1965, 7). Thus Aristotle would treat "equals," but not everyone, in the same way.

The modern rendition of the idea is that you should give the same (or at least "like" or "similar") treatment to those who are similarly situated, although not to everyone. This is not quite as cryptic as Aristotle's statement, but it still leaves you facing a problem. How do you decide who are similarly situated? Are men and women similarly situated with respect to potential service in the armed forces? Are a black and a white applicant for a job similarly situated, when the black belongs to a class of persons who have historically been the victims of discrimination and the white does not?

The point is that in making decisions about who are similarly situated, you must choose the considerations to take into account, and you are likely to be influenced by your conception of the desirable—your values. Moreover, someone else may be influenced by different values, and so you face disagreement about what the rule of equal treatment requires. I hasten to add that every sensible conception of equal treatment requires a consideration of values and so invites disagreement, but the rule about the similarly situated encourages the illusion that an objective decision is being made.

An Alternative Conception

Benn and Peters offer an alternative conception. Their rule is that "all are to be treated alike until relevant grounds are established for treating them differently" (Benn and Peters 1959, 137). In other words, you start with the presumption that people are to be treated in the same way, but the presumption is rebuttable. You rebut the presumption by advancing relevant grounds (good reasons) for differentiating. And if you find differentiation that is unsupported by good reasons, you are justified in condemning it as discrimination.

As Benn and Peters point out, the negative approach—that is, the condemnation of differentiation that is unsupported by good reasons—has played a major role.

> Egalitarians have always been concerned to deny the legitimacy of certain sorts of discrimination resting on given differences, i.e. they have challenged established criteria as unreasonable, and irrelevant to the purposes for which they were employed. Claims to equality are thus, in a sense, always negative, denying the propriety of certain existing inequalities (Benn and Peters 1959, 131).

The Benn and Peters conception of the rule of equal treatment gives a somewhat clearer basis than the others for what is called the "reasonable classification principle," which is basic to political and judicial practice in the United States and which I will outline below.

Differentiation for Good Reasons

It is important to note at the outset that government differentiates in almost everything it does. It differentiates in hiring some but not others as civil servants. It differentiates in the taxes that it imposes. It differentiates through its criminal laws. It differentiates when it builds a road or lets a contract. It differentiates in granting drivers' licenses and in regulating traffic. And so on and on. Government could not function without differentiating, and since this is the case it would be preposterous to suppose that the rule of equal treatment prohibits differentiation. Potentially, at least, the rule permits government to classify people and give different treatment to those in the different classes.

But the classification must be reasonable, and to be judged reasonable it must meet both negative and positive requirements. The negative requirement is that the classification must not differentiate between persons in an arbitrary or capricious way. It must not be based simply on bias or prejudice. And the positive requirement is that it be for the public good.

Tussman and tenBroek express both aspects of the requirement in a statement about the equal protection clause in the American constitution—the clause saying that no state shall deny to any person the equal protection of the laws. This prohibition of discrimination, they say,

> is a demand for purity of motive. It erects a constitutional barrier against legislative motives of hate, prejudice, vengeance, hostility, or, alternatively, of favoritism, and partiality. The imposition of special burdens, the granting of special benefits, must always be justified. They can only be justified as being directed at the elimination of some social evil, the achievement of some public good (1949, 358).

The comparable statement by Sunstein is that "the function of the [Equal Protection] Clause is to prohibit unprincipled distributions of resources and opportunities. Distributions are unprincipled when they are not an effort to serve a public value, but reflect the view that it is intrinsically desirable to treat one person better than another" (1982, 128).

The term *value* refers here to a conception of the desirable, and the term *interest* to a stake in a condition, practice, or event. If you desire something, you value it. If you have a stake in something, you have an interest in it. The two words overlap in meaning. My conception of the desirable may call for the protection or promotion of an interest; and if I protect or promote an interest I am pursuing a value.

No exhaustive, definitive, and binding list of public values and interests exists. You can make up your list, and I can make up mine, and each of us can try to get the support of others for the stand that we take, presumably using legitimate, persuasive means. If you get enough support in the right places, your view prevails; but I can still believe that my view is the right one. And perhaps some time I can turn tables, getting enough support for my view to make it prevail.

Neither of us can prove categorically that we are right.

Nevertheless, a considerable measure of agreement exists on a socially desirable set of values and interests. Various public documents record the agreement. Thus the Declaration of Independence, after proclaiming that all men are created equal, goes on to say that they are endowed with rights to life, liberty, and the pursuit of happiness. The constitution endorses a longer list. Its introduction speaks of establishing justice, insuring domestic tranquillity, providing for the common defense, promoting the general welfare, and securing the blessings of liberty. Various articles of the constitution and amendments to it add to the list. The right to vote (the right of political participation) is a value; so is fairness in the administration of justice; so is free speech and freedom of religion. The rule that no state shall deny the equal protection of the laws is accompanied by another saying that no state shall deprive any person of life, liberty, or property without due process of law. And so on.

You can also find agreed values and interests in the Charter of the United Nations, and you can find even more in the Covenants on human rights adopted by the General Assembly of the United Nations.

Theorists and philosophers name fundamental values and interests too. They cite consideration and respect, speaking perhaps of the principle of, or the right to, equal consideration and respect. They speak of self-actualization or self-fulfillment, the view being that we all do or should have an interest in, and attach value to, the fullest possible development and use of our talents. They speak of autonomy; that is, they attach value to an arrangement of affairs maximizing the probability that each of us can independently and rationally decide what we will do and how we will live. As a rule, too, those who endorse any of these values and interests likewise endorse the idea of equality of opportunity.

Especially on the basis of the paragraph just above, it may seem to you that no significant distinction exists between public values and those that are private or personal, and in a sense that is the case. After all, according to the almost universally accepted view, it is one of the functions of government to promote and uphold the moral and material well-being of the people, so the differentiation in which government engages may serve private interests. The point is, however, that it must serve the public interest too. The private interest is to be served only if it is done on the basis of general principles, impartially applied. The justification of governmental differentiation must be that the purpose or effect is to serve a public or social good.

Judicial Tests of Equal Treatment

The rules given above for deciding whether differentiation is discriminatory come from academic sources. American courts also face the problem, for they hear numerous cases based on a claim that government is denying the equal protection of the laws. In making decisions on this issue, the justices on the Supreme Court differ somewhat in the tests that they apply, but it is not far wrong to say that the principal ones are the "rational relationship" test and the test of "strict scrutiny" (Choper 1987; Schwarz 1987).

The Rational Relationship Test

This test asks whether a rational relationship exists between a differentiating measure and a public value or interest.

Most differentiating measures easily meet the test. To illustrate: a rational relationship surely exists between compulsory education for the young and a desire to promote the general welfare, but the rational relationship disappears if the proposal is to require everyone to go to school all his life. Thus classification and differentiation are justified and do not deny equal treatment. In some circumstances, a rational relationship exists between the conscription of young men and the public interest in national defense, but the relationship disappears if the proposal is to conscript grandmothers too.

Note that the burden or cost imposed on those required to attend school is relatively light; in fact, school attendance is assumed to be to their long run advantage. It is thus easy to justify the curtailment of liberty that is involved. In contrast, the cost imposed on a young man who is conscripted and sent into battle is potentially extreme, making justification more difficult. What the contrast suggests is that the greater the burden on the individual, the more urgent the justifying public interest must be. A sense of proportion is involved, a balancing of values, a cost-gain ratio.

In applying the rational relationship test, the courts start with a presumption that all governmental measures meet it, else they would not have been adopted, and they put the burden of proof on anyone who claims otherwise.

The "Strict Scrutiny" Test

When a differentiating measure is based on a criterion of classification that the courts regard as "suspect" or as affecting a "fundamental interest," they are not satisfied with the "rational relationship" test or with the presumption that the measure is justified. Instead, they proceed to "strict scrutiny," and place the burden of proof—the burden of justification—on the party responsible for the differentiation.

The idea that some measures call for "strict scrutiny" traces back to the musings of one of the justices of the Supreme Court in 1938. He spoke of "statutes directed at particular religious . . . or national . . . or racial minorities," and of "prejudice against discrete and insular minorities"—prejudice that "tends seriously to curtail the operation of those political processes ordinarily to be relied upon to protect them " (*United States v. Carolene Products Co. 1938*). His thought was that cases involving such matters might call for more exacting judicial scrutiny than other kinds of cases.

Then in a subsequent case concerning the relocation of the Japanese-Americans in World War II, another justice took the view that "all legal restrictions which curtail the civil rights of a single racial group are immediately suspect. . . . [C]ourts must subject them to the most rigid scrutiny." Thus the idea of *suspect* criteria of classification was born, coupled with the idea that any use of such criteria should lead to *strict scrutiny*.

The Supreme Court has never explicitly said what the basis is for deciding whether a criterion of classification is "suspect." The idea of extending protection to "discrete and insular minorities" is suggestive, although that expression is vague. A somewhat fuller statement is that a criterion is suspect if it sets apart a class of people who need "extraordinary protection from the majoritarian political process" because they have been saddled with disabilities, or subjected to a history of purposeful unequal treatment, or relegated to a position of political powerlessness (*San Antonio School Dist. v. Rodriguez 1973*).

In line with these considerations, the Court regards as suspect any classification by race, religion, national origin, or (in some connections) alien status. This suggests that a criterion is suspect if it is historically associated with measures that maintain or accentuate the disadvantage of a racial or ethnic group that is already weak and disadvantaged.

Differentiation on the basis of a suspect trait is likely to be *invidious*, and, if so, strict scrutiny is sure to be fatal. *Invidious* differentation is hateful, obnoxious, tending to degrade or demean. It involves the treatment of people not on the basis of their personal characteristics but rather as members of a group to which undesirable traits are ascribed. It imposes a badge of opprobrium on the members of that group, denying them equal respect and perhaps condemning them as inferior. It attaches stigma to them, or reinforces the stigma under which they already live.

Given a suspect criterion and strict scrutiny, the Court, as noted above, rejects any initial presumption that the classification and differentiation are rationally related to the promotion of a public good. In fact it adopts the opposite presumption, and puts the burden of proof on those who wish to argue on behalf of the legislation or the policy in question. Different justices employ somewhat different words in stating the rule. One of the statements is that those arguing for a "suspect" measure must show that a "compelling [or overriding] governmental interest" is at stake and that the measure is "narrowly tailored" and "necessary" to serve that interest (Choper 1987, 260-63).

The interpretation of these requirements calls for judgment, and the guidelines are loose. If an interest is named in the constitution, it is no doubt "compelling," but what the other criteria are for deciding that question remains unclear. Presumably the differentiating measure is "necessary" only if no alternative way of serving the compelling interest is available. Whether a differentiating measure is invidious may be perfectly clear, but the eye of the beholder may play a significant role too.

For example, think of a municipal ordinance aimed at reducing racial friction by requiring residential segregation: blacks in one part of town and whites in another. Since race is the criterion of classification, the ordinance is automatically suspect and must come under strict scrutiny. The municipality involved can easily establish that the interest of the government in reducing or averting racial friction is compelling; and it has a fair chance of establishing a rational relationship between this compelling interest and the method employed. Moreover, it can claim that the measure is even-handed and not invidious, imposing comparable limitations on each racial community.

Nevertheless, at the individual level there is an obvious inequality: a black may reside where a white cannot, and vice versa. The liberties and opportunities of individual persons are thus at stake. And the segregationist measure has an element of the invidious about it in that it stems from a history of white supremacy and was adopted by a municipal government under white control. Thus, applying "strict scrutiny," the Court asks whether the residential segregation is necessary as a means of reducing or averting racial friction. How serious is the prospective friction? Can't a more acceptable way of handling the problem be found? Isn't the segregation invidious? Such considerations have in fact led to the judgment that a municipal ordinance of the sort described denies the equal protection of the laws.

I note above that strict scrutiny is regularly fatal to racial differentiation when judges agree that it is invidious. When the differentiation is benign or remedial, the outcome is not so predictable, as subsequent chapters will show.

In the light of the above, think of the following statement by Justice Powell: "The guarantee of equal protection cannot mean one thing when applied to one individual and something else when applied to a person of another color. If both are not accorded the same protection, then it is not equal" (*University of California Regents v. Bakke* 1978). Do you accept this as an absolute rule, or would you qualify it in some way?

Differentiation by Sex

The main current problem about suspect criteria is that sex is not included on the list. In one case, four of the justices of the Supreme Court took the stand that sex should be added, but five said no.

Nevertheless, the Court is not satisfied with the rational relationship test in judging differentiation by sex. Instead, it has adopted an intermediate standard, holding that differentiation by sex is justifiable only if it is "substantially related" to an "important" governmental interest (*Craig v. Boren* 1976). The strict scrutiny standard, in comparison, would require it to be "necessary" to the promotion of a "compelling" (or "overriding") governmental interest.

The Court has also come to say that differentiation by a few other traits (age and handicap, for example) are quasi-suspect, calling for "heightened scrutiny."

These various terms and categories (suspect, quasi-suspect, not suspect; strict scrutiny, heightened scrutiny, and rational relationship) are obviously useful, but don't be fooled into thinking that they assure judicial objectivity. Issues don't come with labels already attached. A court selects the labels to employ, and inevitably does so on the basis of values considered relevant—on the basis of a sense of the relative importance of the considerations at stake. The judicial process is a balancing process, with subjective judgments playing a significant role.

Fundamental Rights and Interests

As noted earlier, "strict scrutiny" is triggered not only by the use of a "suspect" criterion of classification but also by differentiation that impinges on a fundamental right or interest. But how do you decide which rights or interests are fundamental?

The clear and succinct answer turns out to be incomplete. It is that any right or interest is fundamental if it is named in the constitution. But what if a right or interest that is not named has constitutional importance nevertheless? For example, even though the constitution does not say who has a right to vote, it is clear that voting has constitutional importance. And you can argue that education has constitutional importance too, even though the constitution does not speak of it, because it is essential to free speech and good citizenship.

The examples illustrate the problem of identifying "fundamental" rights and interests. General agreement exists that voting is fundamental, so measures impinging on it get strict scrutiny. But the situation with respect to education is confused. The Supreme Court takes the view that the silence of the constitution about education is fatal to the argument that it is a fundamental right or interest. This might lead you to expect that the naming of education as a right, or as a governmental duty, in state constitutions would lead state courts to make a different judgment. In fact, in some cases it does, but in others it does not. And the situation is further confused by the question whether, regardless of the terms of any constitution, the very social importance of an interest or right should not make it "fundamental."

What this means is that the courts are still groping for clear criteria for selecting the rights or interests to count as fundamental and thus to protect with strict scrutiny.

Underinclusion and Overinclusion

When government classifies as a basis for differentiation, it must act reasonably and not arbitrarily. Classification must be based on criteria that are relevant to the legitimate public purpose that is being pursued. Like cases must get like treatment, which means that everyone should get into the category where she belongs and no one should get into a category where she does not belong. This requirement is ordinarily discussed in terms of overinclusion and underinclusion, which is to be avoided, or at least kept at a minimum.

The relocation of Japanese-Americans during World War II provides an illustration. The public interest officially pursued was to protect the country against sabotage and espionage. If the government had had reliable criteria for identifying potential saboteurs and spies, it would have been reasonable to treat them as similar cases and to differentiate between them and others. But it was not reasonable to suppose that literally all Japanese-Americans were potential traitors.

Nevertheless, the government treated all Japanese-Americans alike, relocating them all. The classification was overinclusive.

From another point of view, the classification was underinclusive, for the same logic that called for the relocation of persons of Japanese ancestry should have called for the relocation of persons of German ancestry.

During the war the Supreme Court refused to find that the Japanese-Americans were denied the equal protection of the laws, but few defend that judgment today. Congress has in effect apologized, offering the Japanese-Americans token reparation.

To anticipate a question concerning possible underinclusion that will be discussed in Chapter 8, I might mention the fact that women have not been required to register for the draft along with men, nor have they been drafted. And when they volunteer they are not given combat assignments. What public value or interest, if any, justifies such classification and differentiation? Should the armed forces regard men and women as similar cases and give them like treatment? What about persons who are heterosexual and persons who are homosexual?

Intent v. Effect

I say above that for differentiation to be acceptable the purpose or effect must be to serve a public value or interest.

For many years the Supreme Court seemed to focus on effects. For example, in 1971 it considered the screening devices of the Duke Power Company in recruiting and promoting employees, which had a disproportionate adverse impact on blacks. Like the lower courts, the Supreme Court cleared the company of discriminatory intent, but that did not lead to a dismissal of the case. Instead, the Court raised the question whether the screening devices employed were related to job performance. "[G]ood intent or absence of discriminatory intent does not redeem employment procedures or testing mechanisms that operate as 'built-in headwinds' for minority groups and are unrelated to measuring job capability" (*Griggs v. Duke Power Co. 1971*). It was effects that counted.

In the following years, however, the Court began emphasizing intent or purpose, and in 1977, in a case in which race was the issue, it asserted that "proof of racially discriminatory intent or purpose is required to show a violation of the Equal Protection Clause" (*Arlington Heights v. Metropolitan Housing Corp. 1977*).

The Court did not explicitly acknowledge or explain the shift. A few years later, when intent v. impact was the issue in another case, it pointed out that large numbers of governmental measures affect great classes of people differently; and it apparently wanted to avoid being swamped with complaints about discrimination. One way to do this was to require that those who seek to prove a denial of equal treatment must be able to trace it to a discriminatory purpose.

In some cases, of course, intent may be crucial to a judgment. An obvious illustration concerns the firing of a black teacher. The fact of what happens does not tell you whether the firing was for good cause. You need to look at the underlying intent or purpose. In many other kinds of cases, too, an inquiry into intent may be helpful in deciding whether the constitution has been violated.

But as the Court itself held in numerous cases, including *Griggs*, a denial of equal treatment may occur in practice regardless of intent. Moreover, intent or purpose is not always easy to determine. When many persons join in an action (and government can scarcely act unless a number are involved), they may have different purposes in mind. The same action may serve two or more purposes, leaving it uncertain which of them to count or what relative weight to give them. Official claims concerning purpose may be hypocritical, the "real" purpose being unavowed or denied. Even though those who originally adopt a given measure may have intentions that are pure, those who fail to change it when times change may have motives that are not, raising in a different way the question whose intentions count. And if a measure denies a constitutional right, paramount importance should surely attach to the effect and not the intent.

The courts accept the view that intent may be inferred from the totality of circumstances surrounding an action, and thus they show a degree of flexibility, but it is odd to insist that a violation of the equal protection clause occurs "only" if discriminatory intent can be proved.

I might recall the references above to overinclusion and underinclusion. This problem concerns effects. Although ulterior private motives no doubt influenced the decision to relocate the Japanese-Americans during World War II, the official intent was to serve an important public good. Nevertheless, the effect was to deprive large numbers of their liberty without good reason. That is the basis for saying that the measure denied the equal protection of the laws. Presumably no such denial would have occurred if those relocated had been selected individually because of special characteristics or behavior.

Another illustration of the problem of intent versus effect may be helpful. It concerns Massachusetts, which grants preferential treatment to veterans. Veterans who apply for civil service positions and who meet the basic qualifications go automatically to the top of the eligibility list, and for many years about 98 per cent of the veterans have been men. Because of the preference for veterans, Helen Feeney failed to get a position for which she applied, and she went to court claiming sex discrimination (*Personnel Administrator v. Feeney 1979*).

No one can be entirely sure about the intentions of those who enacted the veterans preference law. It was plainly open to challenge. It did not even benefit all veterans, but only those who sought civil service positions; and it obviously disadvantaged almost all women who applied. Those adopting the scheme surely knew that this would happen, and those who failed to repeal or modify the law knew just as surely that it was happening.

But Massachusetts claimed innocence so far as sex discrimination is concerned. Its law was neutral as to sex. The disadvantage that women suffered was not intended, but was simply an incidental by-product of an effort to reward and encourage patriotic service.

Helen Feeney's claim, of course, was that, regardless of intent, the effect of the law was to favor men over women. Those who believe that the armed forces should treat men and women alike find the bias all the more galling in that it accentuated the disadvantages (the discrimination?) associated with differentiation by the military.

The Supreme Court sided with Massachusetts. It noted that most laws classify and that many affect different groups unevenly. And it went on to say that "when the basic classification is rationally based, uneven effects upon particular groups . . . are ordinarily of no constitutional concern. . . . [T]he Fourteenth Amendment guarantees equal laws, not equal results."

Subsequently cases have come into the courts involving the question of intent v. effect in connection with statutory rather than constitutional law. The focus has been on the Civil Rights Act of 1964, which bars discrimination in several of its titles. In these cases, the Court has split badly, leaving it uncertain whether discriminatory intent is essential to prove discrimination or whether disparate impact may be enough (*Guardians Assn. v. Civil Service Comm'n, N.Y.C. 1983. Alexander v. Choate 1985*).

Suppose that a public building is so constructed that persons in wheel chairs cannot get in. The architect and builders had no intent to exclude them, but simply did not think of the problem. Should this count as a denial of equal treatment?

Differentiation and Discrimination

I have been speaking of both *differentiation* and *discrimination*. Lest this cause confusion, let me give definitions. I use *differentiation* as a neutral term describing a matter of fact. It indicates that a distinction is made but does not say whether the distinction violates the rule of equal treatment.

The word *discrimination* presents more difficulties, for according to common usage, discrimination may be either good or bad, depending on the reasons for it. On the one hand, for example, we want government to be discriminating when it recruits civil servants, selecting those best qualified. But on the other hand, we do not want government to discriminate in the sense of rejecting an applicant arbitrarily, perhaps because of her color. This means that discrimination may be either compatible or incompatible with the requirement of equal treatment.

Unless I tell you differently, however, I use *discrimination* as a judgmental and pejorative term, meaning that equal treatment is denied. To say that a differentiating measure is discriminatory is to say that it ought to be condemned. Perhaps the classification and differentiation do not serve a public value or interest, or perhaps the social gain is insufficient to justify whatever costs or burdens are involved.

A teacher differentiates when she assigns different grades to different students. The presumption is that the differentiation is compatible with equal treatment, for it occurs in the pursuit of a legitimate purpose and on the basis of grounds that are relevant to that purpose. But we can all think of possible reasons for differentiation that would make it discriminatory.

Active and Passive Discrimination

Up to now, I have been speaking of active discrimination, but I should acknowledge the existence of passive or latent discrimination too. Suppose for example that it is a matter of tradition, or a matter of common knowledge, that certain jobs or careers are for whites and not for blacks, or for men and not for women. Suppose further that people in all these categories guide their behavior accordingly. Blacks do not apply for "white" jobs, and women do not apply for jobs that are supposed to be for men. Does discrimination occur?

If you have only active discrimination in mind, the answer must be no. You cannot point to a specific, concrete denial of equal treatment. You cannot name either a guilty person or a victim. But though this is the truth, it is obviously not the whole truth. Discrimination may occur without being overt. It occurs on a passive or latent basis when arbitrary treatment is so generally expected that no one comes forward and asks for equal treatment. Moreover, its effects may be extensive and enduring, as when blacks or women fail to prepare themselves for careers from which they expect to be barred orin which they expect their prospects to be blighted.

We will run into the problem of passive discrimination later on.

The Equal Enjoyment of Human Rights

The international convention on racial discrimination, sponsored by the United Nations and ratified by more than half the states of the world, contains a definition of equal treatment—or, more strictly, a definition of discrimination—that is relatively simple. It holds that differentiation is to be considered discriminatory only if its purpose or effect is to deny the equal enjoyment of human rights; otherwise, it is compatible with the requirement of equal treatment.

The formula is instructive and potentially useful, though not fundamentally different in its import from the line of thought developed in this chapter. Its principal merit is that it specifies a general goal: the equal enjoyment of human rights. It thus in effect points to a list of the values, interests, or purposes that need to be considered in making judgments. Differentiation that has the purpose or effect of promoting or upholding the equal enjoyment of human rights is compatible with equal treatment, whereas differentiation that has the opposite purpose or effect is not. Human rights cover a high proportion (all?) of the values, interests, or purposes that are significant to questions about discrimination.

In addition to identifying the values to be considered in making judgments about discrimination, the convention is clearer than American law in giving a green light to affirmative action. Differentiation that imposes short-term burdens on some for the benefit of others is permissible so long as the purpose or effect is to promote the equal enjoyment of human rights.

3 Equal Treatment: For Whom? Why?

This chapter takes up two questions: Who is entitled to equal treatment? Why?

Part of the answer to the first question is simple. According to the fourteenth amendment, and also according to the International Covenant on Civil and Political Rights, equal treatment is for *persons*. The Universal Declaration of Human Rights speaks of equal treatment for *human beings*.

Thus equal treatment is for *persons* or for *human beings*. So the question that is left concerns the criteria for deciding who count as persons or human beings. The chapter includes a brief aside too, because of stirring claims that animals also have rights.

Then the question is why. Why should persons or human beings be accorded equal treatment? The question is surprisingly troublesome.

Who Is Entitled to Equality?

For the most part, the question who counts as a person or human being causes little difficulty. Babies are born, and count as persons or human beings from that time until they die. Questions arise not so much about this central fact as about cases at the margins.

Should a zygote, embryo, fetus, or anencephalic infant count as a person or a human being? Does someone who has suffered brain death continue to count as a person as long as his heart beats? Should a claim to equal consideration be conceded to any animals? Should a collective entity, like a nation or a people, be said to have a claim to any kind of equality?

A zygote is a fertilized egg. An anencephalic infant lacks a brain. A person suffers brain death when the brain ceases to produce waves—when all activity of the brain comes to a permanent end.

I will take up the first three questions in this chapter and reserve the fourth for Chapter 17.

Abortion and Brain Death

In *Roe v. Wade* (1973) the Supreme Court took the position that a person or human being comes into existence only when a live birth occurs. The zygote, embryo, or fetus has no claim to the equal protection of the laws.

The Court faced the same question in *Webster v. Reproductive Health Services* (1989), when considering a Missouri law that seems to take a different stand. The preamble of the law specifies that "the life of each human being begins at conception," and "the unborn child at every stage of development [has] all the rights, privileges, and immunities available to other persons. . . ." Qualifications of uncertain import follow.

This time the Court held that it did not need to answer the question in order to rule on the issues before it. However, Justice Stevens in his separate opinion pointed out that "no member of this Court has ever questioned the holding in Roe . . . that a fetus is not a person within the meaning of the Fourteenth Amendment." Stevens went on to say that even the most vigorous anti-abortionists on the Court are willing to let the states decide whether to permit abortion, which implies a denial of the view that the fetus is a person.

The question is difficult, unlikely to be definitively settled in the visible future. Horan and Balch surely misconceive the problem when they speak of "the strictly scientific question of when a human being comes into existence" (Horan, Grant and Cunningham 1987, 75). What we face is not a scientific question but rather a question about the definition of words. To say that the question whether a human being exists is purely scientific is to assume that we already know what the term means—what crucial qualities a system of living cells must have in order to be called a person. But this is the very issue that is unsettled.

Disagreement even exists on the meaning of conception, some saying that it occurs when the egg is fertilized and others when the fertilized egg gets implanted in the uterus about six days later. In any event, from the moment of conception, growth and change go on minute by minute. It is difficult to think of a zygote—a microscopic bit of protoplasm—as a person, but in due course that bit of protoplasm begins to look like a human being. A heart forms and starts to beat, and movement occurs. Immediately prior to birth the fetus looks the same as the baby that is born. The selection of any one moment in this process as the moment when a person comes into existence has an element of the arbitrary about it, but the selection of birth as the crucial moment is at least understandable, not only because the event is so dramatic but also because only then does a visibly separate being exist outside the womb.

At the same time, the position that a person comes into existence only when a live birth occurs is not inevitable. The courts have repeatedly displayed creative imagination in giving meaning to words, holding, for example, that a corporation—a totally inanimate organization—can be considered a person. This suggests that those who wish may claim similar license in determining whether to count a zygote as a person.

Apart from the question when a person comes into existence, the abortion issue is debated in terms that are largely irrelevant here. One of the major issues is whether the pregnant woman has a right to privacy and whether or when the interest of the state in the potentiality of life justifies limitations on that right. Another issue, to be discussed in Chapter 9, is whether a government that offers medical and related services to a woman who carries the fetus to term is free to deny such services to a woman who wants an abortion.

Although I will not pursue the matter here, I should note the question whether even live birth necessarily brings a person into existence. In rare cases, as noted above, an infant is anencephalic. Born literally without a brain. No brain waves. Is that infant a person?

The question needs to be considered in conjunction with the fact that brain death has come to be widely recognized. The heart in the body lying there continues to beat and the lungs continue to breathe, but the brain ceases to function: no sign of any brain waves. In such circumstances, if brain death is recognized, the body is no longer a person, and nothing need be done to keep the heart beating.

Now if a person ceases to exist at the time of brain death, the obvious question is whether a person comes into existence in the absence of brain birth. The heart of an anencephalic infant will stop beating within a week or two in any case, but do moral or legal considerations require that it be kept functioning as long as possible? When can the organs of such an infant be taken in order to be transplanted?

If an anencephalic infant is a person, then it surely counts as handicapped, and laws concerning the equal treatment of the handicapped apply. This question too will come up later—in Chapter 9.

Another question is also unusual. Some take the view that even babies with brains do not become persons until they develop more, and perhaps they go on to argue that, in principle, infanticide may in some circumstances be justifiable.

The prevailing view, of course, rejects infanticide, and the problem of anencephalic infants has not been much debated. On the other questions no consensus is in sight. Religious faith or dogma might theoretically provide answers, but questions of faith and dogma divide people about as much as they unite them. In any event, the constitutional prohibition of the establishment of religion presumably bars the acceptance of a religious doctrine on the question when a person comes into existence.

We are thus left with political struggle as the means of handling the issues. Who can win the most support in the electorate and in legislative bodies, and who can control appointments to the courts, particularly to the Supreme Court? Theoretically, of course, the political struggle can be informed and conditioned by reason and prudence.

If the decision should ever be that a person or a human being comes into existence prior to a live birth, problems will ensue. The unborn person will then be entitled to equal treatment along with the pregnant woman nurturing it. If she has an abortion, terminating the life of the unborn, will she be liable to criminal prosecution? Will any others who assisted her? Should a woman who has a zygote removed from her body go to prison? In what circumstances, if any, would you permit the woman to plead self-defense? If the rule that a zygote is a person leads to the birth of an unwanted child to an indigent mother, should government assume any responsibility for the health and well-being of the child? If a zygote, embryo, or fetus is injured or killed in circumstances having nothing to do with an abortion, what legal rights and obligations come into play? What of a fertilized ovum in a laboratory dish? Is a laboratory assistant who disposes of it guilty of murder? Should the census count the unborn for purposes of representation in Congress? Should the age of a person be counted from the moment of conception rather than from the moment of live birth, and should people thus become eligible to vote and to receive social security benefits nine months earlier than heretofore? Should a zygote provide a basis for a tax deduction just like a child? Should a zygote count as an heir of a deceased father, equal in rights to other heirs?

The abortion issue is often discussed in terms of the question when life begins, but this is a biased question, which could take you back in time indefinitely. After all, the sperm and the egg are both alive prior to conception. The issue is also often discussed in terms of the right to life, but this is a slogan, and like most slogans it is vague. The proper question is whether a zygote, embryo, or fetus should be considered a person or be conceded a right to become a person.

Animal Rights

Peter Singer is prominent among those who argue that equal treatment for persons really means the equal consideration of their interests—that is, a consideration of interests uninfluenced by the identity of the person who has them. And Singer goes on to argue that equal consideration should go to the interests of nonhuman animals.

> If a being suffers, there can be no moral justification for refusing to take that suffering into consideration. No matter what the nature of the being, the principle of equality requires that its suffering be counted equally with the like suffering—in so far as rough comparisons can be made—of any other being. . . . This is why the limit of sentience (using that term as a convenient, if not strictly accurate, shorthand for the capacity to suffer or experience enjoyment or happiness) is the only defensible boundary of concern for the interests of others (Singer 1979, 50).

According to Singer, then, it is not simply human beings but sentient beings that are entitled to have their interests given equal consideration. Singer quotes Jeremy Bentham (d. 1832) to the effect that

> a full grown horse or dog is beyond comparison a more rational, as well as a more conversable animal, than an infant of a day, or a week, or even a month, old. . . . The question is not, Can they reason? nor Can they talk? but, Can they suffer (Singer 1979, 50)?

I am not going to pursue this argument, for I want this to be a short book. If you are intrigued by the question of the rights of animals, you will do well to read Singer's *Practical Ethics* (1979). For the purposes of this book, I am simply going to assume that equality is for human beings, individually or collectively.

In doing this, I follow the example of John Rawls, author of *A Theory of Justice*. His concern is for "moral persons." Such persons, he says, are characterized by two moral powers.

> The first power is the capacity for an effective sense of justice, that is, the capacity to understand, to apply and to act from (and not merely in accordance with) the principles of justice. The second moral power is the capacity to form, to revise, and rationally to pursue a conception of the good (Rawls 1980, 525).

Rawls acknowledges problems with his position. Normal babies and imbeciles are human beings, but do not have a capacity for a sense of justice or a conception of the good. Rawls's choice is to put this problem aside, not on the ground that it is inconsequential but on the ground that other problems are more urgent.

The Universe Within Which Comparisons Occur

The idea of equality or equal treatment necessarily calls for comparisons. But what is the universe within which the comparisons are made?

If we think entirely in terms of the constitution of the United States, the answer looks easy. The fourteenth amendment says that no state is to deny to any person *within its jurisdiction* the equal protection of the laws; and the Court has held that the federal government is under the same obligation by virtue of the due process clause of the fifth amendment (*Weinberger v. Wiesenfeld 1975*). Thus questions about equal treatment are to be decided on the basis of comparisons within each state or within the United States as a whole. The comparisons are between persons, whether or not they are citizens.

The above answer has troubling features, for at both the state and the federal level differential treatment that is questionable is sometimes tolerated. Thus a crime that brings life imprisonment in one state may bring capital punishment in another, with no violation of the constitution. And the educational and other benefits that people receive from government in different states may vary depending on the tax base on which government rests and the choices of those who make the laws.

If we take an international perspective the problem is even more troubling. Human rights, including the right to equal treatment, are for all human beings, and presumably the rights are the same for all. Not that the least developed country is expected forthwith to honor the rights (for example, the right to education) as fully as the most advanced. That would be a manifest impossibility, and people have no right to the impossible.

But the goal of those who believe in human rights is a common standard over the entire world, and they want governments to make progress going in that direction. Governments are in fact doing so, both unilaterally and through international organizations, but progress is slow. Those seeking to promote equal treatment can get little comfort from comparisons between Ecuador, England, and Ethiopia, or Chile, Chad, and China.

Why Persons Should Get Equal Treatment

Why should government be obliged to treat persons (human beings) equally?

Answers are not as incisive as they might be, for the tendency is to talk in terms of equality and to make statements that might refer either to equal treatment or to equality of condition or result. My concern is with equal treatment, and I will try to limit myself to answers that relate to it.

These answers vary. Some authors seem to endorse equal treatment arbitrarily, giving no supporting rationale at all. Some endorse it as a matter of faith or intuition, claiming that it reflects God's will or that a right to equal treatment derives from a state of nature or a mythical social contract. Some seek to give equal treatment an intellectual basis, postulating one or more values and holding that a commitment to these values requires acceptance of the equality principle. And some make it a matter of expediency or convenience. I will take up these answers in turn.

Arbitrary Endorsements of Equal Treatment

The Declaration of Independence declares it "self-evident" that all men are created equal; and the Declaration goes on to say that they are endowed by their Creator with certain rights. For the moment, at least, I am classifying the reference to self-evidence as an arbitrary endorsement of a right to equal treatment, that is, an endorsement that is given without any attempt at justification.

A statement by John Locke also appeals to the idea of self-evidence. There is, he said,

> nothing more evident than that creatures of the same species and rank, promiscuously born to all the same advantages of nature and the use of the same faculties, should also be equal one amongst another without subordination or subjection (Quoted by Gutmann 1980, 28).

On occasion, Isaiah Berlin likewise seems to regard it as self-evident that people should get equal treatment.

> The assumption is that equality needs no reasons, only inequality does so; that uniformity, regularity, similarity, symmetry . . . need not be specially accounted for, whereas differences, unsystematic behaviour, change in conduct, need explanation and, as a rule justification (Berlin 1956, 305).

Berlin also describes equal treatment as an end that "cannot . . . be

defended or justified, for it is itself that which justifies other acts—
means taken towards its realization" (p. 326).

William Frankena is similarly arbitrary in saying that "all men
are to be treated as equals, not because they are equal in any respect
but simply because they are human." He also says that human beings
are to be treated as equals because they are "similarly capable of
enjoying a good life," that is, a happy or satisfactory life (Brandt 1962,
19). I take this to be an arbitrary position. If a capacity to enjoy a good
life is the crucial consideration in awarding equal treatment, many pet
dogs would surely qualify.

Ronald Dworkin also takes a position arbitrarily. His main
emphasis in *Taking Rights Seriously* is on the proposition that all
human beings are entitled to equal concern and respect. But he does
not develop an argument supporting the proposition. Instead, he
describes it as "axiomatic" (p. xv) and as a postulate (p. 273).

After invoking self-evidence, Jefferson (in the Declaration of
Independence) goes on to say that men are *created* equal, endowed by
their Creator with rights. Similarly the Christian tradition stresses the
fatherhood of God and the brotherhood of man, with the implication
that brothers are equal in the eyes of God (Veatch 1986, 21-76). In
practice, of course, seemingly good Christians have found it possible
to deny equal treatment. Moreover, some (for example, some of those
responsible for policies of apartheid in South Africa) have denied it in
principle too, arguing that God intends inequality. The requirements
of Christianity are thus variously interpreted. But the dominant strain
of the tradition, and certainly the dominant Christian view today,
supports the principle of human equality.

An appeal to the idea of a state of nature is similar to an appeal
to God's will in that it is speculative and a matter of faith. But the
same result ordinarily follows. That is, those who appeal to the idea
of a state of nature generally assume that in it men had equal rights
and liberties and that at least some of these natural rights and liberties
could never have been forsworn. Thus they are still possessed. And
those who believe in natural law believe that human equality is "its
first and essential tenet" (Passerin d'Entreves 1951, 22).

Postulated Values and Equal Treatment

Another common practice is to postulate one or more values and then
to explore the relationships between them and equal treatment. This
is what Rawls does. The values that he stresses are self-respect and
reasonableness or rationality. To him, "self-respect and a sure confidence in the sense of one's own worth is perhaps the most important
primary good" (1971, 396).

> We may define self-respect (or self-esteem) as having two aspects. First of all, . . . it includes a person's sense of his own value, his secure conviction that his conception of his good, his plan of life, is worth carrying out. And second, self-respect implies a confidence in one's ability, so far as it is within one's power, to fulfill one's intentions (1971, 440).

Rawls likewise places great stress on reasonableness or rationality. In fact, he describes himself as advancing a theory of rational choice.

Rawls starts with a number of persons in what he calls an original position, charged with working out the principles of justice. He makes crucial assumptions at the outset. One is that the parties in the original position are equal. This assumption, he says, seems reasonable (1971, 19). Another is that the parties "wish to avoid at almost any cost the social conditions that undermine self-respect" (1971, 440). Still another is that the parties are reasonable or rational. And the final assumption is that they are behind a "veil of ignorance," meaning that they have no knowledge that helps them predict their own fate under the rules that they develop. Their reasonableness or rationality can thus be pure—undistorted by any thought of shaping the rules to their own personal advantage.

Given these assumptions, the principles of justice that follow put stress on the ideas of equal treatment and equality. The first principle is that

> each person is to have an equal right to the most extensive total system of equal basic liberties compatible with a similar system of liberty for all.

And the second principle is that

> social and economic inequalities are to be arranged so that they are both (a) to the greatest benefit of the least advantaged . . . and (b) attached to offices and positions open to all under conditions of fair equality of opportunity (1971, 302).

Note that the idea of equal treatment or equality appears here several times. All are to enjoy equal basic liberties. (Any denial of equal liberty, Rawls says, "would . . . be humiliating and destructive of self-esteem" [1971, 545]). It is not equality but inequality that needs to be justified. And when inequalities are accepted, it is because the arrangement is better for the least advantaged than any available alternative.

This does not necessarily mean that the gap between the least and the most advantaged will be reduced, but it does mean that the least advantaged will gain. "Injustice," according to Rawls, "is simply inequalities that are not to the benefit of all" (1971, 62). There is to be "fair equality of opportunity," a requirement that I will discuss in the next chapter.

I should note that, although Rawls stresses the vital importance of equal basic liberties, he does little to assure that they will be of equal worth to different persons (1971, 545). So long as arrangements making for inequality are to the greatest benefit of the least advantaged, they are permissible, even if the least advantaged are left too badly off to make effective use of their liberty.

The main point here is that the rationale for equal treatment or equality that Rawls develops rests on his assumptions concerning the commitment of people to the values of self-respect and reasonableness or rationality.

The fact that some consider it self-evident that persons should have equal rights raises the question what makes it self-evident. One possibility is that they are implicitly assuming what Rawls makes explicit: that self-esteem and reasonableness or rationality are prime values, and that concern for them makes it imperative to endorse the equality principle.

You perhaps noted that in a statement quoted above Rawls calls for "*fair* equality of opportunity." This suggests that *fairness* may serve as a postulated value and lead to an emphasis on equal treatment. It calls for approximately the same kind of behavior as reasonableness. Isaiah Berlin uses an illustration that makes the point. Imagine a situation in which you have a pie that you are to divide among six persons. If you divide the pie into six equal pieces and give one piece to each person, neither you nor anyone else is likely to think that you need to justify what you do. Everyone takes it for granted that it is reasonable or natural or fair to treat people alike in the absence of any reason to treat them differently.

In contrast, if you cut the pie into five unequal pieces and give them to five of the persons, with nothing for the sixth, you yourself will feel that you need to justify what you do and virtually every observer will ask, at least to himself, what the justification is.

Berlin goes on to point to the widespread reliance on rules. We need rules as guides and in order to make behavior predictable and habitual. Without rules, personal relationships would be chaotic and it is doubtful whether we could speak of a social order. To try to proceed in any complex undertaking without rules would be irrational. Rational behavior is governed by rules.

Now of course a rule may itself call for inequality. Nevertheless, "what is meant by saying that a given rule exists is that it should be fully, i.e., equally fully, obeyed by those who fall under it, and that any inequality in obedience would constitute an exception, i.e., an offence against the rules" (Berlin 1956, 306).

A commitment to reasonableness or rationality likewise calls for consistency. Those who are reasonable or rational want to avoid being caught in logical contradictions. A rational government that classifies and differentiates, therefore, wants to do it for good reasons and not arbitrarily. It wants to make it as sure as can be that like cases get like treatment.

The Golden Rule should be mentioned too as a possible postulate. You can scarcely believe in that rule without accepting the rule of equal treatment as a necessary corollary.

Equal Treatment as a Matter of Expediency or Convenience

A purely pragmatic consideration suggests the need to make equal treatment a principle of public policy: the principle is necessary if the public peace is to be preserved and if the loyalty of the people to the political system is to be maintained.

The idea of the importance of self-respect, stressed above, has its counterpart in the resentment commonly aroused if people are made to feel inferior. They do not like to be humiliated. They find it galling to be treated as second class and second rate, to have to defer always to others and to accept subservience to others. Their pride is at stake. Reasonable differentiation is understandable and acceptable, but arbitrary subordination is regarded as an injustice and an insult.

At any one time, the offended may be unable to take effective action, but a political system obviously courts trouble if any substantial portion of the population resents one of its fundamental features. History shows that before the idea of human equality gained wide currency people reconciled themselves to subordination in a hierarchy. But now that equality has come to be endorsed on so nearly a universal basis, it is not to be expected that a political system could long survive if it deliberately and explicitly based itself on inequality. That would be tantamount to an announcement of support for injustice and unfairness. The ruling white party in South Africa is facing the force of these truths.

Carl Cohen offers a different expediential consideration in support of equal treatment. He cites two hypothetical principles that contrast with each other: "(1) In the absence of good grounds for discriminating among men it is reasonable to treat them as equal. (2) In the absence of good grounds for treating men as equal, it is reasonable to treat them as unequal" (1971, 264). He grants that neither proposition can be established conclusively, but he considers the first of them "the more plausible and the more natural." He thinks that in the absence of good ground for discriminating, it follows that the people involved should be regarded as equal, at least in the context at hand. And he points out that the rule of equal treatment provides useful guidance in a multitude of situations, whereas a rule of unequal treatment gives relatively little guidance, saying nothing about the standards that are to be applied.

Equal Treatment as a Residual

It is possible to reach the rule of equal treatment without a supporting theory, that is, on a negative rather than on a positive basis. The possibility is implicit in a statement by Benn and Peters, quoted in the preceding chapter. The statement is to the effect that egalitarians have never really demanded that all persons be treated alike. Instead, they have put the stress on kinds of differentiation they regard as unacceptable, agitating against differentiation based on certain specific grounds, like birth, religion, and race. Equal treatment thus turns out to be what prevails after particular kinds of differentiation are eliminated. The crucial role is played not by a rationale explaining and justifying equality but by a rationale for attacking a particular form of inequality. This suggests the question what kind of differentiation that is now accepted is most likely to be regarded in the future as discriminatory.

You can choose among these theories concerning equal treatment, or perhaps you will wish to develop a theory of your own. My own inclination is toward the view that belief in equal treatment necessarily goes with belief in a whole set of traditional values: liberty for individuals; fraternity among them; reasonableness and rationality; fairness; the fullest opportunity for all to develop their talents; self-respect for all; a stable and orderly society; and so on. It is difficult to see how such values can be upheld unless equal treatment is made the rule.

4 Equality of Opportunity

Almost everyone endorses equality of opportunity. Under one interpretation or another, it fits with virtually every political outlook, from right to left. On the one hand, those who think in terms of a competitive world in which people are rewarded according to merit see equality of opportunity as the ideal. On the other hand, those who think in terms of a fraternal world of cooperation and compassion likewise see it as at least acceptable. More broadly, all those who believe in fairness—and almost everyone says that he does—must endorse equality of opportunity. Those speaking and writing on the subject tend to invoke the idea of a common starting point in a race or the idea of a level field of play; and they assume a common set of rules applied impartially to all competitors.

The obvious explanation of the widespread endorsement of equality of opportunity is that the expression has different meanings, and almost everyone can find a meaning that he accepts. The appearance of agreement is thus deceptive.

My main purpose in this chapter is to identify the various meanings; and in doing that I will also point to some of the related problems and policy implications.

I will deal in turn with three definitions, and with variations on them. The conceptions that they reflect are cumulative; that is, the second incorporates the first and builds on it; and the third incorporates the first two and adds more.

The first is that equality of opportunity is simply what exists for individuals in the absence of discrimination against them. The second is that equality of opportunity is what exists not only in the absence of discrimination but also in the absence of any kind of disadvantage or handicap for which government or society is responsible.

The third goes farther. It recognizes the fact that some individuals suffer disadvantages for which neither they nor anyone else is responsible. They just have not done well in the "natural lottery"—a term that I get from John Rawls. For example, they were born with less talent than others, or born with poorer motor skills, or born into an economically and culturally deprived home. How then can they enjoy equality of opportunity? The third definition answers the question by adding to the requirements of the first two: government (or "society") must do what it can to make up for the disadvantages for which the individual is not responsible. (Cf., Goldman 1979, 170-75; O'Neill in Vetterling-Braggin, Elliston, and English 1977, 177-89). The third definition thus calls for equality of life chances and suggests that equality of condition or result should ideally be made attainable, depending only on how well different persons take advantage of their opportunities.

The Absence of Discrimination

The first definition is the simplest and the least demanding. It is that equality of opportunity is what exists in the absence of discrimination, that is, in the absence of unreasonable (arbitrary) differentiation. Equal treatment alone assures equality of opportunity. Nothing more is required.

This definition responds to major historical problems, in the United States and abroad. To a large extent the struggle for equality has been a struggle to eliminate discrimination, that is, to eliminate differentiation based on traits that are arbitrarily selected, traits that ought to be regarded as irrelevant to the matter at hand, mainly birth, race, sex, language, and religion.

The definition implies a policy recommendation: government itself must refrain from discriminating, and it should act to reduce nongovernmental (societal) discrimination.

This last requirement leads to a problem. It is undesirable and impractical for government to try to eliminate all discrimination in private life. Anyone who wants to differentiate by race, sex, language, or religion in choosing her friends should be free to do so. The woman arranging a dinner party in her home should be free to select her guests on whatever basis she pleases. If you do not want to enter an elevator with a person of another religion, that is your business.

The right to liberty includes the right to make such choices. But how about the hotel keeper or storekeeper or the manager of a restaurant? Should she be free to discriminate in hiring and in deciding whom to serve? How about the manager of a factory or any large business enterprise?

These questions assume that a distinction should be made within the nongovernmental realm between the activities that should be regarded as private and others that should be considered public, that is, "affected by a public interest." The distinction developed in medieval England, and is fuzzy. You do not apply a foreordained standard and discover what is affected by a public interest. Rather, you make a judgment. And your judgment may differ from those that others make. This means that the issue may become political, to be resolved by voting. And it means that different rules may prevail at different times.

The main general rule that has developed is that places of public accommodation—enterprises that offer goods and services to the public—should be regarded as affected by a public interest. So, further, should other enterprises that involve sizeable numbers of people and that operate more or less impersonally. I will explore this distinction more fully in Chapter 12. It leads to difficult problems, illustrated by the distinction between a hotel keeper and Mrs. Murphy, who takes in three boarders. And it is illustrated by the distinction between large, impersonal service clubs, like Rotary, and little intimate bridge clubs.

The consensus among those devoted to the idea of equality of opportunity is that government should act against discrimination in the public realm—that is, in connection with its own activities and in connection with activities affected by a public interest. Otherwise the opportunities open to one or another element of the population will be curtailed.

The view is deceptive in that it makes the problem look relatively simple. I will be pointing to problems throughout the book, but will give you a foretaste here. Suppose that a teenage girl loses in her gamble and becomes pregnant, though she does not want to be. A baby would jeopardize her future. If you think that it should be illegal for her to have an abortion, what implications are you accepting concerning her entitlement to equality of opportunity?

Alternatively, assume that the girl is indigent and that a governmental program exists offering free medical care to her and others like her. You favor that program, but you want an exception made in the case of abortion: the girl may have free medical care if she carries her baby to term, but not if she has an abortion. What are the implications of this stand for her enjoyment of equality of opportunity?

Disadvantages for Which Society Is Responsible

In addition to practical questions attending the first definition, a question of principle arises too. What is the relationship between equality of opportunity, on the one hand, and a historic record of governmental and societal discrimination, on the other?

Think, for example, in terms of the blacks of the United States. They differ among themselves, of course, just as the members of all other large groups do, so no generalization is true of them all. Still, it is to be expected that some of them are scarred and disadvantaged by the long history of slavery and discrimination. In comparison with whites, a smaller proportion have behind them a history of self-respect and family achievement. A higher proportion come from poor homes and have gone to poor schools. The black culture in which they are steeped is no doubt shaped in part by the long record of racial subordination, exploitation, and oppression. And individual living blacks have suffered personal discrimination.

Now turn the page and think of the whites. Differences exist among them too. With respect to racial matters, some are no doubt blameless. Nevertheless, it is whites who have practiced racial discrimination and who have enjoyed the preferential treatment that is its counterpart. Some proportion of them are relatively advantaged by the racial discrimination of the past, and some continue to have racist attitudes.

A metaphorical response to these considerations is common. As noted earlier, it conceives life as a race, and it asks whether the termination of discrimination alone will bring the black to the same starting point as the white and thus give him equality of opportunity. The question invites a negative answer; and it invites the judgment that government should take special action on behalf of the blacks. In the name of promoting equality of opportunity, it should seek, as a minimum, to undo the effects of the discrimination for which it is itself directly responsible; and perhaps it should also do something about the effects for which it is indirectly responsible. The argument is that it has an indirect responsibility for denials of equal treatment in places of public accommodation, for it failed to enforce necessary rules, and that it even has a degree of responsibility for historic discrimination in the private realm because of the influence of its example.

This line of thought has had effects, although it has obviously not triumphed fully. Thus with respect to segregation in the public schools, government requires not simply that it should end but that integration should occur. Government has adopted "head start" programs at the pre-school level, and remedial opportunities at higher levels. It makes affirmative action mandatory for a variety of purposes: to induce more of the disadvantaged to continue their education or to take specialized training, and to help make it possible for them to do so; to induce employers, including government itself, to recruit a higher proportion of their employees from among the disadvantaged groups; and to bring it about somehow that blacks are duly represented not only in jobs at the lower levels but also at managerial levels and in the professions; and so on.

I focus above on American blacks, but could focus approximately as well on governmental or societal responsibility for the historic discrimination against women, Hispanics, Indians, the handicapped, or other groups that have been the victims of discrimination.

Again there are problems, for the second definition of equality of opportunity calls for what you can describe either as affirmative action or as reverse discrimination, depending on whether you are for or against it. I will discuss it more in Chapters 8 and 13.

Disadvantages for Which the Individual Is Not Responsible

The third definition goes farther. In its extreme form, it suggests that equality of opportunity exists only when all the minorities and women are proportionately represented in the different pursuits. Thus if blacks comprise twelve percent of the population, they should also comprise twelve percent of the lawyers, medical doctors, university professors, cabinet makers, and so on (English 1978, 270).

The extreme form of the third definition can scarcely be defended. After all, people with the same opportunities are sure to differ in their tastes, their talents, and their industry, so they can be expected to make different choices and to succeed or fail at different rates. The natural result is that, even in the absence of discrimination, different groups, racial and other, will be differently represented in different pursuits.

Further, the life chances of different persons are bound to differ depending on the home into which they are born. Critics of the third definition point out that the equality of opportunity that is envisaged could be achieved, if at all, only if babies are taken from the home at birth and are then all nurtured in the same environment. Morever, they tend to point out not only that some are born physically handicapped while others are not but also that people are born with different motor skills and mental abilities.

Advocates of the third definition must perforce acknowledge

these considerations, but they nevertheless call for measures that, at the very least, reduce the gaps between the life chances of different persons. The ideal is to free individuals from constraints that limit their opportunities but are beyond their control.

Like the second definition, the third is accepted in part. A number of the progressive measures of American history reflect it. The very existence of a system of public education tends to promote equality of opportunity for those born into families with low incomes. The Homestead Act opened up opportunity to those unable to buy land. The more recent program of governmental aid for families with dependent children contributes, however modestly, to the promotion of equality of opportunity. So do Head Start and training or retraining programs.

John Rawls adopts a variation of the third definition. He cites what he calls the liberal interpretation of "fair equality of opportunity," and wants to go beyond it (1971, 73). The liberal interpretation specifies that "those who are at the same level of talent and ability, and have the same willingness to use them, should have the same prospects of success regardless of their initial place in the social system, that is, irrespective of the income class into which they are born"; that is, they should have the same life chances (1971, 73). This interpretation is inadequate, he thinks, because it does nothing to correct for the inequalities of the natural lottery. It "permits the distribution of wealth and income to be determined by the natural distribution of abilities and talents." This is arbitrary, and thus, he says, reasonable persons should not accept it as definitive.

According to Rawls, the equal and reasonable persons in the original position, who work out the principles of justice, would adopt the principle that "undeserved inequalities call for redress." "Since inequalities of birth and natural endowments are undeserved, these inequalities are to be somehow compensated for." Thus, he holds, "in order to treat all persons equally, to provide genuine equality of opportunity, society must give more attention to those with fewer native assets and to those born into the less favorable social positions" (1971, 100).

Rawls provides for redress in the rule that, to be acceptable, inequalities must be to the advantage of the least fortunate. "Those who have been favored by nature, whoever they are, may gain from their own good fortune only on terms that improve the situation of those who have lost out" (1971, 101). Rawls does not want equality of opportunity to be interpreted simply as an equal opportunity to leave the less fortunate behind (1971, 106).

Norman Daniels, in *Just Health Care* (1985), also advances a variation of the third definition of equality of opportunity. He points out that Rawls's *Theory of Justice* offers no prescription for just health care, for Rawls does not recognize that anyone gets sick. In an effort to meet the need, Daniels develops the idea of a normal range of opportunity that should be open to all, depending on their various skills and talents. He goes much beyond most others in speaking of a social obligation to *guarantee* fair equality of opportunity.

In Daniels's view, disease and disability deny fair equality of opportunity in about the same way as discrimination based on the morally irrelevant traits, such as race, and he proposes that the moral function of the health care system is to prevent this from happening (pp. 38-42). If fair equality of opportunity for any person is threatened by health problems, he argues, government should step in to provide the necessary care.

To a greater degree than the others, the third definition involves a danger. It is that we will forget that equality of opportunity is not the only value that people cherish. The extreme illustration is the hypothetical proposal mentioned above that, if equality of opportunity is to be achieved, babies must be removed from home at birth and must then be nurtured in the same environment (Fishkin 1983, 106-7). Obviously, this would undermine values that, for most of us, are more important than equality of opportunity, so we dismiss the proposal as preposterous. The point is significant, indicating that, at least in practice, concern for a variety of other values influences the interpretation that people are willing to put on equality of opportunity.

PART

2 GOVERN-MENTAL PROGRAMS AND ACTIVITIES

5   **Elections**

Scarcely anyone explicitly challenges the rule that people are entitled to participate in politics as equals, but issues arise nevertheless. In the United States, the issues of the past have mainly concerned the suffrage and the equal population principle (that is, apportionment and malapportionment). Currently the principal issues concern gerrymandering and at-large elections. An interesting question has arisen, too, about deliberate attempts to facilitate or assure the election of candidates according to their race or sex. I will take up these issues in turn, postponing until Chapter 16 the discussion of another issue that may loom larger in the future: political equality v. economic inequality.

The Suffrage

Historically a variety of qualifications for voting kept the suffrage limited, but most of them have been eliminated. Property, income, tax, and sex qualifications are all gone. Age, citizenship, and residence qualifications remain, generating little controversy. Requirements concerning registration generate more, but the major problems in recent times have concerned race and language.

Race

The fifteenth amendment, which went into effect in 1870, forbids the denial of the right to vote on account of race, but in the southern states, where slavery had existed and where the blacks were most numerous, the whites were determined to exclude the blacks anyway.

What they did was to resort to subterfuges, adopting various methods of denying the vote without naming race as the reason. They permitted a person to vote only if his grandfather had been eligible to vote, or only if he paid a poll tax (perhaps including poll taxes unpaid in earlier years), or only if he passed a literacy test that they administered prejudicially, or only if he could prove that he was of good moral character. And they used other devices to keep the blacks away from the polls or to otherwise deny them equal participation in the political process. If one measure was stricken down as unconstitutional, the whites were ingenious in finding a substitute.

Further, in many communities whites topped off the official measures with economic pressures, intimidation, and violence, confident that the white sheriff and the white prosecutor would look the other way when they broke the law. In some jurisdictions a few blacks managed to vote, but for many decades through almost all of the South, government was an instrument in the hands of the whites.

During the decades of the white political monopoly, blacks won skirmishes now and then, mainly in the courts, and the number voting increased; but sweeping change did not occur until the 1960s. Then the civil rights movement developed, initiated and managed mainly by blacks, but with considerable white support. The movement was both an appeal to the public conscience and a warning that change was imperative if an orderly society was to be maintained. It led to the Civil Rights Act of 1964, which made a start toward change in the suffrage, and to the Voting Rights Act of 1965, extended and amended in later years, especially in 1982 (McDonald 1989; Foster 1985).

As amended, the Voting Rights Act prohibits requirements whose purpose or effect is to deny or abridge the right to vote because of race, color, or membership in a minority language group. Political processes associated with nominations and elections are to be equally open to members of racial and linguistic minorities who seek to participate (Hester 1982, 826).

In addition, the Voting Rights Act fixes criteria for identifying jurisdictions with a pronounced record of discrimination and puts them under special controls. If they seek to make any change in their rules or arrangements for elections, they must obtain "preclearance" either from the federal district court of the District of Columbia or from the Attorney General. The court can give a preclearance only if it finds that the proposed change does not have the purpose and will not have the effect of denying or abridging the right to vote on one of the forbidden grounds; and the Attorney General can give preclearance by default, that is, by failing to object within sixty days. A denial of preclearance by the court, or an objection by the Attorney General, is a veto. The consequences of decades of exclusion do not quickly disappear. Blacks are voting and are putting some of their candidates into office, but they are not voting in as high a proportion as the whites nor are they represented in office in proportion to their numbers.

Language

Language has also been an issue in connection with elections, and the influx of people from Puerto Rico and Mexico is making it more important.

In the past a language requirement was linked to a literacy test. As recently as the 1960s, twenty states of the United States had such a test, and in eighteen of them literacy had to be in English.

Attacks on the requirement developed especially in the 1960s in conjunction with the movement against racial discrimination. In many cases the test was administered so as to keep blacks from voting, and in addition it denied the vote to citizens who, although perhaps literate in their native tongue, were illiterate in English (many Puerto Ricans in New York, for example).

Congress acted first on behalf of the Puerto Ricans, specifically for the purpose of enforcing the equal protection clause. It prohibited an English-language requirement in the case of those with six years of education in American-flag schools in which the predominant classroom language was other than English. The Supreme Court upheld the right of Congress to enact such legislation without itself interpreting the equal protection clause (*Katzenbach v. Morgan 1966*).

In a companion case, two of the justices made it a point to declare that the equal protection clause alone, independently of any congresssional action, forbids the distinction that New York was making between Spanish- and English-speaking citizens (*Cardona v. Power 1966*). Similarly, the Supreme Court of California ruled that an English language requirement for voting denies equal protection; it rejected the claim that a knowledge of English could reasonably be required as a means of promoting more intelligent voting (*Castro v. State 1970*).

In renewing the Voting Rights Act in 1975, Congress acted in more sweeping fashion. Finding that "voting discrimination against citizens of language minorities is pervasive and national in scope," it extended to them the same protections that it had adopted for the benefit of blacks ten years earlier, and it required that elections be bilingual in any voting district in which members of a single language minority constitute more than 5 percent of the citizens of voting age; in other words, whenever anything is provided to the voters in English (e.g., notices, instructions, assistance, ballots), it must also be provided in the language of the minority (Guerra 1988; Leibowitz 1982, 6-15).

Political Parties as Private Clubs

As noted in Chapter 2, the ban on discrimination applies only to governmental activities and to those private activities that are "affected by a public interest." Clubs classified as private may discriminate as they please.

Some decades ago in a number of states, whites seized on this principle as an additional basis for a racial monopoly. They claimed that a political party is a private organization, free to exclude blacks from its primaries and its other activities; and they adopted a number of stratagems to bring exclusion about.

Texas illustrates the extremes. First it adopted legislation saying that "in no event shall a Negro be eligible to participate in a Democratic Party primary . . . ." When the courts declared this to be a state action that denied the equal protection of the laws, the government of Texas simply washed its hands of the matter, leaving decisions to the political parties themselves. This led to the so-called Jaybird pre-primary, in which whites agreed among themselves who the candidates should be before holding the official primary.

All such stratagems eventually failed, the courts holding that "political parties have become in effect state institutions" rather than private clubs. Given the principle that state action is involved, equal treatment has to be afforded, to blacks and others (Abernathy 1977, 572-77; Grossman and Wells 1988, 317-30).

More recent stratagems have run up against the preclearance requirement—for example, changes making offices appointive that previously were elective or making it more difficult for those who seek to run as independents (Parker 1987, 681).

The Equal Population Principle

The rule is that all votes count the same; they all count as one. Superficially, that seems adequate to assure equality.

Think, however, of an election to the lower house of a state legislature with one hundred members, elected from one hundred electoral districts. Suppose that one of the districts includes only 50,000 persons whereas another includes 500,000. Every vote counts as one, of course, but if 50,000 persons get as much representation as 500,000, an obvious inequality exists. A vote in the smaller district has something like ten times the weight (or value or efficacy) of a vote in the larger district.

Situations of this sort may develop gradually, as population grows and shifts, or they may be created deliberately. Whatever the explanation, they deny equal treatment, leading the courts to speak of the "dilution" or "debasement" of the votes in the larger districts. And those who emphasize the right of equal treatment speak of malapportionment.

The problem has plagued American politics for many decades. For long the assumption was that the issue was not suitable for judicial settlement and that change could come only through legislatures; but in many of the legislatures those who derived advantage from malapportionment, or who thought they did, had the political power to block change.

Change finally came through the courts. Appeals to them began after World War II and brought decisive action in the early 1960s. Crucial statements of the Supreme Court go as follows:

> The fundamental principle of representative government in this country is one of equal representation for equal numbers of people, without regard to race, sex, economic status, or place of residence within a state. . . . The Equal Protection Clause requires that a state make an honest and good faith effort to construct districts, in both houses of its Legislature, as nearly of equal population as is practicable. [The] overriding objective must be substantial equality of population among the various districts, so that the vote of any citizen is approximately equal in weight to that of any other citizen in the state (*Reynolds v. Sims* 1964).

The decision pertained to a state legislature, but once the principle—the equal population principle—was established in one connection it had to be followed in other connections too. Thus to the rule of one person one vote is added the rule of one vote one value.

The most recent major Supreme Court decision insisting on the equal population principle relates to New York City. It is being obliged to revise its governmental structure in order to bring to an end the debasement of the votes of people in some of its boroughs (*Board of Estimate of City of New York v. Morris* 1989).

The historic bargain giving each state two seats in the Senate violates the equal population principle, but it is enshrined in the constitution and so, as a practical matter, is untouchable. Comparable arrangements in the states have had to be abandoned.

Gerrymandering

The word *gerrymander* comes out of American history. In the early 1800s a political leader named Gerry (later Vice President) had a hand in delimiting electoral districts. He did it so as to enable his party to win in as many districts as possible, which meant that he ended up with oddly shaped districts, one of them looking like a salamander. So "Gerry" and "salamander" were combined to get "gerrymander." The word refers to the drawing of the boundary lines of electoral districts so as to maximize the political strength of one group and minimize the strength of another. The groups in question are ordinarily either political parties or racial communities, so the usual references are to partisan and racial gerrymandering.

I will speak mainly of racial gerrymandering, leaving it to you to apply what is said to partisan gerrymandering. Two main strategies are involved. One is to divide or disperse the blacks so that they have little or no chance of winning anywhere (Parker 1984, 89). Sometimes this is called "fracturing." For example, a black community that is large and compact enough to comprise an electoral district by itself may be split up, the different parts becoming minorities in districts that whites can control.

The second strategy is to concentrate the blacks into as few districts as possible, conceding those districts to black control but making whites dominant everywhere else. Sometimes this is called "packing."

The term *gerrymandering* is also applied to other strategies, all having about the same purpose. Some municipalities have annexed territory in order to add to the number of white voters within the city limits or have disgorged territory in order to reduce the number of black voters. Many jurisdictions have resorted to at-large elections, to be discussed in a moment.

When blacks are submerged in districts controlled by whites, or when they are packed into one or a few districts with many surplus votes, their individual votes still count as one, but their collective, communal political power is minimized. The courts speak of this as an impairment of their access to the political process, and, as in the case of malapportionment, they speak of the "dilution" or "debasement" of the vote (Parker 1987, 684-85).

Note an underlying assumption: that voting is racially polarized. If people voted without regard to race, no reason for racial gerrymandering would exist. But when members of any racial group vote as a bloc, gerrymandering may be the crucial factor in determining who wins.

The question whether a gerrymander has occurred is not always easy to answer. Think, for example, in terms of a city with a sizeable black population, almost all of whom live in one area. Assume that if electoral districts are delimited in a certain way, the blacks will comprise 65 percent of the population in at least two electoral districts. Suppose, however, that boundary lines are drawn so that the blacks comprise, say, 54 percent in three districts. Those drawing the lines say that they have provided for black majorities in the maximum possible number of districts and on this basis plead not guilty to a charge of gerrymandering. Do you concede their innocence?

A negative argument usually prevails. The argument is that age distributions differ in the black and white communities: a higher proportion of blacks are ordinarily below the voting age. Thus when blacks comprise 54 percent of the population of an electoral district they are likely to be less than 50 percent of the voting age population.

Further, blacks tend to register and to go to the polls in smaller proportion than whites, and the argument is that this should be regarded as the result of decades of discrimination: their education has, in general, been poorer; a higher proportion of them have been unemployed or only partially employed or confined to jobs that do not pay well; they have been intimidated; their belief that what they do may make a difference has been undermined; black leaders, on the whole, have had less political experience than their white counterparts and may have less money to spend.

Thus, the argument continues, to draw lines so that blacks comprise only 54 percent of the population of a district is to carry the sins of the past into the present and future, condemning the blacks to defeat and denying them equal access to the political system. The rule has been suggested, and is widely accepted, that blacks must comprise at least 65 percent of the population of a district—or 60 percent of the voting age population—if they are to have effective access to the political process (Parker 1984, 108-11; *Ketchum v. Byrne 1984*). If lines are drawn to give them less than these percentages, the question is whether gerrymandering has not occurred.

In conjunction with the rule against racial gerrymandering, a non-retrogression rule has developed. That is, boundary lines are not to be redrawn in such a way as to reduce the number of districts in which the blacks or Latinos can win.

At-Large Elections

Elections may occur in either single- or multi-member districts. For example, think again of a legislature with one hundred members. To employ the single-member district plan is to divide the state into one hundred districts and to have each district elect one legislator. To employ a multi-member district plan is to divide the state into a smaller number of districts and to have some or all of them elect two or more legislators; the state might be divided, for example, into twenty districts, with each district electing five legislators. In each of the twenty districts, according to the usual arrangement, all the voters would be entitled to vote for five candidates. In that kind of situation, the election is said to be at-large.

The use of at-large elections in multi-member districts can have the same purpose or effect as gerrymandering; in fact it is sometimes listed as one of the methods of gerrymandering. A black community that might elect its own representative if it were in a single-member district may be submerged and rendered politically impotent in a multi-member district with at-large elections.

Given multi-member districts, associated rules can either help or hurt the blacks. If single-shot voting is permitted, it potentially helps them. Single-shot voting occurs when voters who are invited to vote for, say, five candidates for the legislature actually vote for only one. The favored candidate thus gets relatively more votes than the others, and this might make the difference between victory and defeat.

However, if whites are in control, they may prohibit single-shot voting; speaking more strictly, they may specify that a ballot will not be counted unless votes are cast for the prescribed number of candidates. Or the whites can adopt the numbered post system, which means that opposing candidates are paired off on a head-to-head basis, leaving voters with nothing to gain by withholding votes. Or they can adopt a staggered term system so that, at the extreme, only one seat is filled at each election. And the whites can adopt other devices to prevent the blacks from escaping the normal implications of at-large voting.

Conversely, rules associated with at-large elections in multi-member districts may make it easier for minorities to obtain representation. Limited voting and cumulative voting are the most likely possibilities (Karlan 1989, 223-36).

Limited voting occurs when each voter has fewer votes than there are offices to be filled. For example, in a district that is to elect three representatives, suppose that each voter has only one vote. The three candidates who get the most votes are elected even though none of them get a majority. Assume that the whites put up three candidates and divide their votes evenly among them, and assume that the blacks put up one candidate and vote for her as a bloc. It works out that if the blacks cast more than 25 percent of the votes, they will elect their candidate. If each voter has two votes, with three candidates to be elected, it works out that blacks could elect their candidate with slightly more than 40 percent of the votes (Grofman and Lijphart 1986, 157). Theoretically a minority might do much better, depending on how prudent the majority party is in deciding on the number of candidates to support and in allocating votes.

Cumulative voting occurs when each voter has as many votes are there are offices to fill, and when she can allocate them as she pleases, perhaps giving them all to one candidate. Illinois used this system in electing the lower house of its legislature from 1870 to 1980. In 1987 Alamogordo, New Mexico, adopted the system for its municipal elections in a deliberate attempt to give Mexican-American voters a better chance to obtain representation (Engstrom, Taebel, and Cole 1989). The percentages guaranteeing that a minority can elect its candidate are the same as in limited voting.

When single-member districts are used, minorities need to be geographically concentrated in order to achieve success. In contrast, given limited or cumulative voting, a dispersed minority can do as well as one that is concentrated.

Tests of Dilution

As noted in Chapter 2, it has not always been clear whether decisions about the denial of equal protection should turn on the intent or the effect of an action. The issue has come up in connection with various practices, including the use of at-large elections.

Mobile, Alabama, adopted such elections in 1911 along with the commission system of government, and the Supreme Court passed judgment on the resulting issue in 1980. Blacks comprised a sizeable proportion of the population of Mobile (35 percent in 1970), but had never been able to elect a black to the city commission. In contrast, had Mobile been divided into electoral districts, with one commissioner elected from each district, the election of at least one commissioner supported by blacks would have been highly probable. The results of at-large elections were thus eloquent, but the Court held that they were not enough to prove a denial of the equal protection of the laws. In its judgment, "an illicit purpose must be proved before a constitutional violation can be found." Discriminatory intent was the "ultimate question" (*Mobile v. Bolden 1980*).

Congress was unhappy with this judgment, and when it renewed the Voting Rights Act in 1982 it adopted an amendment providing that a claim might be based either on purpose or on results.

Nevertheless, the tendency is for those attacking at-large elections to stress purpose. The reason is fairly clear. How would you go about proving that at-large elections result in a dilution of the black vote? To do this, you must be able to say what would have happened under different electoral arrangements—perhaps in single-member districts. This would be difficult. Even if you are confident that some degree of racial polarization occurred, it probably was not complete; and how can you tell what proportion of the members of each racial community crossed racial lines in voting?

In contrast with the difficulties of using results as a basis for proof, it may in some circumstances be relatively easy to find evidence concerning purpose. Time and again public discussion leading up to the choice of an electoral system has included open appeals to racial considerations. In the Mobile case itself, when it was reconsidered in a lower court after being remanded by the Supreme Court, counsel for the blacks demonstrated that the whites had a racial purpose in mind in 1911 in choosing at-large elections, even though the number of blacks who voted then was extremely small (*Bolden v. City of Mobile 1982*). And the result was a court order that Mobile change its voting system.

When a claim is made that an electoral system is intended to debase votes, it is obviously best if direct and explicit supporting evidence can be produced; but this is not essential. The courts accept inferences that are properly drawn from "the totality of circum-stances" (*Lodge v. Buxton 1981*; Derfner 1984, 157-59; *Thornburg v. Gingles 1986*).

Interestingly enough, whites are appealing against the use of at-large elections in a few communities where they find themselves in a minority.

As I have noted already, gerrymandering and at-large elections may serve a partisan rather than a racial purpose. A political party in control may draw electoral boundary lines or adopt at-large elections so as to maximize its own strength and minimize that of a competing party. As in the case of malapportionment, the assumption for long was that this was a political matter, not suitable for action by the courts. In principle, that assumption is no longer valid. The Voting Rights Act does not touch the issue, being concerned only with discrimination based on race and language, but in 1986 the Supreme Court held that partisan gerrymandering (including the adoption of at-large elections) is properly justifiable under the equal protection clause.

At the same time, the Court fixed difficult requirements if partisan gerrymandering is to be proved. Proof must relate both to intent and effect. Neither will suffice without the other. Further, the effect must relate not simply to one election but to a series of elections, and it must be "sufficiently serious" to call for judicial intervention. In the case before it, the court held that these conditions were not met (*Davis v. Bandemer 1986*). In how many future cases they can be met remains to be seen.

Election by Race or Sex

The most obvious way of assuring representation to blacks and other minorities would be to employ a system of proportional representation (PR). In each of its versions, PR requires that elections occur in multi-member districts (or in one country-wide district), and assumes that each minority or other kind of group will support its own political party; each party then gets offices in proportion to its voting strength.

The problem is that PR is not a part of the American tradition. Moreover, to adopt it as a means of assuring representation to racial groups would be to abandon the theory that the focus should be on individual persons, regardless of race, and it might institutionalize racial struggle. So we are in the paradoxical position of trying to maintain an officially nonracial electoral system while being sensitive to its racial consequences; and a few communities adopt half-measures like limited or cumulative voting. Racial communities are not to be assured of PR, but neither are they to be denied fair access to the political process.

Not only is PR unacceptable but so are other arrangements that would recognize racial communities in a more or less official fashion. Various episodes illustrate the point. Louisiana once raised the question by having the race of candidates indicated on ballots, and the Supreme Court interposed a veto. According to the Court, the designation of the race of candidates on ballots was not "reasonably designed to meet legitimate governmental interests . . . ," for the race of candidates had no bearing on their qualifications for office. The requirement, the Court went on, encouraged voters to discriminate on grounds of race, putting "the power of the State behind a racial classification that induces racial prejudice at the polls." The Court did not explicitly base its judgment on the equal protection clause, but this is the most obvious possibility (*Anderson v. Martin 1964*).

Nor is benign discrimination on the basis of race or sex to occur. This question came into the courts, interestingly enough, from the University of North Carolina, where the constitution for student government assured "protective representation" to blacks and to women. It required that the student Governing Council include at least two blacks, two women, and two men; and it specified that if elections failed to produce such representation, the President of the Student Body should make appointments to bring it about. The constitution further specified that at least four of the seven members of an Honor Court must be of the same race or sex as the student being tried.

Two students went to court about the matter, appealing not only to the equal protection clause but to various statutes, including Title VI of the Civil Rights Act, which bans discrimination on grounds of race, color, or national origin in any program or activity receiving federal financial assistance. (Title IX includes a similar ban on sex discrimination.) Although the ruling pertained only to the university, the principles no doubt apply to public elections and office-holding generally.

The courts used strong language in striking the arrangement down. According to one of them, it "blatantly fouls the letter and spirit of both the Civil Rights Act and the Fourteenth Amendment." According to another, the explicit emphasis on race was "a preposterous defiance" of these measures. To add appointed members to an elected body was to reduce its representative character. To adopt the view that race might influence the judgment of an Honor Court was to diminish confidence in its integrity. If such measures were to be justified, the state would have to show that "its purpose or interest is both constitutionally permissible and substantial, and that its use of the classification is 'necessary . . . to the accomplishment' of its purpose or the safeguarding of its interest." The arrangement failed to meet this test. The proper policy, according to the courts, was to eliminate attention to race, not to accentuate it. The court made no mention of discrimination as to sex (*Uzzell v. Friday 1977; Uzzell v. Friday 1979*).

The judgment is plausible, but it would also have been plausible had it gone the other way. After all, the arrangement was benign, not stigmatizing, and it was obviously designed to combat a racist and sexist tradition. No doubt exists at all that racial considerations have influenced many elections and that they have influenced the actions of criminal courts. To appear to deny this is itself preposterous. It is quite thinkable that the courts might have found the arrangements reasonable, justified by a compelling public interest.

At the same time, the official goal has become the development of a nonracial society (that is, a society in which racial differences are of no consequence), and it is arguable that the arrangements for the student government were not carefully tailored to promote this goal. Further, those arrangements could be interpreted to recognize blacks (and women?) as a distinctive political community, giving them representation as a collective entity; and this would have marked a departure from the principle that it is persons who are entitled to the equal protection of the laws. More on this in Chapter 17.

A comparable issue came into the courts a decade later concerning a requirement fixed by the Democratic Party for its 1984 convention. The requirement was that state delegations to the party's national convention consist 50/50 of men and women. In electing a delegation of eight persons in its primary, Maryland therefore classified candidates by sex on the ballots and instructed voters to vote for no more than four men and four women.

A voter challenged the arrangement, claiming that it unduly limited his choices and that the classification of candidates by sex violates the equal protection clause. The federal district court agreed with him on both counts. The court granted that the representation of women at the convention was an interest, but not compelling enough an interest to override the voter's right to free choice. "Just as a state can no longer encourage voters to cast ballots on the basis of race, . . . so, too, a state cannot explicitly encourage and require voting on the basis of gender" (Bachur v. Democratic Nat. Party 1987).

The court put its position in an odd light by suggesting that the Democratic Party might accomplish its purpose by methods other than elections: it might appoint delegates to the convention, or decree that they be selected in caucuses. Only if the constitutional right to vote was involved would affirmative action based on sex be forbidden. Again, as in the case of the University of North Carolina, the question is whether the court might not have attached greater importance to the public interest in involving women more fully in American political life.

Think of the following contrast. The courts strike down the arrangement at the University of North Carolina to assure representation by race and sex, and at the same time they order the redrawing of boundary lines and the abandonment of at-large elections so as to give a minority community a better chance of obtaining representation. Is there a contradiction?

In seeking an answer you might consider the separate opinion of a district court justice in United States v. Dallas County Comm'n (1988) concerning the at-large election of members of a school board. The justice was caustic. He felt compelled to go along with the judgment of the court ordering a shift to single-member districts, but in his view this amounted to rigging arrangements so as to provide the blacks with safe seats. Moreover, in his view the effect was to reward the blacks for choosing and maintaining residential segregation. He might have added that the court was going in the direction of assuring that the blacks would get something approaching PR.

The objection is challenging. What it neglects is the fact of racial polarization in so many areas and the fact that whites have so commonly sought to manipulate electoral arrangements for their own advantage. The problem is to protect the black community against the designs of the dominant white community without taking race into account—a problem that is beset with obvious difficulties.

Although the courts have in many cases tried to protect black communities against the debasement of their votes, they have never insisted that black communities elect black candidates. Their actions thus contrast with adoption of racial and sexual quotas in connection with student government at the University of North Carolina.

I might note that a UN subcommission on political discrimination once adopted a resolution specifying that special measures taken to assure the "adequate" or "balanced" representation of different elements in the population shall not be considered discriminatory (Van Dyke 1985, 10).

6 Education: Race

Education has been front and center in the United States in the struggle over equal treatment, and race has been the most prominent problem. I take up that problem in this chapter, reserving until the next chapter other problems relating to education—those stemming from differences of economic class, sex, language, and handicap.

Where race is concerned, questions about equal treatment come up with respect to: (1) elementary and secondary education; (2) higher education; (3) and disappointment with integration as the solution.

Racial Differences and Elementary and Secondary Education

Racism lies in the background—and sometimes in the foreground—of the struggle over equal treatment in the field of education. Whites who assume their own superiority have had difficulty adjusting to the requirement of the fourteenth amendment that no person, regardless of race, is to be denied the equal protection of the laws.

That amendment was adopted after the Civil War, more than a century ago. In the following decades, it was clear that whites must permit blacks to ride in trains, but it was not clear that they had to accept blacks as fellow passengers in the same coach. It was clear, too, that if government provided schools for white children it must do the same for blacks, but it was not clear that white and black children must be under the same roof. And, especially in the former slave states, the whites chose segregation.

Inevitably the choice was challenged. It came before the Supreme Court in *Plessy v. Ferguson* (1896), with separate railway coaches as the issue; and the court took the view that separate treatment was permissible so long as it was equal. The principle naturally extended to the public schools: separate but equal.

Whites rarely took the "but equal" part of the principle seriously. Legal battles thus continued, the early cases relating to admission to professional schools. In one of them the ruling of the Court was that a state government denied equal protection when it refused to admit a black to its own law school, though offering to pay his tuition to a law school in another state (*Missouri ex rel. Gaines v. Canada 1938*). In another the ruling was that the creation of a separate law school for blacks denied equal protection, for students at a newly created black school would necessarily lack various advantages that students at the established white law school enjoyed (*Sweatt v. Painter 1950*).

The great breakthrough for the blacks and for the rule of equal protection, however, came in *Brown v. Board of Education of Topeka 1954*. The case involved an attack on the principle of segregation as such, it being conceded that the black schools in Topeka were equal to those for whites.

The attack was successful. The Supreme Court reversed *Plessy*. It endorsed the statement of a lower court that "'segregation with the sanction of law . . . has a tendency to [retard] the educational and mental development of negro [sic] children.'"

> To separate them from others of similar age and qualifications solely because of their race generates a feeling of inferiority as to their status in the community that may affect their hearts and minds in a way unlikely ever to be undone. . . . We conclude that in the field of public education the doctrine of 'separate but equal' has no place. Separate educational facilities are inherently unequal.

A year after *Brown I* the Court decided *Brown II*, on the question what rule should replace "separate but equal." The Court gave a minimal answer, requiring simply that admission to the public schools be put on a racially nondiscriminatory basis "with all deliberate speed." This confirmed that students were not to be segregated by race, but it did little more to specify the meaning of equal protection. And few school boards wanted instruction from the courts anyway, preferring to avoid change. Some white political leaders were openly defiant of the new judicial doctrine. Racist attitudes and policies continued.

Not until 1968 did the Court become more explicit. Then, in

Green v. School Board of New Kent County, it held that school boards had "an affirmative duty to take whatever steps might be necessary to convert to a unitary system in which racial discrimination would be eliminated root and branch," and they were to perform this duty not "with all deliberate speed," but "now." They were to "convert promptly to a system without a 'white' school and a 'Negro' school, but just schools."

Underlying the *Green* decision was the belief that, since government had been denying equal treatment to the blacks and thus accentuating the disadvantage under which they lived, it was obligated in equity not simply to stop doing it but also, in so far as possible, to prevent the wrongs of the past from being carried into the future. Little or nothing could be done to provide redress to the blacks who had suffered poor schooling, but their children and grandchildren could be saved from a similar fate.

Between *Brown* and *Green,* Congress entered the picture in a major way. First, in the Civil Rights Act of 1964, it prohibited discrimination on the basis of race, color, or national origin in any program or activity receiving federal financial assistance. And then, mainly as an aspect of President Johnson's "war on poverty," it adopted the Elementary and Secondary Education Act of 1965, providing for federal financial assistance to schools attended by children of low-income families. This gave the federal government another weapon in its effort to enforce *Brown* and *Green*: it could withhold financial aid from those who dragged their feet about changing "white" schools and "black" schools into "just schools" (Revised Criteria 1978, 6659).

But what test should a school meet in order to be classified as integrated? Was it enough if the school authorities gave students "freedom of choice" about the school to attend? The courts said no, predicting that the racial character of schools would not be much changed. Was it enough if students simply attended the school nearest to their home—the "neighborhood school?" Again the answer was no, though a qualified no, for roughly the same reason. In many cases, public policies had contributed to residential segregation, and school buildings had been located so as to serve one or the other racial community. A neighborhood school policy would thus not ordinarily remove the vestiges of segregation, but would carry the effects of unconstitutional policies into the future.

If racial discrimination was to be eliminated root and branch, a mixing of the races was obviously imperative, but (at the elementary and secondary levels) how many blacks had to attend a previously white school and how many whites had to attend a previously black school? Could the courts require bussing and impose the attendant costs? What should be required concerning the racial composition of the faculty and the administrative staff?

The question concerning students came to be answered with the rule that the ratio of blacks and whites in each school should be the same as the ratio of blacks and whites in the population of the school district, and that if bussing was necessary to achieve this result, so be it. With respect to faculties and staffs, one of the rules prescribed was that the ratio of blacks and whites in each school should be the same as their ratio in the school system as a whole. Another was that the ratio should be the same as in the pool from which recruiting occurs.

Suppose, however, that a city is 90 percent black, with surrounding suburbs that are 90 percent white. And suppose that this division results in part from white flight—the movement of whites out of the city so that white children do not have to go to school with so many blacks. Should shoulders be shrugged about this, or should the courts require that the different school districts merge in order to make meaningful integration possible?

The question arouses controversy. You can argue that a state government should not be permitted to frustrate integration by failing to adjust boundary lines. This argument generally prevails where it is clear that a separate school district was created for a segregative purpose. But if the lines reflect anything other than a segregative purpose, they are likely to be respected. Schools in a city that is overwhelmingly black will thus themselves be overwhelmingly black.

Suppose that after a school district has been integrated, so many people move across district lines that distinctly black and white schools emerge. Must school boards keep compensating for the movement of population to maintain integration? Here the answer of the courts is no. The requirement is simply that government should undo the effects of deliberate, official segregation, but does not have to compensate for private, voluntary choices that lead to a separation of the races.

Obviously, the root and branch elimination of discrimination includes the elimination of any discrimination in the distribution of financial support: the goal is that, regardless of race, the schools should be equal in terms of the quality of the teachers, the administrative staff, the curriculum, and the physical facilities.

The conception of integration reflected above concerns the tangible and the more or less measurable, saying nothing of the spirit prevailing in an integrated system and nothing of the accompanying symbolism. It ignores the question of the relationship between successful integration and the attitudes of those involved. It avoids the question whether integration of a worth while sort is to be expected when, no doubt in varying degrees, those involved are steeped in racism—influenced by assumptions concerning superiority and inferiority. I will take up these questions later.

Higher Education

The states that segregated the races at the elementary and secondary levels did the same at the college and university level, so they faced the requirement of dismantling the segregated system there too. The courts made short shrift of the claim that *Brown* and *Green* applied only to the lower levels.

But the problem is manifestly different in higher education, raising questions about (1) achieving other race participation, (2) the continued existence of identifiably black colleges and universities, and (3) preferential admissions.

Other Race Participation

For some years after *Brown* many of the white state colleges and universities that had barred blacks continued to do so; and when at last they concluded that change was unavoidable, they tended to shift simply to an open admission policy, permitting freedom of choice.

As a rule, the courts have found this insufficient. Thus a federal district court ruled in 1968 that an open admission policy by itself "does not discharge the affirmative duty imposed upon the State by the constitution where, under the policy, there is no genuine progress toward desegregation and no genuine prospect of progress" (*Sanders v. Ellington 1968*). And twenty years later another federal district court held that "when open admissions alone fail to disestablish a segregated school system, be it a primary/secondary school system or a college system, then something more is required" (*United States v. State of La. 1988*).

But what should the "something more" be? And how rapidly must integration be achieved? The answers remain vague. Steps toward the development of answers scarcely began until after 1972, when the advocates of integration got an injunction requiring HEW to enforce Title VI of the Civil Rights Act of 1964 against ten southern states—that is, requiring it to withhold federal funds from the public systems of higher education until, in addition to terminating discrimination, they took affirmative action to remove its vestiges (*Adams v. Richardson 1972*; Prestage 1982).

The result was that HEW required the target states to submit plans for desegregation, and it published a set of criteria for judging the plans (Revised Criteria 1978). Each of the state systems as a whole was to adopt various goals, some pertaining to student enrollment and others pertaining to the composition of faculties, administrative staffs, and governing boards.

With respect to student enrollment, one of the goals was that, among high school graduates, the proportion of blacks going on to college should become at least equal to the proportion of whites. Another was an annual increase in other race attendance (but how much of an increase?) at the traditionally white and black institutions. Still another was to reduce the disparity between the rates at which white and black students graduate. Annual progress toward meeting the goals was to be "substantial," but the Revised Criteria fixed no time limit. With respect to faculties and other academic and non-academic personnel, the Revised Criteria distinguished between traditionally white and traditionally black institutions. I will deal with the provisions concerning black institutions later. Goals for the white institutions are stated in several different ways, the general principle being that the proportion of blacks in the various kinds of positions should at least equal their proportion in the relevant labor market area; and a greater number of blacks should be appointed to governing boards so as to make them "more representative of the racial population of the state or of the area served."

Enforcement of desegregation in higher education remains a problem. Political pressures have been and remain powerful, and sympathies strong. The Court itself weakened enforcement efforts in 1984, when it interpreted the prohibition of discrimination in any "program or activity" receiving federal financial assistance. Until 1984 the assumption was that funds must be withheld from an entire institution if any part of it was guilty of discriminating, but the Court narrowed the application down, saying that funds should be withheld only from the guilty part (*Grove City College v. Bell 1984*). Congress overrode this decision (and Reagan's veto) in 1988, but it is still uncertain how vigorous enforcement efforts will be. In 1988 the Department of Education took the view that four of the southern states had substantially met the goals of desegregation in higher education but that six had not. The six were required to give assurances that they would take additional steps.

Federal district courts take differing stands. Contrary to the rulings cited above, a judgment in 1987 relating to Mississippi was that freedom of choice is an adequate policy. "As long as qualified students, black and white, can attend the type and quality of available institutions they choose, there is no denial of equal protection" (*Ayers v. Allain 1987*). That decision is being appealed.

In 1989 another district court, considering Louisiana's problems, reverted to the earlier principle. It ordered both that the system of higher education be placed under a new, unified governing board and that the new board develop a program to "substantially increase" other race personnel on the various campuses, with the goal of eliminating their racial identifiability (*United States v. State of La. 1989*). Moreover, it specified that if "substantial progress" is not shown within five years a monitoring committee shall recommend solutions. The court rejected the suggestion that a quota of seats on the new governing board be earmarked for blacks, but insisted that their representation be appropriate nevertheless.

A different issue should be noted: whether it is permissible to make changes in one institution that tend to thwart the efforts of another to bring about an increase in other race participation. The clearest illustration of the possibility relates to Nashville, Tennessee, where the state government supported both an extension center of the University of Tennessee (traditionally white) and Tennessee State University (traditionally black). At the very time when each campus was expected to increase other race enrollment, the state took steps to transform the extension center, which had a two-year program, into a four year college. Holding that this would tend to thwart the desegregation of TSU, the federal court ordered that, instead, the extension center should be merged into TSU.

Even more serious difficulties arise with respect to new buildings and new programs, for they are bound to have an effect on the prospects of integration. Those who emphasize quality and economy are likely to favor policies that have a Matthew effect: to him that hath shall be given. New programs are somewhat more likely to flourish in institutions that have a broad base on which to build. But those who emphasize other race participation are likely to want to place new programs in, and even to transfer established programs to, black institutions that have hitherto been neglected. This dilemma has been at the center of numerous controversies.

Should Black Institutions Cease to Be Black?

Whether the goal should be the elimination of the racial identifiability of the black colleges and universities is an important question that has not been much debated.

White institutions do not face the problem, for they can draw their professors, administrators, staff, and students proportionately from the various population groups and still remain predominantly white. But if similar proportional representation is achieved in the historically black institutions, they necessarily lose their racial identity.

Derrick A. Bell, Jr., illustrates the predominant black reaction to the prospect. Bell was a staff lawyer of the Legal Defense Fund from 1960 to 1966, when, he says, he handled or supervised almost 300 school desegregation cases. Later he was Deputy Director of HEW's Office for Civil Rights (Bell 1980, 136). He is the author of *And We Are Not Saved* (1987). His concern for the well-being of blacks is plain.

Bell is troubled by what he calls the "desegregation dilemma"— that once you champion desegregation at the elementary and secondary levels you may have to accept it at the college and university level too. With evident sympathy he quotes the president of one of the distinguished black universities (Morgan State) as saying that those seeking the desegregation of the black institutions have a conception that requires a white majority, with the blacks always a minority.

> They don't quite say this explicitly. But what they say is they want a non-racial system. They want a unitary system. They want to abolish the racial identifiability of institutions (Bell 1979, 951).

In other words, Bell and the president of Morgan State—and others— question the principle that the traditionally black colleges and universities should cease to be "black schools" and become "just schools."

Several considerations relating to equal opportunity support their point of view. Some black high school graduates may be more inclined to go on to college if they can go to one that is identifiably black. They may expect a fuller and more sympathetic understanding of their problems and needs in predominantly black than in predominantly white institutions. And once in college, they may get more encouragement to persist until they graduate.

Moreover, to the extent that a distinctive black culture exists, it is reasonable for those who share the culture to want to maintain and develop it, and institutions of higher education may serve that end. Kenneth S. Tollett of Howard University advances this argument.

> It is desirable for most, if not all, groups to have institutions and mechanisms for discovering, recording, and preserving their heritage and experiences. Predominantly Black colleges and universities are uniquely qualified for and capable of doing this for Blacks. Thus, many of these institutions serve as excellent repositories of the Black cultural heritage. . . . The dismantlement, elimination, or radical transformation

of these institutions (racially) would be a perversion of the spirit and meaning of the equal protection clause (Tollett 1981).

The president of Tuskegee University shows a similar concern.

I believe we need black colleges for the same reason that Roman Catholics need a Fordham or a Notre Dame, Jews need a Brandeis, or the Mormons need a Brigham Young. This is a society which consists not of a sandpile of isolated individuals. We live in communities and require strong community institutions to nurture individual growth and development (U. S. Senate Hearings on Reauthorization of the Higher Education Act, 1985, 173).

Some of the black institutions are sources of black pride. The desirability of fostering black pride is, of course, open to argument. From a strictly nonracial point of view, neither black nor white pride should exist, but only pride in being American or human. But the question is whether this is a realistic point of view and whether the actual alternative to black pride is not low self-esteem and alienation.

Another argument addresses the practical problem that, on the average, black students are not as well prepared for college as their white counterparts, with a higher proportion of them unable to meet admission requirements in white institutions. One possible reaction is that standards are standards, that students who can't meet them should be allowed to suffer their fate, and that institutions that can't meet them should be closed down. A different reaction, and the one that so far prevails, is that black institutions should be regarded as serving a special purpose and that they should thus be supported even while every reasonable effort is made to upgrade both them and the preparatory education that black students receive.

The president of Tuskegee, in claiming that racial identifiability has advantages, found his analogies in institutions identified by religion. In Canada and in some of the countries of Europe, governments maintain schools so identified, perhaps along with schools that are purely secular. Admission is ordinarily open, no child being denied admission to any school because of religion, but parents customarily send their children to schools that reflect their own faith or outlook, government allocating funds to the schools in proportion to their enrollment. The constitutional rule against the establishment of religion is interpreted to prevent this in the United States, but it is a good question whether the equal protection clause should be interpreted to permit something like it in the case of the traditionally black institutions.

The question gains added point in that the differentiation would be for the benefit of a minority. The relevant favorable precedent in the United States concerns the Bureau of Indian Affairs, which

employs Indians preferentially in jobs in or near reservations. Moreover, at least some schools for Indians employ Indians preferentially
for teaching and administrative posts.

Governmental agencies react differently to the question whether
desegregation requires that the traditionally black institutions lose
their identity. The Revised Criteria, mentioned above, deal with the
problem in a gingerly way. On the one hand, they declare that these
institutions are under the same legal obligations as the white institutions to operate without discrimination or segregation. But on the
other hand, they stress the "unique role" of the traditionally black
colleges and declare that "the transition to a unitary system must not
be accomplished by placing a disproportionate burden upon black
students, faculty, or institutions or by reducing the educational
opportunities currently available to blacks."

Further, the Revised Criteria endorse "the objective of strengthening the traditionally black colleges." And, although they say that
white institutions should recruit blacks for the various academic and
non-academic positions according to their proportion in the relevant
labor market area, they are silent about a comparable rule for the
black institutions.

The courts are not of one mind on the subject either. Perhaps
the most extreme stand is the one that a federal district court took in
1970 concerning Alabama's system of junior colleges and trade
schools. In that case, the court ordered a shift in employment policies
so as to "abolish the racial identifiability" of the schools. Among other
things, the court required the assignment of teaching and administrative staff in the various schools so that the black/white ratio would
be substantially the same as in the state as a whole (*Lee v. Macon
County Board of Education 1970*).

The courts have treated Louisiana somewhat differently. A
consent decree of 1981, fixing goals to be pursued for the following six
years, called for increases in other race participation but fell far short
of any suggestion that the traditionally black schools must lose their
racial identity.

Provisions concerning governing boards and faculties are indic-
ative. For white institutions, the goal was that their governing boards
should reflect the racial composition of the population of the state (70
percent white, 30 percent black), whereas for black institutions the
goal was that their governing boards should reflect that racial
composition inversely. And for white institutions the goal was that
blacks should be represented on their administration, faculty, and
staff in the same proportion as blacks with the required credentials
are represented in the relevant labor market area. In contrast, for

black institutions the goal is simply that the proportion of white administrators, faculty, and staff should increase.

To be sure, as indicated earlier, the federal district court in 1989 took a somewhat different position. After noting that none of the then-existing college and university governing boards was an exponent of racial integration, and after naming the Southern board as one that "vigorously seeks to preserve [the] separate identity" of the (black) institution that it served, the court rebuffed such attitudes and declared the elimination of racial identifiability to be the ultimate goal. Moreover, it called for the immediate establishment of a single system of higher education with one governing board for all institutions in the system, hoping that one governing board would be more likely than a series of separate boards to bring integration about. It itself ordered the merger of the law schools associated with Louisiana State and Southern, both located in Baton Rouge. But it declined to order other mergers. And its language in referring to the goal of eliminating racial identifiability seemed perfunctory.

What "merger" will mean in the case of the law schools is not clear. The problems are suggested by the hypothetical possibility that the faculty and staff of one school might simply be dismissed, the students being told to seek admission to the other school.

Other courts, facing the narrower issue of policies relating to hiring, promoting, and firing professors have taken stands consistent with the view that colleges and universities are not free to seek to preserve their racial identity. Thus Tennessee State University, with an imbalance in favor of blacks on its faculty, was ordered to recruit whites preferentially "unless there [is] a superior black applicant" (*Geier v. University of Tennessee 1979*). Two other district courts found that Dillard University and Jackson State University, both predominantly black, had discriminated against white faculty members in firing them or failing to renew their contracts; and both institutions had to pay damages (*Fisher v. Dillard University 1980; Whiting v. Jackson State University 1980*).

Congress puts more stress on strengthening the black institutions than on any effort to eliminate their racial identifiability. In reauthorizing its program of financial aid for black colleges and universities in 1986, it shifted away from its earlier euphemisticreference to "developing" institutions and became race-specific. It found that

> the current state of Black colleges and universities is partly attributable to the discriminatory action of the States and the Federal Government and this discriminatory action requires the remedy of enhancement of Black postsecondary institutions to ensure their continuation and

participation in fulfilling the Federal mission of equality of educational
opportunity (Public Law 99-498, October 17, 1986).

On this basis, Congress appropriates money for the specific purpose
of helping to meet the needs of black institutions as such.

In Chapter 16 I will explore the question of conceding status and
rights to collective entities such as racial minorities. If the black
community were conceded to have rights, rights in the field of
education would surely be among them.

Preferential Admissions

Countrywide, the greatest public controversy relating to higher
education has been over the preferential admission of minority
students to traditionally white schools. The issue came to a head in
Bakke—second only to *Brown* in the amount of attention it has
received (*University of California Regents v. Bakke 1978*). Bakke, a white,
applied for admission to the medical school at the University of
California at Davis, where the policy was to admit one hundred
students each year, with sixteen of the places reserved for minority
applicants. He was rejected, though his composite score on the
various admission tests was higher than the scores of some of the
minority students admitted. He claimed that he was denied equal
treatment, and the case went up through the judicial hierarchy to the
Supreme Court.

The Court split badly on the issue. Four justices took the view
that the preferential policy at Davis violated Title VI of the Civil Rights
Act. On the face of it, the view looks well-founded. Title VI, you will
recall, says that no person on the ground of race shall be excluded
from participation in any program or activity receiving federal financial assistance. Bakke was excluded, contrary to the plain words of the
law.

Nevertheless, the issue is not necessarily that simple. Four other
justices pointed to past racial discrimination and refused to take the
view that either the law or the constitution prevents measures of
redress. As a matter of equity, they voted to uphold the medical
school in its effort to contribute toward redress.

That redress is morally imperative also looks plain, but you
might think that the argument is vulnerable in the Bakke case. It is
vulnerable if you adhere to the theory of "victim specificity"—that is,
the theory that an institution may provide redress only to the specific
victims of its own earlier acts of discrimination. The medical school
was itself not accused of past racial discrimination, so according to the
theory of victim specificity it had no occasion to provide redress. And

even if there had been prior discrimination, Bakke was not responsible for it. You can argue, therefore, that the rule followed by the medical school favored the undeserving at the expense of the innocent.

But you can also mount an argument going in the other direction. You can point out that blacks will get little redress if the only institutions that can provide it are those that are themselves guilty of discriminating and if they can provide it only to their own specific victims. After all, a high proportion of the discrimination of the past has been passive or latent—that is, it has reflected customary practices that blacks did not dare challenge. Much of the discrimination occurred against blacks now dead, but their children and grandchildren still suffer from its effects. And many of the living persons who have in fact suffered overt discrimination would find it difficult or impossible to prove their claims.

In any event, you can argue, judgment of the relative merits of different applicants for admission to a school can only be approximate, and Bakke's score was not so much above the scores of the minority candidates to be decisive, given the other reasonable considerations that can appropriately be taken into account.

You can add another point to the argument if you wish: that whites in the past did not examine the personal histories of the blacks to whom they did harm, but did harm to any and all indiscriminately. They rewarded the undeserving at the expense of the innocent in wholesale fashion. In other words, whites have historically followed communal rather than individualistic principles in race relations, putting the whole black community down.

The record thus suggests the need for special remedial measures to advance the community to the place in American society that it would have gained in the absence of discrimination, and further suggests that the most highly qualified blacks should now be selected for preferential treatment. This should not be shocking in view of the preferential treatment on which whites insisted for themselves during many decades. What is shocking is that so many whites have become champions of ostensibly nonracial individualistic "justice" only after this has come to serve the advantage of the white community.

As to the claim that Bakke's innocence should preclude placing any burden on him, the most telling response is that this kind of practice is common. The most extreme illustration is that, in time of war, we compel some persons but not others to risk their very lives, even though they have no personal responsibility for bringing the war on. A compelling public interest is judged to justify the differentiation.

The four justices who voted to uphold the medical school's policy did not spell out all of the above line of argument, but it fits with their views.

The ninth justice, Powell, agreed in part with each of the groups of four. He was skeptical of the claim that preferential treatment is necessarily benign, fearing that it reinforces the stereotype that blacks cannot achieve success on their merit. And he pointed to the inequity in forcing innocent persons like Bakke to bear the burden of redressing grievances not of their making. In sum, he did not approve an effort by the medical school to remedy "societal [nongovernmental] discrimination," which he described as "an amorphous concept of injury that may be ageless in its reach into the past."

At the same time, Justice Powell took the view that the medical school could legitimately seek diversity in its student body so as to promote an "atmosphere of 'speculation, experiment, and creation.'" This, he held, is an aspect of academic freedom, a special concern of the first amendment. The search for diversity is not to be on a quota basis, but when the personal merits of individual applicants are considered, race can count as a plus, and thus perhaps as the deciding factor.

Cogent arguments about preferential admissions can thus be advanced on each side. In *Bakke*, the consideration that tipped the balance is that institutions can legitimately seek diversity in their student bodies, and may thus take race into account in deciding which applicants to admit.

Subsequently a similar issue came up in Tennessee. As an aspect of an affirmative action program, judicially approved in a consent decree, Tennessee started selecting seventy-five blacks at the sophomore level each year for special grooming, with a view to their eventual admission to graduate programs in law, medicine, veterinary medicine, dentistry, and pharmacy. This led to an official protest from William Bradford Reynolds, who spoke for Reagan's Department of Justice and who will figure in later chapters also in connection with questions of equal treatment.

Reynolds granted the principle of remedial action. Speaking of employment situations rather than of students, he said that affirmative remedies should be available designed to restore the victims of discrimination to their "'rightful place'—that is, to the position they would have attained but for the discrimination."

> Moreover, this 'rightful place' relief is, in our view, available not only to those applicants turned away on account of race but also to those qualified individuals shown to have been discouraged from ever

applying for employment because of their knowledge of the employer's unlawful discrimination (Reynolds 1983, p. 261).

But Reynolds claimed virtue not by championing remedial action but by restricting it narrowly. It should occur only for the benefit of those who could prove that they were victims of discrimination; in other words, he endorsed the theory of "victim specificity" referred to above. Remedial action was to be a rare exception to the rule that "race is an impermissible basis on which to allocate resources or penalties (1983, 259, 261). Reynolds wrote a whole article on "Securing Equal Liberty in an Egalitarian Age" without even mentioning the question of redress (Reynolds 1987). He held that classification by race is not simply "suspect," it is automatically unconstitutional. The purpose of the civil war amendments was "to end forever a system which determined legal rights, measured status, and allocated opportunities on the basis of race . . . ." He praised the statement of a dissenting justice in *Plessy* that the constitution is color blind—a position that the courts have consistently rejected (Reynolds 1984).

In line with these views, Reynolds pointed out that the University of Tennessee did not require the selected black students to prove that the professional school to which they hoped to go had ever discriminated against them, and he held that it was therefore unconstitutional to give them preferential treatment. For a university to favor individuals whom it had not itself wronged was to shift from an individualistic emphasis on persons to a concern for equality of results for groups.

In taking these stands, Reynolds in effect asked the Court to go against a series of earlier decisions, including the *Bakke* decision and others that I will deal with in later chapters. But the Court rebuffed his plea. Citing the various precedents, it reaffirmed the view that a compelling public interest may justify differentiation by race; and it also reaffirmed the view that an institution's program of affirmative action may legitimately benefit persons in a disadvantaged group other than the victims of its own past discriminatory practices (*Geier v. Alexander 1986*).

Disappointment with Integration

Disappointment with integration is widespread. At the elementary and secondary levels, the disappointment is due in part to the fact that not enough whites live in some cities or school districts to make significant integration possible. In 1980—twenty-six years after *Brown*—a third of all blacks were in schools in which minority students comprised more than 90 percent of the student body, and 63 percent were in schools in which they comprised more than half (Hochschild 1984, 30). If the courts were willing to order the consolidation of city and suburban school districts, more integration could be brought about, but, as noted above, the courts have been unwilling to do this except where school districts were created with segregative intent.

Other reasons for disappointment are probably more significant, raising the question whether it was not naive to suppose that equal treatment would follow almost automatically if black and white students were put under the same roof. After all, the attitudes and practices associated with slavery and Jim Crow could scarcely be expected to disappear the moment a black child walked through the door into a hitherto all white school. We can imagine a number of circumstances that would maintain the unequal treatment of blacks even after integration occurred.

Suppose, for example, that white administrators, teachers, and students are infected with racism ranging from the mild to the gross. They also resent integration. Political leaders and school authorities do no more than they are explicitly required to do and delay every move as long as they can. Their attachment is to the white school, and they attempt to maintain its character despite the requirements concerning blacks. They hire black teachers and black administrators reluctantly if at all, and they keep any who are hired in the lowest possible status. They regard black students as unwelcome intruders and make this attitude clear.

Suppose that some or all of the teachers look on black children as inferior. They are confident that white children can learn, but have low expectations in attempting to teach blacks. Administrators and teachers do little or nothing in the school or the community to bring about the discussion of ethnic and racial attitudes and to combat racial prejudice.

Suppose that students differ in their socioeconomic background. A substantial portion of the whites have parents who are middle-class—educated and with above average incomes—while a substantial portion of the blacks have parents who are less well educated and whose incomes are low; perhaps many of the blacks come from single-parent families living in poverty, which implies differences in levels of nutrition and health, and perhaps differences in levels of motivation and hope. At each grade level, the blacks on the average are less advanced than the whites.

Suppose that a substantial portion of the black students speak "black English" rather than standard English. The teachers could, of course, take the view that "black English" is a distinct language that is being spoken correctly, but actually they take the view that the black students are simply making mistakes and deserve to be graded down accordingly.

Suppose that administrators and teachers take the view that tracking is desirable. That is, students are separated on the basis of their apparent ability, the best students being put on one track and the poorest students on another. Perhaps some are rated as mentally retarded and are put on a third track. When this policy is followed, the usual result is that whites are disproportionately represented on the upper track and blacks are disproportionately represented on the lower tracks. Those on the lower tracks may be failed year after year, though required by law to stay in school until they reach a specified age.

Suppose that disciplinary problems arise more frequently with blacks than with whites. And suppose that some degree of racism influences the responses of the school authorities.

Suppose that it is the ambition of every first rate administrator and teacher to become associated with the better schools and to get away from the worse schools. The result is a self-reinforcing tendency for the better schools to become still better and the poorer schools to become still poorer as the sifting and shifting of administrators and teachers goes on. The result is accentuated if parents are free to choose the school to which to send their children.

Suppose, too, as is likely, that blacks have attitudes unfavorable to successful integration. They resent the humiliations that they suffer, whether at the hands of administrators, teachers, or other students. They resent white authority. And some show their resentment in attitudes and acts of defiance. Some do not favor integration, preferring the company of other blacks and perhaps adhering to the ideas of black nationalism.

I do not mean to suggest that all of the above attitudes and circumstances have prevailed in every case where integration has been attempted. It is clear that they have not. Even where they existed, it has been possible in some cases to counteract them effectively. But in many other cases most or all of the problems sketched out above were neither avoided nor solved, with the result that high hopes associated with integration have been disappointed.

A book edited by Derrick Bell (*Shades of Brown*, 1980) evidences the disappointment. Bell is mentioned above in the discussion of the integration of black colleges. He holds that desegregation "has in large part failed" (Bell 1980, 92). Discrimination continues, he says, despite integration. He speaks of "resegregation within desegregated schools, the loss of black faculty and administrators, suspensions and expulsions [of blacks] at much higher rates than white students, and varying forms of racial harassment ranging from exclusion from extracurricular activities to physical violence." And he wants the emphasis shifted to "real educational effectiveness," whether or not in integrated schools (Bell 1980, 100-101).

The fact that integration has been successful in some cases suggests that it theoretically could be in many more. Hochschild has analyzed the conditions of success. She stresses that democratic procedures are not likely to suffice and that authoritarian measures are likely to be necessary, that action must be relatively speedy and drastic rather than slow and incremental, that desegregation plans should include entire metropolitan areas whenever possible, that the staff of an integrated school must itself be integrated, with some blacks in positions of authority over some whites, that the school must give up its previous racial identity through interracial agreement on new symbols and customs, that staff and teachers must fix their expectations and maintain their standards regardless of race, that active interracial measures must be taken to change racist attitudes, that fair rules of discipline must be fairly enforced, and so on.

> *When fully and carefully carried out*, mandatory desegregation reduces racial isolation, enhances minority achievement, improves race relations, promotes educational quality, opens new opportunities, and maintains citizens support. *When fully and carefully carried out*, mandatory desegregation does not harm (and may improve) white achievement. It need not increase (and may decrease) violence and vandalism in the schools. It promotes reforms in educational structure and processes, and it may expand educational opportunities. . . . Desegregation can teach students to respect, understand, and even like people different from themselves, and it prepares them for life in an increasingly multiracial nation (Hochschild 1984, 177).

In another publication Hochschild draws comparable conclusions:

> . . . a successful school desegregation plan begins to break down the cumulative inequalities of race, class, and power. . . . By bringing blacks and whites into mutually respectful contact and by treating all students in similar ways, good plans exchange racism for individualism. By channeling resources to poor schools and broadening the horizons of poor students, successful plans equalize opportunities and diminish class barriers. By increasing black influence in white society and involving parents in the schools, good plans enhance political equality and reduce power disparities. Above all, successfully desegregated schools take rights seriously, and confront head-on the normative conflict between liberal democracy for some and liberal democracy for all (Hochschild 1986, 314-15).

Hochschild herself italicizes *"when fully and carefully carried out."* Given widespread attitudes of a racist sort, the question is in what proportion of the cases it is realistic to expect that mandatory desegregation will meet this condition.

The most likely alternative to the kind of integration that Hochschild envisages is to muddle along, more or less unsatisfactorily.

7 Education: Non-Racial Distinctions

Questions about equal treatment in the field of education arise not only with respect to race, but also with respect to other matters. This chapter deals with those relating to financing the schools and to differentiation as to sex, language, handicap, and the number of years of schooling provided.

Financing the Schools

Decentralization in education inevitably leads to differences. Different states adopt different policies, and within each state further differences stem from the delegation of powers to local governments or local school districts. The quality of the education provided is bound to differ.

Some of the differences trace back to the various characteristics of administrative and teaching personnel. To meet this problem as well as possible, states fix minimum standards of training that those who want to teach must meet. Beyond that, the problem is in the hands of those who recruit and who decide questions about salary and promotion.

Other differences trace back to money. States and localities differ in their emphasis on education and their financial ability to support it. The usual rule is that school districts depend at least in part on a local property tax, and the assessed valuation of property in different districts is bound to differ, sometimes substantially. Differences can be reduced by any of several strategies—by consolidating school districts, by adjusting the tax rates, or by arranging subsidies of an equalizing sort from the state or federal government. But inequalities are likely to remain.

The leading case on the issue is *San Antonio School District v. Rodriguez* (1973). It was based on the fact that reliance on the local property tax led to substantial differences in the number of dollars per pupil devoted to the schools in different school districts. Faced with a claim that this involved a denial of the equal protection of the laws, the Supreme Court split badly, reaching a five to four decision.

The district court had assumed that the discrimination was against "the poor," and that "the poor" constituted a "suspect" class. The Supreme Court rejected both positions. It pointed out that no predictable relationship exists between assessed property values in a district and the average income of the residents. In any case, it held that classification by wealth is not necessarily suspect. "Where wealth is involved," it said, "the Equal Protection Clause does not require absolute equality or precisely equal advantages." Assuming that all pupils get "an adequate education," the fact that some fare better than others does not violate the equal protection requirement. Anyway, the Court held, it is an "unsettled question" whether the quality of the education offered is determined by the amount of money expended for it.

From hindsight, it is odd that any claim was advanced on behalf of "the poor." Had the question been whether geographically delimited sets of persons were treated differently, the answer would have been a foregone conclusion; and this is the kind of question that suffices in connection with gerrymandering and at-large elections.

But in connection with gerrymandering and at-large elections, the Supreme Court takes the view that a "fundamental" right is at stake—the right to vote—whereas it rejects this view with respect to education. In *Rodriguez*, it based the rejection on the fact that the federal constitution does not mention education, and it was unmoved by the contribution that education makes to the exercise of such constitutional rights as free speech and political participation.

Justice Powell, who wrote the majority opinion, was clearly influenced by the potential ramifications of a different judgment. He pointed out that if it was unconstitutional to base education on the varying proceeds of a property tax, then it would presumably also be unconstitutional to base other local governmental activities on that tax; and he drew back from the potentially sweeping consequences. "It has simply never been within the constitutional prerogative of this Court to nullify statewide measures for financing public services merely because the burdens or benefits thereof fall unevenly depending upon the relative wealth of the political subdivisions in which citizens live."

The dissenting justices attacked the view that education is not a "fundamental" interest. According to Brennan the test is not whether education is mentioned in the constitution but how much it helps to uphold the various rights that are mentioned. And according to Marshall, "fundamentality" is a function of "the importance of the interests at stake." Marshall scorned the view that inequalities over and above an "adequate" education do not matter: "The Equal Protection Clause is not addressed to the minimal sufficiency but rather to the unjustifiable inequalities of state action."

Issues concerning the financing of the schools have also come up in a number of other states, with mixed results. Galie says that by the mid-1980s approximately thirty states had revised their formulas for state aid to school districts so as to reduce financial disparities (In Friedelbaum 1988, 105). He speaks of twenty-seven challenges in state courts, of which a third have been successful (p. 113).

California's Supreme Court has held both that wealth is a suspect classification and that the state constitution makes education a fundamental interest. On this basis it further held that California's system for financing its schools violated the state's own equal protection requirement (*Serrano v. Priest 1977*).

New Jersey's Supreme Court once closed down the whole public school system until the state legislature revised the system for financing it (Lehne 1978, 155). And the revised plan too has been held to violate the state constitution in that it does not go far enough in eliminating financial disparities between affluent suburban and poor urban school districts (*Abbott v. Burke 1985; New York Times*, August 26, 1988, 7:4). This judgment is being appealed.

In Texas itself the state Supreme Court has in effect rejected the *Rodriguez* judgment. It found that the property wealth per student in the richest school district was 700 times that in the poorest district, and that the average property wealth in the 100 wealthiest districts was more than twenty times greater than the average in the 100 poorest districts. Basing its judgment on a requirement of the state constitution that the legislature should make "suitable provision" for an "efficient system of public free schools," it held that "districts must have substantially equal access to similar revenues per pupil at similar levels of tax effort. Children who live in poor districts and children who live in rich districts must be afforded a substantially equal opportunity to have access to educational funds" (*Edgewood Independent School District v. Kirby 1989*).

In contrast, the courts in some states have simply followed the precedent set by the Supreme Court in *Rodriguez*—despite the fact that most state constitutions use language justifying the conclusion that education is a "fundamental" right. Thus the requirements of equal treatment in education vary from state to state.

Sex

Questions about sex discrimination in education have to be considered against the background of public policy on the treatment of women. My first purpose here is to sketch out that background, and then I will take up the question of single-sex schools and of sex discrimination in sports.

General Public Policy

As you know, the reference in the fourteenth amendment is to *persons*. No state is to deny to any person the equal protection of the laws. It thus seems to preclude differentiation by sex. But, as you also know, the rule of equal treatment is interpreted in the light of other values that are also precious. A number of these other values have in the past been construed to call for the differential treatment of women, and some still are.

For decades after the adoption of the fourteenth amendment, the general assumption was that it had no bearing on the treatment of women. They were thought to have a separate and special social role, a proper place, and to need special protection in some respects. A judge in Illinois expressed the view in 1872, when he upheld the refusal of the state to grant a woman a license to practice law.

> The civil law, as well as nature herself, has always recognized a wide difference in the respective spheres and destinies of man and woman. Man is, or should be, woman's protector and defender. The natural and proper timidity and delicacy which belongs to the female sex evidently unfits it for many of the occupations of civil life. The constitution of the family organization, which is founded in the divine ordinance, as well as the nature of things, indicates the domestic sphere as that which properly belongs to the domain and functions of womanhood. The harmony, not to say identity of interests and view which belong, or should belong, to the family institution is repugnant to the idea of a woman adopting a distinct and independent career from that of her husband (*Bradwell v. The State 1872*).

Through the years various legislative and judicial actions nibbled away at discrimination against women. Some of the state legislatures enfranchised women, and the nineteenth amendment

(1920) assured their enfranchisement over the whole country. A number of other measures adopted at the state and federal levels also reflected a concern for equal treatment.

But change came slowly, and the more impatient advocates of women's rights decided not to rely on the fourteenth amendment but to champion another. The Judiciary Committee of the House of Representatives first considered a proposed new amendment in 1923, and Congress has had the issue more or less under consideration ever since. In 1972 it adopted what by then was called the Equal Rights Amendment (ERA) and referred it to the states: "Equality of rights under the law shall not be denied or abridged by the United States or by any state on account of sex." Many of the same forces that gave strength to the civil rights movement and to agitation over racial discrimination contributed to the campaign for the ERA, which clearly influenced public opinion.

To those supporting the women's movement, the results were disappointing: not enough states ratified the ERA it to bring it into effect.

Nevertheless, the decades of agitation for the ERA made legislative and judicial bodies at every level more sensitive to sex discrimination. Although on a piecemeal and incomplete basis, sexist laws got amended and judicial decisions began to call for change. A number of states added ERAs to their own constitutions. Finally in 1971, for the first time, the Supreme Court itself struck down a law because of sex discrimination. The law in question said that if a father and mother had an equal claim to serve as the administrator of the estate of a minor, the father should be preferred. The court held that this was arbitrary, denying equal protection to the mother.

Although views on the Supreme Court have been changing, the Court still refuses to treat sex along with race as a "suspect" basis for classification. Instead it has adopted what is usually described as an intermediate standard of review, holding that differentiation as to sex, if it is to be justified, "must serve important governmental objectives and must be substantially related to the achievement of those objectives" (*Craig v. Boren 1976*). In contrast, differentiation by race survives only if it is "necessary" to the promotion of a "compelling" or "overriding" governmental interest.

Single Sex Schools

The *Brown* decision, saying that separate is inherently unequal, related to race and is not necessarily conclusive with respect to other traits. As to differentiation by sex in a variety of contexts, Congress and the courts take several different stands. Sometimes they insist that treatment be the same, with no differentiation. Sometimes they endorse the separate but equal rule. And sometimes they require or permit treatment to be separate and unequal—as in registration for the draft and the assignment of military personnel. This last subject comes up in the next chapter.

In education it is the first two rules that prevail. Congress provides illustrations. In Title IX of the Education Amendments of 1972 it extended to sex the same rule that already applied to race. It said that, in educational programs and activities receiving federal financial assistance, no person shall be subject to discrimination on the basis of sex; and in 1974 it added a finding that "the maintenance of dual school systems in which students are assigned to schools solely on the basis of race, color, sex, or national origin denies to those students the equal protection of the laws."

But Congress permits exceptions. The rule against differentiation by sex does not apply to institutions of higher undergraduate education that have traditionally and continually followed a single-sex policy; they may maintain the policy. And the rule does not apply to institutions controlled by a religious organization if a policy of coeducation is inconsistent with its religious tenets. No such exceptions are granted for differentiation by race.

Apart from such exceptions, the presumption is that educational institutions—above all those with governmental support—will be open to both sexes. The experience of the University of Virginia illustrates the point. It once admitted only men at the undergraduate level, but then four women who were denied admission went into court, and won. The court declined to say that the equal protection clause prohibits single-sex education, but it held that no other Virginia institution gave educational opportunities to women equal to those offered to men at the university. Separate was not equal, and the implication was that separate could scarcely be equal (*Kirstein v. Rector and Visitors of the University of Virginia 1970*). Prior to the judgment of the court, the university had already made plans to abandon the men-only rule.

The Supreme Court decided a comparable case in 1981. The case arose from an attack by a man on the women-only rule of the school of nursing at the Mississippi University for Women (MUW). The Supreme Court held that, though the man involved could have gotten the training he wanted at two other state institutions, the refusal to admit him at MUW denied him equal protection. According to the Court, the women-only rule did not serve any legitimate governmental purpose; moreover, the exclusion of men tended "to perpetuate the stereotyped view of nursing as an exclusively woman's job" (*Mississippi University for Women v. Hogan 1981*).

The experience of two special high schools in Philadelphia is also instructive. Until 1983 one was for boys and the other for girls. Both had stringent admission standards. Considering a challenge to the arrangement in 1976, a Circuit Court put emphasis on the finding that, though the education provided was separate, it was equal; and on this basis it refused to find a denial of the equal protection of the laws (*Vorcheimer v. School Dist. of Philadelphia 1976*). On appeal, the Supreme Court divided equally on the issue, which meant that the decision of the Circuit Court was confirmed.

In 1983, however, a Pennsylvania state court reached the opposite judgment. It acted on the basis of both the fourteenth amendment and the ERA that Pennsylvania had adopted. In connection with the fourteenth amendment, it invoked the standard of review that the Supreme Court enunciated in *Craig v. Boren*, cited above. It held that no substantial relationship existed between the separation of the sexes in schools and any important governmental interest. Further, it held that the education provided in the two schools was not in fact equal, and that in any case separate schooling was not compatible with Pennsylvania's ERA (Salomone 1986, 120-21; *Newberg v. Bd. of Pub. Ed. 1983*).

Discrimination in Sports

At all levels of education the tradition in sports is one of discrimination against women. New conceptions of the requirements of equal protection attack that tradition, and so do the requirements of Title IX and of the Equal Pay Act. But what kinds of issues arise, and what is the related reasoning?

The most common issue is whether a person of one sex is eligible for a team designated for the opposite sex. For example, should girls be permitted to compete with boys in a body contact sport such as football? The main argument against it is that, on the average, girls are smaller and weaker and thus more liable to injury, but courts reject the argument, pointing out that some girls are bigger and stronger than some boys. The equal protection clause and Title IX both preclude a boys-only rule when it obviously implies inequality (*Lantz by Lantz v. Ambach 1985*; Hetzel 1987, 289-90).

Suppose, however, that a school has a girls-only volleyball team and that a boy wants to try out. You might say that this raises the same question, but the parallel is not exact. You can open a football team to girls and still be confident that few boys will be displaced; moreover, in allowing girls to try out for the team you are attacking the tradition of discrimination against them. But if you open the volleyball team to boys, they are likely to dominate, displacing a considerable proportion of the girls who might otherwise make the team. Thus instead of promoting equality for girls you will keep them under a disadvantage. Moreover, a girl who tries out for the football team is voluntarily accepting the risks of injury, but if you admit boys to the girls' team you are yourself imposing risks. The probability is that the courts would uphold the rule excluding boys from the team (*Clark, Etc. v. Arizona Interscholastic Ass'n 1982*; Hetzel 1987, 284; Wade and Hay 1988, 47).

I am assuming above that the school has no football team for girls and no volleyball team for boys. Suppose, however, that a school argues that volleyball is the girls' equivalent of football, and that the arrangement is an implementation of the separate but equal rule. Court decisions have gone both ways on this issue (Wade and Hay 1988, 21, 27).

Suppose that a school adopts the separate but equal principle in a more straightforward manner and has, say, separate basketball teams. What should happen if a girl says that she wants to try out for the boys' team, seeking the tougher competition and the enhanced opportunity to develop and display her skills? Here you have a real problem. The girl can say that both the constitution and Title IX protect the rights of individual persons and that she wants to be treated as an individual person, not as a member of a group or class. She wants her rights.

You will presumably hesitate. If you permit the girl to play on the boys' team, you will find it difficult to deny the same permission to a boy who wants to play on the girls' team, and then the consequences may follow that are mentioned above in connection with volleyball: the girls end up under a disadvantage. What usually happens is that the separate but equal rule is enforced, regardless of the question of the personal rights of the individual girl. The argument is that government has an interest in promoting the equal treatment of girls as a class and an interest in bringing the system of discrimination to an end; and the argument further is that these are important interests, justifying differentiation by sex (Wong 1988, 451).

The sports that I mention above all classify as contact sports. The separate but equal rule is also acceptable for noncontact sports; but if only one team exists, the rule is that both sexes must be allowed to compete for places on it (Wong 1988, 421).

Note that the idea of redress enters into some of the arguments described above. Rarely is it a question of redress to a particular person for prior discrimination against him or her. Instead, redress goes to girls as a class, and emphasis on the class is more suggestive of the idea of group rights than of the personal rights of individuals. The idea of "victim specificity" is scarcely relevant.

The Disparate Impact of the SAT

Female high school students in New York went to court in 1988 against the State Education Department, claiming that its exclusive reliance on SAT scores in awarding scholarships discriminated against them contrary both to the equal protection clause and to Title IX. They proved their point. Over a number of years males had consistently outscored females by from 40 to 60 points, and the court held that the probability of this happening in the absence of sex discrimination was nearly zero. Moreover, the court also held that disparate impact was enough to establish the women's case, proof of discriminatory intent being unnecessary. The suggested solution is that the Education Department shift to the consideration of high school GPAs as well as the SAT scores in awarding its scholarships (*Sharif by Salahuddin v. New York State Educ. Dept. 1989*).

Language

Problems about equal treatment are inevitable in communities where more than one language is spoken, above all when, as in the United States, one of the languages is dominant. To have equal opportunities in life, those who speak a minority language must learn English, which puts a burden on them that others do not share. At the same time, the need to learn English raises questions about arranging for language instruction in the schools. And if minority language students are treated separately, the question of segregation may arise too.

Speakers of Chinese comprise one of the smaller language minorities in the country, yet initiated the leading Supreme Court case on the problem (*Lau v. Nichols 1974*). In San Francisco, children speaking only Chinese showed up in school. One of them, pointing to the fact that classmates were taught in a language that they could understand whereas he was not, claimed to be a victim of discrimination. He did not ask to be taught in Chinese, but sought some appropriate remedy.

The Latinos are the largest language minority, and have had difficulties analogous to those of the Chinese. Texas provides illustrations. Some Texan communities once thought it best to put Mexican-Americans in separate schools, which looked reasonable in that the students had special needs in common. But then the tendency was to neglect the "Mexican schools," just as schools for blacks were neglected. Moreover, when integration became mandatory, some Texan communities achieved it by counting Mexican-Americans as white and mixing them with the blacks, leaving Anglos with their own separate schools.

Other problems have arisen where Mexican-Americans and Anglos are in the same school. Given their language problem, Mexican-American children have tended not to progress as rapidly as Anglo children, and so have been held disproportionately in the same grade for more than one year. Or they have been treated as retarded or put on the slow track or assigned to the lowest of the ability groupings. Drop-out rates among Mexican-Americans have been high, and the proportion of high school graduates going on to college has been low.

Where students have special language problems, the position might be that government is not responsible. San Francisco took this position in the case mentioned above. Its argument was that responsibility belonged to the parents: they should see to it that their children learned English in order to take advantage of the education that the city was offering.

Both the federal district court and the Circuit Court endorsed San Francisco's position. The Circuit Court pointed out that "every student brings to the starting line of his educational career different advantages and disadvantages . . . ." And it went on to absolve the city of any responsibility for the disadvantages unless they stemmed from past governmental discrimination (*Lau v. Nichols 1973*). A dissenting judge, however, scorned the view that the "equal treatment of unequals satisfies the demands of equal protection." He said that "the Equal Protection Clause is not washed away because the able bodied and the paraplegic are given the same state command to walk."

The Supreme Court sided in effect with the dissenting judge. It acted on the basis of the Civil Rights Act of 1964, barring discrimination in any program or activity receiving federal financial assistance. To teach a child in a language he did not understand, the Court held, was to discriminate against him, denying him "meaningful education." The Court cited an HEW guideline to the effect that schools must take "affirmative steps" to rectify the language deficiencies of students in order to make possible their "effective participation" in the educational program. This rules out "immersion" as a policy, that is, putting minority language students into classes taught exclusively in English.

The view of the Court is suggestive of the third of the definitions of equality of opportunity described in Chapter 4. To uphold equality of opportunity, it is not enough for government to refrain from discriminating. Nor does it do its full duty if it simply seeks to counteract the effects of disadvantages and handicaps for which it is responsible. At least in some connections and to some extent, it must also seek to counteract the effects of disadvantages and handicaps for which the individual is not responsible.

Although calling for "affirmative steps," HEW did not specify what they should be. Nor does the law. Congress in effect confirmed the vague HEW guideline in the Equal Educational Opportunities Act of 1974, but it refrained from being more specific. It simply declared that a state that failed to take "appropriate action" to overcome the language problems of students would be denying equality of educational opportunity.

In the case of the Chinese students, the solution was to give them special instruction in English. Nevertheless, in general Congress supports bilingual education. Its bilingual education act of 1968 offers subsidies to states that adopt programs of an approved sort, and it has periodically reauthorized such support.

Transitional bilingual education (TBE) is preferred. Its object is to help the student make the transition from her native tongue to English. The typical program lasts three years, beginning with kindergarten or the first grade. The teacher must know both English and the native language of the students. She first uses the students' native tongue as the language of instruction and makes English one of the subjects taught, and then she switches to English when the students know it well enough. Between 1975 and 1980, following the *Lau* decision, the Office of Civil Rights (OCR) of HEW negotiated plans for bilingual education with over five hundred individual school districts (Rossell and Ross 1986, 388). Problems arise, of course, when Spanish-speaking students transfer into a school at a grade level not covered by the bilingual program. Then special instruction in English becomes imperative.

The Reagan administration showed little enthusiasm for bilingual education. It gave special emphasis to an escape clause that Congress included in the revised legislation adopted in 1984—a clause authorizing the use of a limited percentage of the appropriated funds in special alternative programs of an experimental sort. The Reagan administration even sought to remove the limit, wanting to leave it to the states to choose among the possible policies (U. S. Department of Education 1986, vii).

Affirmative steps to help those with limited proficiency in English require that they be grouped together, but the law prohibits segregation by language, and the language minorities, as a rule, do not want it (*Desegregation and Education Concerns of the Hispanic Community*, 1977: 62). At the same time, problems arise. The solution is sought by putting those with special language needs together in the same classes while keeping them in the same school building with others.

Problems concerning discrimination against language minorities are not limited to the elementary and secondary schools. In 1987 various organizations that championed the interests of Mexican-Americans in Texas went into court accusing the state of Texas of violating its own constitution and laws through policies that favor Anglos and discriminate against both blacks and Mexican-Americans. Texas has allegedly located its academic programs and facilities unfavorably to Mexican-Americans and has allegedly funded at lower levels those institutions that Mexican-Americans attend. And it is accused of failing sufficiently to encourage and assist Mexican-Americans who wish to enter graduate and professional programs.

The accusation that Texas denies equal protection to Mexican-Americans is not new. Not many years ago, a case came into the courts because Texas was refusing to provide funds for the education of children who had not been "legally admitted" into the United States. The court pointed out that, according to the fourteenth amendment, no state is to deny equal protection to *any person within its jurisdiction*. The right is not restricted to citizens, or to those legally admitted (*Plyler v. Doe 1982*).

As noted in Chapter 5, a number of states in recent years have declared English to be their official language—without specifying what the consequences of the declaration should be. Litigation over the issue seems likely. A note in the *Harvard Law Review* argues that, regardless of English-only declarations, the "courts should find that the presence of established federal programs and the equal protection clause of the fourteenth amendment prohibit state action limiting the rights of language minorities" ("Official English," 987: 1362).

Handicaps

The problem of children with handicaps raises with special force the question of the meaning of equal treatment and equality of opportunity. (Following federal law, I use the term *handicap* to cover all sorts of impairments and disabilities.)

Government has traditionally neglected the handicapped, doing little or nothing to assure them equal treatment or equality of opportunity. Those without handicap have generally found it more comfortable if the handicapped, especially the severely handicapped, were simply kept out of sight, or at least ignored. But such neglect has not survived the increased concern for equality in recent decades.

A federal district court made one of the first relevant pronouncements in 1972, declaring that "all children, regardless of any handicap or other disability, have a right to publicly-supported education suited to their needs . . ." (*Mills v. Bd. of Ed. of D.C. 1972*). Shortly thereafter, Congress endorsed the principle. It applied to the handicapped the rule that it had included in the Civil Rights Act of 1964: no handicapped person who is otherwise qualified shall be subjected to discrimination in any program or activity receiving federal financial assistance. And it offered grants-in-aid to states to help them provide "free, appropriate public education" to handicapped children in the "least restrictive environment."

The reference to the "least restrictive environment" is reasonably clear, but problems arise. Handicapped children are to be "mainstreamed" whenever possible—sent into classrooms along with others. One of the implications is that (where federal funds are involved) buildings and rooms within them must be made accessible—for example, to persons in wheel chairs. Another implication is that support services are to be provided. Support services do not include medical care, but they do include such care as a qualified school nurse can provide, including intermittent catheterization when necessary.

In one of the leading cases the question was whether a public school is obliged to provide a sign-language interpreter for a student with impaired hearing. You might argue that if instruction in a language that the student does not understand denies equal treatment, so does instruction in a voice that the student cannot hear. The answer to the argument, I suppose, must turn on numbers and therefore on costs. The number of students with a language problem far exceeds the number with a hearing impairment, and the per pupil costs of meeting the problem are much less. Moreover, language difficulties can be overcome within a few months, or a few years, while hearing impairments are likely to last for a lifetime.

In court, the decision concerning a sign language interpreter turned not on such considerations but on the question what constitutes an "appropriate" education. The law is not clear on the point. Does access to the classroom automatically assure an "appropriate" education? Or is education appropriate only when the outcome enables the student to participate in society as fully as can reasonably be expected in the light of his handicap, or only when it enables the student to achieve her full potential?

The vague answer of the district court was that education is "appropriate" only when it gives the student "an opportunity to achieve [her] full potential commensurate with the opportunity provided to other children." On this basis the district court said that the school should provide the sign language interpreter, and the Circuit Court agreed.

But the Supreme Court reversed. According to it, Congress did not mean to require that schools must "maximize each handicapped child's potential." Further, a standard requiring "equal" educational opportunities would be "unworkable . . ., requiring impossible measurements and comparisons." What Congress wanted to assure was simply equal access to an education that was "sufficient to confer some . . . benefit . . ., reasonably calculated to enable the child to achieve passing marks and advance from grade to grade." Since the hearing-impaired child in question was meeting this standard, the school did not need to provide a sign language interpreter (*Hendrick Hudson Dist. Bd. of Ed. v. Rowley 1982*).

In case it is not feasible to have a handicapped child attend school, personalized instruction in the home is to be arranged, which has led to the question whether such instruction can be limited to the normal school year.

As intimated above, these principles have financial implications. The costs of meeting the needs of handicapped students may be high, raising the question whether there are limits beyond which the government and taxpayers should not be expected to go in providing for equal treatment. Perhaps you might want to argue that equal treatment is accorded when per pupil expenditures are the same, with nothing extra spent because of any special needs of the handicapped.

Further, the principle that education is to be adjusted to the needs of individual students has extensive possible ramifications (Cf. Bastian et al. 1986). Some kind of a balance obviously has to be struck between that principle and the meeting of other needs.

Note that the above rules relate to government itself and to programs and activities receiving federal funds. Congress is considering, and seems likely to adopt, a bill concerning the equal treatment of the handicapped by enterprises "affected with a public interest."

Years of Schooling

Several studies relating to equality in education focus on the number of years of schooling that different persons get. Substantial differences in this respect are obvious. Many drop out of school as soon as the law permits, which usually means that they do not go through high school. Others go on to college and perhaps beyond.

Differences in the number of years of schooling indicate inequality, of course, but those who focus on the problem may be concerned about something other than the equal protection of the laws. Weaver, for example, is concerned with the relationship between education and the class structure, or between education and the distribution of privilege in society. He uses the escalator metaphor: as more of the poor got an elementary education, more of the rich started getting a secondary education; and as more of the poor started getting a secondary education, more of the rich went on to college. In his eyes, one of the functions of education is thus to maintain the social gap, that is, to maintain inequality between the classes (Weaver 1982, 41-67).

Alternatively, some focus on cost/benefit ratios. In education, do people come out even, or do some subsidize others? And if inequality exists, what should be done about it?

At the elementary and secondary levels, education is presumably redistributive. Many taxpayers subsidize the education of other people's children; and where per pupil costs in different school districts are evened out through an equalization formula, the rich presumably subsidize the poor.

The situation with respect to publicly supported higher education is different. Although not free, it is subsidized, and attendance is not universal. Students come preponderantly from the middle and upper classes, and these classes tend to be represented with special disproportion in the major state universities, where the subsidies per student are highest. Thus, in a sense, the poor pay taxes to help those in the middle and upper classes maintain the advantage they already have (Hansen 1974; Moynihan 1972).

Jencks once made what he called a "crude estimate" that "the most extensively educated fifth of the population received about 75 percent more than their share of the nation's educational resources, while the least extensively educated fifth received about half their share" (Jencks 1972, 26).

The striking feature of this statement is the reference to "their share," as if everyone has an entitlement to a given share, presumably an equal share, of the educational resources available. It is as if treatment is equal only when it is the same. To rectify the presumed inequality Jencks goes on to suggest a method by which those who get more than "their share" would pay accordingly. While in school they would get free tuition and "a living stipend," but then through life they would pay a surcharge on their income taxes (Jencks 1972, 260).

Whether this is desirable as a matter of policy is debatable. The thought that each person should pay for the benefits that he or she receives is of course appealing. At the same time, it may be to the general social advantage to encourage those who are so inclined to enhance their knowledge and develop their talents. The encouragement should occur, of course, without regard to race, sex, or socio-economic class. If those who respond to the encouragement get the special benefits that higher education provides, the appeal can be to the principle stated by John Rawls: that inequalities are justified when they are to the advantage of the least fortunate.

It is a different question whether arrangements for financing higher education deny the equal protection of the laws. The answer is probably in the negative, since individual choices that at least nominally are free play a central role. It is not a matter of law that students from the lower socio-economic class tend not to pursue a higher education and that students from the middle and upper classes therefore get disproportionate benefit. Further, it would be difficult for persons from the lower socio-economic class to prove that the law imposes damage on them. Still, the law fixes the framework within which the various choices are made.

8 Personnel Policies

This chapter concerns the personnel policies of government. That is, it concerns the civil service, mainly at the state and local levels, where discrimination as to race is the main issue. And it concerns the military services, where discrimination as to sex and sexual orientation is the main issue.

The Civil Service

As I have noted several times already, the equal protection clause says that no state is to deny to any *person* the equal protection of the laws. The right belongs to individuals, although as noted in the preceding chapter you may find that if you consider individuals one by one you are less able to protect their rights than if you consider them as a class. I will take up that vexing problem more carefully in Chapter 17. Here the point is that the equal protection clause does not require that blacks or women or any other group be represented in the civil service or, for that matter, anywhere in government. Even where explicitly representative bodies are concerned, the courts (as indicated in Chapter 5) have ruled out measures designed to assure representation by race or sex.

But what happens if, despite the constitution, a governmental agency has in the past clearly followed discriminatory policies, denying employment or promotion on the basis of race?

Alabama faced the question a quarter century ago. A federal district court found that its Personnel Department had "engaged in a blatant and continuous pattern and practice of discrimination in hiring in the Department of Public Safety both as to troopers and supporting personnel. In the thirty-seven year history of the patrol there has never been a black trooper and the only Negroes ever employed by the department have been nonmerit system laborers" (*NAACP v. Allen 1972*).

Facing this record, the court ordered the Department to give every other new appointment to a black until blacks comprised 25 percent of the trooper force; and it imposed the same rule with respect to the appointment of supporting personnel. The assumption was that blacks comprised at least 25 percent of the qualified persons in the relevant labor market.

Not many years later a similar case was in the courts, deriving from the fact that, though the Personnel Department had hired blacks, it discriminated on a racial basis in its promotion policies. In 1984, of 131 state troopers above the rank of corporal, not one was black. Of 66 corporals, the only blacks were the four who had been appointed following a court order.

The Supreme Court rendered the final judgment in this case. It reaffirmed the principle that government has a compelling interest in remedying past and present discrimination by a state and it ordered the Personnel Department to develop promotion policies that did not have an adverse impact on blacks. And it specified that meantime one out of every two troopers promoted must be a black, assuming the availability of qualified black candidates (*United States v. Paradise 1987*).

The courts have acted similarly in many other cases. In one of them, concerning San Francisco, the court came close to calling for the representation of minority groups on the police force, as if a group right exists.

> All citizens profit when the city achieves a racially integrated police force of qualified individuals who are knowledgeable of the diverse problems of different ethnic groups and who are not prey to destructive hostility from minorities who feel excluded from full participation in the city government life. Clearly, the general harmony of the community is enhanced by the city's obtaining a police force representative of its population (*Officers for Justice v. Civil S. Com'n C. & C. San Francisco 1973*).

In this case the court specified that its aim was to require the hiring of minorities at a rate that would bring the percentage of minority policemen "closer to the percentage of minorities in the population within a relatively short period of time."

Court orders for ratio-hiring do not call for the hiring of the unqualified. Nevertheless, the probable result, at least in some instances, is that a less qualified person is appointed while a more qualified person is passed over.

Since I sketched out the main pro and con arguments on this issue when describing the Bakke case in Chapter 6, and since I will take the issue up more thoroughly in Chapter 15, I will simply raise a few questions here, relating to Alabama's Personnel Department. The questions need to be considered against the assumption that its discrimination was largely of the passive kind, meaning that the record gave the blacks good reason to believe that they would not be hired and that they therefore rarely applied.

Assuming the above, were the courts on good ground in requiring change in the policies followed? Would it have been enough simply to require that the department make known its willingness to employ blacks, without specifying the proportion of subsequent appointments that should go to them? Should the courts have adhered to the principle of "victim specificity," limiting preferential employment and promotion to blacks who could prove that the Personnel Department had discriminated against them? Or were the courts justified in doing approximately what they did?

Problems arise over civil service exams. Exams ought to be fair, of course; and scores should be reasonably good predictors of a capacity to learn how to do the job if not of actual performance on the job. But these criteria are not always easy to meet. Complaints occur of cultural bias that makes an exam easier for whites than for blacks or Hispanics, and perhaps easier for men than for women. And the more complex an exam needs to be, the greater the difficulty in developing one that is valid and reliable. If all you need to know is how well an applicant has mastered the three R's (in English!), the problem is relatively simple, but it is much more difficult when more advanced knowledge is required and when personal traits such as motivation, creative imagination, a sense of responsibility, and a capacity to work effectively with others are involved. Moreover, it may take years to determine the extent to which exam scores predict later performance.

The result is that examinations are open to challenge on the ground that they lead to unequal treatment. I noted in the preceding chapter that female high school students in New York successfully challenged exclusive reliance on SAT scores in connection with the awarding of scholarships. Minority persons too may challenge tests. If they can prove discriminatory intent, that is likely to be decisive. If they rely on disparate impact, they must be prepared to demonstrate that the test is somehow unfair. Standards need not be lowered in order that minority persons can pass.

Problems sometimes arise too concerning qualifications for a job. For example, members of police and fire departments, prison guards, and others need to meet certain physical requirements, requirements concerning height and weight among others. But how small may a person be and still do the job effectively? The tendency has been for white men to fix the requirements unnecessarily high, with the result that women and Asians have been disproportionately screened out.

Is it compatible with equal treatment to reserve any civil service positions explicitly on the basis of sex? The answer is yes—but only if sex is a bona fide occupational qualification (bfoq).

But when is sex a bfoq? Women serve successfully as police officers in many cities, and as firefighters in some. Perhaps the most serious question concerns the employment of women as guards in a prison for men, or vice versa. A federal district court has held that Alabama was justified in refusing to hire a woman as a guard in a men's prison, on the ground that she would attract assault. But some other states employ prison guards without regard to sex, and apparently do not encounter major problems (Freedman 1983, 934-36).

You might ask yourself whether the principles that have led the courts to order the ratio-hiring of blacks as state troopers should also lead them to order the ratio-hiring of women. And you might ask yourself whether a woman who is nursing a baby should be eligible to serve in a police or fire department.

Problems have arisen too concerning mandatory retirement based on age. Federal law prohibits it in the case of "employees," granting exceptions where a bfoq is involved. But what should count as a bfoq? Must police and wildlife officers be under 55? Must a judge, appointed to office, retire when he reaches 70? In the first kind of case, the courts say no—that governments imposing an age limit of 55 have been unable to justify it. In the case of a judge who wanted to go on serving after reaching his 70th birthday, the finding of the court was that he was a policy making official, not an "employee" as defined in the federal law; thus he remained unprotected against a state law calling for mandatory retirement (*EEOC v. Massachusetts 1988*).

Cases of discrimination come up in the civil service not only at the state but also at the federal level. Perhaps the most notorious of them concerns the Department of Justice itself—charged with enforcing laws against discrimination. In 1988 a federal district court found that a component of the Department, the FBI, had been discriminating against its Hispanic agents in making job assignments, and that this led to further discrimination with respect to promotions. Moreover, the court ruled that the FBI added to its guilt by retaliating in discriminatory fashion against the particular agent who sought judicial enforcement of his rights (*Perez v. F.B.I. 1988*).

Similarly, a federal court found the Department of State was guilty of discriminating in various ways against female foreign service officers (*Palmer v. Shultz 1987a and 1987b*).

The Military

Explicit race discrimination was the rule in the military until after World War II. President Truman then ordered its elimination, and the more egregious forms seem in fact to have been eliminated. Problems nevertheless persist, for a tradition of racism is difficult to overcome.

More novel and interesting problems, however, relate to the treatment of women and of homosexual persons.

Women

Superficially, the equal protection clause seems to prohibit differentiation by sex, but for long the general tacit assumption was that it applied to racial discrimination alone. In any event, remember that the clause only establishes a presumption in favor of treating persons in the same way. The presumption is rebuttable, and is widely held to be rebutted by the argument that differentiation is desirable and necessary in order to uphold values associated with a special role for women.

Given the vagueness of the requirement of equal treatment, students of the subject differ in their prescriptions concerning the sexes. At the one extreme are those who espouse what is confusingly called the equal treatment model. The assumption is that once you decide what the fourteenth amendment requires with respect to the equal treatment of men, you should simply extend the same (equal) treatment to women (Williams 1984-85, 351-70). You should not even have special rules concerning pregnancy and childbirth, but instead should apply rules relating to disability.

Advocates of this model, however, accept differentiation between the sexes where housing and toilet facilities are involved. For example, even if the armed forces were to adopt the "equal treatment" model, they would not need to put men and women indiscriminately in the same barracks.

At the other extreme are those who espouse a special treatment model, although the question how special the treatment of women should be leads to disagreement. At a minimum, the advocates of this model want to celebrate pregnancy as a unique condition and childbirth as a unique function, and they may favor special treatment for women in other connections too.

Implicitly, Carol Gilligan suggests special treatment for women. Her book *In A Different Voice* (1982) indicates that men tend to be aggressive and competitive, assuming hierarchical relationships, whereas women tend to be compassionate and nurturing, thinking in terms of networks of relationships and seeking to handle problems so that no one is hurt (pp. 62-65).

The government and the armed forces have never chosen clearly between such models. They choose "equal treatment" in some respects and special treatment in others.

Women may of course join the armed forces as volunteers, but so far they have never been conscripted. After World War II Congress even imposed a limit on voluntary enlistments, specifying that women were to comprise no more than two percent of the members of the armed forces. It repealed that limit in 1967 and since then the proportion of women has gradually increased. The figure in 1988 was approximately 10 percent.

Other congressional limitations remain in effect. They permit the Navy to assign women to regular duty only on "hospital ships, transports, and vessels of a similar classification not expected to be assigned combat missions." The Navy may assign women to other vessels only on temporary duty and only if no combat mission is expected during the period of the assignment. Neither the Navy nor the Air Force may send women fliers on combat missions. The Army voluntarily follows comparable policies (Tuten 1982, 255-59).

On the basis of these principles, approximately half of the posts in the armed forces are closed to women (*New York Times*, 11/15/88, 16:1).

Whether the exclusion of women from combat is justified is a matter for debate, and was debated especially when the campaign for the ERA was at its height. The most hard-headed argument supporting the exclusion policy is that women "are substantially inferior to men in the physical requirements of ground combat." Tuten, who makes that assertion, goes on to say, "It is inevitable that divisions and corps with admixtures of women in the CS/CSS [combat support, and combat service support] units will be measurably less combat effective than all-male units." According to him, "Equal opportunity on the battlefield spells defeat" (Tuten 1982, 248, 250-51).

In addition to the hard-headed argument are others based on a conception of the psychological differences between men and women and of the social roles that it is desirable to have them play. Those arguing along this line follow Carol Gilligan in the characteristics that they assign to men and women, and are likely to go on to argue that the social roles of men and women should vary accordingly. If fighting has to occur, it is thus proper that men should do it and that women should be safeguarded from it in so far as possible, maintaining the gentler and more civilized aspects of social life. Women, according to this view, should not be put into a position where they might be wounded or killed—or captured and raped; and they should not be asked to kill others.

As the record demonstrates, nothing about the fourteenth amendment precludes the acceptance of this line of argument. But challenges are advanced. One challenge is that the evidence gives little support to the view that women are ineffective fighters, although it does not prove the opposite either. Opponents of the combat exclusion cite the many instances in which individual women and groups of women have in fact engaged in combat, performing at about the same level as men. And they cite field training exercises in which "the proportion of women in combat support and combat service support units had no effect on measurable unit performance" (Segal 1982, 278. Holm 1982, 337-45. Cf. House Hearings 1983, 393).

Women alone, of course, face the possibility of pregnancy, but, as noted above, pregnancy can be classified as another physical disability, along with those that both men and women suffer (Kornblum 1984, 418; Williams 1982, 193). Even with pregnancy counted, lost time rates in the armed forces tend to be lower for women than for men; this is because women are less likely to go AWOL or to lose time because of alcohol and drug abuse or disciplinary penalties (Holm 1982, 257).

I have not seen a direct refutation of the claim that women speak "in a different voice." But it is obviously possible that, to the extent that they differ from men in their psychological nature, they do so on the basis of cultural conditioning rather than on the basis of anything biological. And if that is the case, the question is not what nature suggests or dictates but what kinds of characteristics should be cultivated in both men and women and what kind of society to strive to maintain or build.

The compromise that permits women to enlist in the armed forces but excludes them from combat roles has implications. It compels the services to employ a quota system based on sex. The reason for this is most obvious in the case of the Navy. Given the rules concerning combat duty, it must be able to man the fighting ships; and it needs to rotate personnel between ship and shore duty. Thus the Navy must not give too high a proportion of the shore billets to women, lest men have to be kept permanently at sea. The Army and Air Force face comparable problems and follow comparable policies (Binkin and Bach 1977, 24-28; Goodman 1979, 252).

Another implication of the combat exclusion is that it restricts the usefulness of women to the armed forces and thus, in principle at least, reduces the incentive to recruit them. It is impossible to say whether or to what extent it reduces their inclination to volunteer. In so far as it does, it restricts the number enjoying the benefits that come with service in the armed forces: the job itself and the pay that comes with it; the educational opportunities during and after the period of military service; the veterans benefits; sheer adventure.

For women who join the armed forces, the combat exclusion reduces the chance for upward mobility in that it denies positions of command that would in turn lead to higher positions (Kornblum 1984, 369). And it reduces the chance that service in the armed forces will give a boost to a subsequent civilian career—for example, in elective office (Goodman 1979, 244-49).

Perhaps even more importantly, exclusion from combat has symbolic significance, implicitly rejecting the "equal treatment" model mentioned above and reflecting the "special treatment" model. From the point of view of those who think that women should be treated like men, the exclusion puts the women who enlist under a handicap, encouraging the view that they constitute supporting personnel, denying them full professional standing, and suggesting that they are not capable of exercising the full obligations of citizenship.

The Defense Advisory Committee on Women in the Services speaks in its several reports of a pervasive bias against women, of policies and attitudes that demean and denigrate them, of skepticism about their professional competence, of abusive behavior toward them as well as paternalistic and patronizing behavior, and of sexual harassment (Davis 1987; New York Times, 2/21/89, 24:1).

Differentiation by sex with respect to combat has not been directly challenged in the courts. In 1981 the Supreme Court heard a case stemming from the fact that the selective service act required only males to register. The Court might have seized on the case to consider the question of a combat role for women, for if the exclusion of women from combat denies them equal protection, it would be difficult to justify the rule that only men shall register for the draft.

But even the dissenting justices were silent on the issue. The Court did not apply the usual tests for determining whether differentiation by sex denies equal treatment but simply deferred to Congress. And the majority concluded that, given the policies that Congress favors, men and women "are simply not similarly situated for purposes of a draft or registration for a draft" (*Rostker v. Goldberg 1981*). And those not similarly situated could be treated differently. The decision suggests the question what the courts would do if a man who is sent into combat should claim that he is being denied the equal protection of the laws.

If the Court were to address itself to the constitutionality of the combat exclusion and not simply defer to Congress on the matter, it would presumably apply tests more or less like those applied in other sex discrimination cases. The questions would be whether the differentiation by sex serves an important governmental purpose and whether it is substantially related to the achievement of that purpose.

Both questions would cause difficulty. The central question might or might not be explicitly acknowledged: whether it is an important governmental purpose to maintain a distinction in the social roles of men and women. As long as Congress and the public say that it is, the Court would presumably reflect the fact. If the Court had to decide on the basis of the question whether "equal opportunity on the battlefield spells defeat," it would be in a more difficult position, for the evidence that women in combat are less effective than men is weak. The fact that, on the average, men are bigger and stronger would not provide an adequate basis for a judgment, for some women are bigger and stronger than some men; and in any event, many military assignments call for qualities that have nothing to do with size or strength.

Those who urge unlimited military opportunity for women need not oppose all differentiation. For example, as noted above, they do not need to favor mixing men and women in the same living quarters. The constitution says nothing explicit about a right to privacy, but the right is widely recognized nevertheless, and can reasonably be taken to guide interpretations of the right to equal treatment. Further, regardless of a right to privacy, the principle that related values are to be given due respect (or that reasonable classification is permissible) can be taken to justify the assignment of men and women to separate quarters.

Pay and perquisites must of course be the same for those of comparable military rank, regardless of sex. An issue relating to this point went into the courts because of a rule of the Air Force concerning special allowances for dependents. If a male officer claimed that his spouse was a dependent, the Air Force accepted the claim without question, but if a female officer made the same claim she was required to prove it. It is perhaps needless to say that the Supreme Court found this to be discriminatory (*Frontiero v. Richardson 1973*).

The adoption of the ERA would not necessarily have resolved the question of the role of women in the armed forces. Recall that, according to it, equality of rights is not to be denied or abridged on account of sex. Adoption of the amendment would have put the courts on notice that the public wanted less differentiation based on sex, but it would not have commanded the elimination of all differentiation. Values relating to privacy, for example, would still have prevailed. And no one can be sure whether values relating to the compassionate, caring, and nurturing role of women would have prevailed too. Moreover, a number of those who favored the ERA expressed the view that it would not affect the freedom of the armed forces to restrict women to noncombat roles if they chose to do so (Mansbridge 1986, 45-66).

In the absence of proof that women fight less effectively than men, two sorts of arguments can be advanced in support of the exclusion of women from combat, and perhaps from the armed forces. One has been intimated already—that women speak in a different voice; that is, that as a general rule they differ from men in their psychological inclinations. And, equally important, that it is socially desirable to recognize and maintain the difference.

The second argument relates not to equal treatment at all but to the militarization of society and the reduction and limitation of armaments. The argument is that the use of women in combat, or in the armed forces, accentuates the militarization of society and that this is to be deplored. Further, given the worldwide tradition against the use of women, it might be possible to secure an international agreement to limit or prohibit their use in the future. The issue is thus whether the denial of equal opportunity to women is justified by a desire to avoid the increased militarization that their mobilization entails. It would be interesting, too, if the proposal of an international agreement to limit or prohibit the use of women in the armed forces were accompanied by a proposal that no man below 40 would be used either.

Homosexual Persons

The armed forces face a problem concerning the treatment of homosexual persons. Some background is appropriate.

Sodomy is practiced by an unknown proportion of heterosexual persons and is the principal form of physical intimacy open to homosexual persons. As of 1961 the laws of all 50 states made it a crime, and as of 1986 the laws of 24 still did. These laws are rarely enforced, but one of them—Georgia's—came into play a few years ago, after two men were found to be engaging in sodomy in the privacy of a bedroom. The District Attorney decided not to press charges, but one of the men took the case to court himself, challenging the constitutionality of the law (*Bowers v. Hardwick 1986*).

The case went up to the Supreme Court and boomeranged (Sunstein 1988; Goldstein 1988). Five justices joined in rejecting Hardwick's claim, and thus spoke for the Court. The five did not mention the question of equal treatment, though Georgia's Attorney General conceded that the law against sodomy would be unconstitutional if applied to a married couple. Instead, the five focused on the question whether Georgia was denying liberty without due process of law or violating a right to privacy. Their stance was conservative, based largely on their understanding of history and tradition: many societies through many centuries have condemned sodomy as illegal or immoral or both, and all the states of the United States made it illegal until 1961. Thus no historic tradition recognized a right to liberty or to privacy where sodomy was involved. Given this record, the five saw nothing to justify Hardwick's claim that Georgia's law was unconstitutional.

Four dissenting justices took the stance of classical liberalism. They dwelt mainly on the "the right to be let alone," encompassing at least a right to liberty and to privacy. They referred also to the equal protection of the laws, protesting the failure of the Court to give it full consideration. Without taking an unequivocal stand, they intimated that a law applied selectively to homosexual persons might deny equal protection; and they also intimated that anti-sodomy laws might deny equal protection even if enforced with nominal evenhandedness, for they call on homosexual persons to conduct their lives without physical intimacy, which involves a burden that heterosexual persons are not required to bear.

Hardwick has important implications. Even if a law prohibiting sodomy is not enforced, it makes the act a crime, and those known to engage in it may be barred from some kinds of employment. Both the Dallas police department and the FBI have refused to hire homosexual persons, and the courts have upheld their stand. In the case of the FBI the court held that "to have agents who engage in conduct criminalized in roughly one-half of the states would undermine the law enforcement credibility of the Bureau" (*Padula v. Webster 1987; Childers v. Dallas Police Dept. 1981*). In some states, homosexual teachers are vulnerable, for conviction of crime may well lead to the revocation of a teaching certificate. California's education code makes this mandatory (Rivera 1979, 860-74).

At the same time, the situation is confused. In the last quarter century 26 states have repealed laws against sodomy, apparently convinced that they reflect prejudice and deny liberty and equal treatment. The Civil Service Commission has dropped its discrimination against homosexual persons, and some municipalities have adopted human rights ordinances that prohibit differentiation based on homosexual orientation or conduct (Mohr 1988, 197).

A decision of the Supreme Court of California in 1979 illustrates the changing view. It declares that "both the state and federal equal protection clauses clearly prohibit the state or any governmental entity from arbitrarily discriminating against any class of individuals in employment decisions . . . . [T]his general constitutional principle applies to homosexuals . . ." (*Gay Law Students Ass'n v. Pacific Tel. & Tel. 1979*).

The District of Columbia likewise illustrates change. It has traditionally made sodomy a crime, but it also has a Human Rights Act that extends its protection to homosexual persons. Among other things, the act prohibits educational institutions from discriminating on the basis of sexual orientation with regard to access to facilities and services. Despite this act, Georgetown University, located in the District, refused in 1979 and in subsequent years to grant "university recognition," and thus access to facilities and services, to a group of gay students, and they sought help from a court.

The resulting judgment of the District of Columbia Court of Appeals was that "the eradication of sexual orientation discrimination is a compelling governmental interest" (*Gay Rights Coalition of Georgetown University Law Center v. Georgetown University 1987*, at 82 [2930]). Thus, according to the court, the District was justified in seeking to prohibit such discrimination, and its prohibition overrides any claim that the university might make in the name of freedom of religion. The court did not insist on the formality of "university recognition" of the gay group, but required that the university extend "facilities and services" lest it lose its tax exempt status.

It is against this mixed background that the policies of the Department of Defense (DOD) need to be considered. At least until 1989 one of these policies was not to accept as a recruit any person, male or female, whose orientation was homosexual, and to discharge any such person who got in. In an article published in 1985, Diamond says that nearly 15,000 were discharged in the preceding ten years (Diamond 1985, 937). Note that the reference was to a homosexual *orientation;* orientation alone, even in the absence of proof of homosexual *conduct*, was enough to bar recruitment or bring about a discharge.

The DOD sought to justify its policy in several ways. It pointed out that many despise and detest persons who are homosexual, making their presence in the armed forces a threat to various interests: the attractiveness of the armed forces to potential recruits, the ability of commissioned and non-commissioned officers to gain and maintain the respect of those whom they command, the prevention of breaches of security, and so on (Diamond 1985, 944; *Beller v. Middendorf 1980; Hatheway v. Secretary of Army 1981*).

The policies of the DOD have been challenged, with results that are significant even if they leave important questions unanswered. In two cases, coming before the Circuit Court in the Ninth Circuit, the decision went clearly in favor of the DOD. Justice Kennedy, subsequently appointed to the Supreme Court, wrote the opinion in one of them. His language leaves the question open whether he would approve *Hardwick*, but he held that "regulations which might infringe constitutional rights in other contexts may survive scrutiny because of military necessities" (*Beller v. Middendorf 1980*).

The next year a different judge explicitly adopted the same standard of review that applies to differentiation as to sex, and reached the conclusion that the differential treatment of homosexual persons in the armed forces "bears a substantial relationship to an important governmental interest." "The government has a compelling interest," the judge said, "in maintaining a strong military force." And he repeated an earlier holding that "those who engage in homosexual acts severely compromise the government's ability to maintain such a force" (*Hatheway v. Secretary of the Army 1981*). Note the reference to *acts* and not simply to *orientation*.

More recent cases are on the other side. One of them concerns a DOD requirement that lesbian and gay applicants for Secret and Top Secret security clearances be subjected to an expanded investigation. The outcome was a stern judicial rebuke. The judge saw no reason for the differential treatment. He pointed to the absence of any record of blackmail based on homosexuality, and he commented that "lesbians and gay men have been the object of some of the deepest prejudice and hatred in American society," that "wholly unfounded, degrading stereotypes about them abound in American society." They "are the type of 'discrete and insular minority' that meeets the . . . test for suspect classification." But "strict scrutiny" was unnecessary, for the DOD's policy did not even meet a rational relationship test. In other words, according to the court, no rational basis exists for subjecting lesbians and gay men to an expanded investigation, so any such investigation denies them the equal protection of the laws (*High Tech Gays v. Defense Indus. Sec. Clear. Off. 1987*).

Watkins v. U.S. Army 1989 presented a similar problem. Watkins admitted to a homosexual orientation when he first enlisted in the Army in 1967, but somehow was accepted and was later permitted to re-enlist. After he had served for 14 years, however, the Army refused to permit him to re-enlist again, and he went to court. The relevant Army regulation made a homosexual *orientation* unacceptable, and the Army made no effort to prove that Watkins had engaged in homosexual *conduct*.

The decision was that the Army was estopped by equitable considerations from barring re-enlistment. It had accepted Watkins originally despite his admission of a homosexual orientation and had permitted him to serve for 14 years, giving him high marks for his various qualities as a soldier. Given that record, the Army could not in fairness reverse its position. Thus Watkins could re-enlist—an outcome significant to Watkins but not contributing any enlightenment about equal treatment.

One of the justices, however, took up the question of equal treatment in a separate opinion, and a second concurred in what he said. He dismissed various earlier cases as irrelevant, including *Hardwick*, because of their focus on *conduct* rather than *orientation* or because of their focus on the due process clause and on the right to privacy rather than on the right to equal protection. He declared that classification according to *orientation* should be regarded as *suspect*, reaching this conclusion on the basis of several considerations: the history of purposeful discrimination against homosexual persons; the invidious nature of the classification—invidious because based on prejudice and inaccurate stereotypes; and the immutability of the trait.

Then the justice pointed out that a "suspect" classification cannot be justified by private bias or by appeal to an alleged social consensus that homosexuality is immoral. The classification could be justified only if it was "*necessary* to promote a *compelling* governmental interest." And the justice held that the Army's policy did not meet this test. Watkins had been a model soldier. His homosexual orientation had caused no problem. If the Army feared that emotional relationships might undermine military discipline, it should develop regulations concerning heterosexual as well as homosexual persons. Since Watkins was open about his homosexual orientation, he was not especially liable to blackmail; in any case, if blackmail was what the Army feared, it could safeguard itself more sensibly by penalizing only those gays who lied about their orientation. Thus, the justice concluded, the Army's Regulations are "constitutionally void on their face."

This separate opinion in *Watkins* became in effect the judgment of the court in *BenShalom v. Marsh 1989*. Miriam BenShalom described herself as a lesbian and was discharged from the Army Reserve solely because of her orientation; she was not accused of homosexual conduct. Again the court declared that the treatment of persons on the basis of their sexual orientation is suspect, but, as in the *High Tech Gays* case cited above, the judge considered "strict scrutiny" unnecessary, for the Army's policy failed even the mildest test: it was "not rationally related to any articulated legitimate government interest." Army regulations must be targeted at *conduct*, not simply at *orientation*.

These judgments will surely lead the Army to revise its regulations. Whether it will simply shift to a focus on conduct or drop any effort to differentiate against homosexual persons remains to be seen.

9 Municipal Services, Medical Services, and Income Support

Government performs functions relating to a variety of matters: police and fire protection; water, sewage, trash; roads and highways; libraries, parks, and playgrounds; health and welfare; housing; and others. In whatever it does, it is bound by the rule of nondiscrimination.

Although the principle is clear, problems arise. In this chapter I will focus on those relating to municipal services, medical services, and income support.

Municipal Services

The town of Shaw, Mississippi, illustrates the problem of equal treatment with respect to municipal services. A Circuit Court considered its practices in 1971 and found that it favored whites and neglected blacks.

> Nearly 98% of all homes that front on unpaved streets in Shaw are occupied by blacks. Ninety-seven percent of the homes not served by sanitary sewers are in black neighborhoods. Further, while the town has acquired a significant number of medium and high intensity mercury vapor street lighting fixtures, every one of them has been installed in white neighborhoods. The record further discloses . . . similar statistical evidence of grave disparities in both the level and kinds of services offered regarding surface water drainage, water mains, fire hydrants, and traffic control apparatus . . . . (*Hawkins v. Town of Shaw 1971*).

The court held that an intent to discriminate need not be proved. In another connection the Supreme Court later rejected this stand, but it permitted intent to be inferred from the totality of relevant circumstances, which meant that the outcome with respect to the town of Shaw could be the same. In any event, the court ordered the town to submit a plan "detailing how it proposes to cure the results of the long history of discrimination which the record reveals." In effect the court held that the distributive and redistributive functions of government are not to be exercised so as to benefit whites at the expense of, or to the neglect of, blacks.

In addition to the discriminatory arrangements and policies that the court mentioned in the Shaw case, we can imagine others. Discrimination might occur simply in decisions about locating public facilities and amenities, like parks, libraries, and fire stations. It might occur in the quality of the facilities and amenities available to those living in different parts of town. It might occur in the police protection afforded. It might occur in the allocation of burdens—most specifically, in the assessment of property for tax purposes. And it might occur in other connections.

Lineberry explores a number of possibilities in relation to San Antonio (Lineberry 1977). He notes that differential treatment may be innocent, and that results may not be a reliable indicator of discrimination. Facilities and amenities in a fixed location automatically confer different advantages and disadvantages on different persons; and what is inevitable should not be regarded as a denial of equal treatment. Moreover, the location of a park, for example, may result from a fortuitous circumstance— perhaps a bequest to the city or the presence of a river—rather than from an intent to favor one community over another. An arrangement of facilities that is equitable at one time may become less equitable as changes occur—for example, as the population of a city grows. In such circumstances, equal protection may perhaps call for the establishment of new parks or the building of branch libraries, for example, but it does not require that the city move parks and libraries periodically to keep them equally accessible to all.

Possibilities of these sorts indicate that what Lineberry calls "unpatterned inequalities" may well exist, that is, inequalities that are not systematically arranged to the advantage of one element in the population and the disadvantage of another. So far as San Antonio is concerned, Lineberry concludes that where a "patterned" differentiation exists, it is likely to be in favor of "the older, near-to-core areas" (Lineberry 1977, 125).

Results are unreliable as a test of discrimination in another way too. Suppose, for example, that one city park is obviously in worse condition than others; or suppose that the crime rate is higher in one section of the city than another. On the one hand, it is possible to argue that the city should devote a higher proportion of its resources to the poorly maintained park and assign a higher proportion of its police officers to the section with the high crime rate. On the other hand, it may be that the city is already devoting resources to the park that are proportionate to its size or proportionate to the number of users, and that differences between parks are due to differences in the amount of vandalism in the different localities; and the number of police officers assigned to the section where the crime rate is high may already be proportionate to the population served.

The question here is whether meeting needs, regardless of their nature, is the test of equal treatment, or whether the allocation of resources is the test. In the case of the vandalized park, the relevant judicial decision was that "the City has satisfied its constitutional obligations by equal input even though, because of conditions for which it is not responsible, it has not achieved the equal results it desires" (*Beal v. Lindsay* 1972).

Another possibility suggests an issue for which no clear answer has been established. Suppose that the state government permits a wealthy suburb to be separately incorporated, enabling it to maintain high quality municipal services on the basis of a low tax rate. At the same time, the adjacent city, including slums, imposes taxes at a high rate and still finds it difficult or impossible to provide minimally adequate municipal services. Does the very structure of the governmental system imply a denial of the equal protection of the laws? Is it compatible with equal protection if the governmental services received vary significantly depending on whether a person lives in the city or in the suburb? Should the suburb be required to merge with the adjacent city (Dimond 1978)?

Issues have also arisen concerning equal treatment by the police. Of course, no one is immune to arrest simply because the police failed to catch someone else who committed the same act. But suppose the law is vague—for example, permitting the arrest of anyone loitering at a bus terminal. On the basis of this law the police arrest any loiterers who look like bums. A New York court has declared such a law unconstitutional, on the ground that it permits arbitrary and discriminatory action.

I might recall that the voting rights cases described in Chapter 5 include references to racial discrimination in governmental services. Thus in *Rogers v. Lodge* the court found that Burke County, Georgia, had been "unresponsive and insensitive to the needs of the black community," and in *Thornburg v. Gingles* it spoke of the "historic

discrimination in education, housing, employment, and health services" for the blacks of North Carolina. In the voting rights cases, of
course, the solution to the problem was sought indirectly—through
assurance to the blacks of their rights of political participation—rather
than through a direct court order pertaining to governmental practices and policies.

In connection with municipal services, the handicapped were
long neglected. The Rehabilitation Act of 1973, however, included a
provision, mentioned before, specifying that no person, solely by
reason of a handicap, may be denied the benefits of or excluded from
participation in any program or activity receiving federal financial
assistance. Among other things, this has led to a judicial decision that
it is not enough if transit authorities provide special vans for the
handicapped; any new buses acquired must be equipped with
wheelchair lifts (*New York Times*, February 15, 1989, 8:4).

Medical Services

In recent decades government has increasingly become involved in
the provision of medical services, and questions concerning equal
treatment have arisen accordingly. Here the focus is on issues relating
to abortion, handicapped infants, general medical care, and the
treatment of the elderly.

Abortion

In Chapter 3 I have already discussed the question when a *person*
comes into existence and when, therefore, the entitlement to equal
protection begins. The generally prevailing position is that the
decisive moment is the moment when a live birth occurs. Since a
zygote, embryo, or fetus is not a person, the equal protection clause
of the fourteenth amendment is irrelevant to it. This position is under
attack, but it survived the Supreme Court's judgment in *Webster* in
1989.

Questions about equal treatment arise, however, when two
pregnant women are treated differently. And questions about equality of opportunity arise when comparisons are made between men
and women.

First as to the differential treatment of pregnant women. I say
"women," but the reference should include teen-age girls, for they
become pregnant too. Suppose that two teen-age girls, or two
women, are pregnant and that they are indigent. May government
pay the medical costs of the one who carries her baby to term without

also paying the costs of the one who has an abortion? You can get opposite answers to this question, depending on where you look.

The Supreme Court of California says no. It holds that once government decides to make a benefit available (such as medical care for indigent women), it faces a heavy burden of justification if it then seeks to withhold the benefit from anyone solely because of the exercise of a constitutional right, including the right to have an abortion during the first trimester. The ruling creates a presumption that if government pays the medical costs of an indigent girl or woman who carries her baby to term, it must also pay the medical costs of another who has an abortion (*Committee to Defend Reprod. Rights v. Myers 1981*).

Through the Hyde amendment relating to the Medicaid program, Congress takes the opposite stand. In the case of indigent women, Congress is willing to have Medicaid funds used to pay the costs of childbirth, but (with rare exceptions) not to pay the costs of an abortion. A Circuit Court held that this violates the equal protection guarantee in that the differentiation serves no legitimate governmental interest, but the Supreme Court overrode the judgment, pointing to the governmental interest in the potentiality of life. "[A]lthough government may not place obstacles in the path of a woman's exercise of her freedom of choice, it need not remove those not of its own creation" (*Harris v. McRae 1980*).

In dissent, Justice Marshall took a stand like that of the California court. Further, he claimed that, in the case of an indigent woman, the "denial of a Medicaid-funded abortion is equivalent to denial of legal abortion altogether," for she is ordinarily unable to pay the costs. He pointed out that the impact on the life and health of a poor woman might be devastating.

The question takes on a different aspect if the comparison is not simply between different indigent women but also between women and men and if the concern is not simply for equal treatment but also for equality of opportunity (Calabresi 1985, 99-106). Think of the fact that nature discriminates against girls and women. Its arrangements for reproduction impose special burdens on them, with no counterpart for boys and men. Pregnancy brings the girl or woman discomfort and illness. It saps her energy. It interferes either with her schooling and education or with her capacity to work, probably affecting her whole career. It impedes her pursuit of happiness while boys and men enjoy their freedom. It even jeopardizes her health and well-being on a long term basis. Moreover, if she gives birth, she then faces the additional burden of caring for and supporting her child, a burden that is all the more onerous if she is a single parent.

The traditional response to the above is a shrug: that's the way it is. But a different response is possible, based on the proposition that girls and women should have equality of opportunity along with boys and men. In other words, they should be able to escape the special burdens of pregnancy. The affluent may be able to arrange this on their own, though government should be willing to provide them with information that might be helpful and to permit them to have an abortion, if they pay for it, in hospitals and other facilities enjoying governmental support. The indigent need more than information; and if government is willing to pay the costs of childbirth it should also be willing to pay the costs of those who want to free themselves at an earlier point from the disadvantage under which they live. Moreover, the promotion of equality of opportunity for the indigent has the added advantage of preventing the development of later problems associated with children who live in poverty and, perhaps, neglect.

Faced with considerations such as these, you need to choose between conflicting values. You balance off your concern for the potential baby with your concern for the well-being and equality of opportunity of the potential mother. As current controversy attests, the choice is not an easy one; and it may shift, depending on whether abortion is sought early or late in a pregnancy.

Handicapped Infants

Defective infants—for example, infants with Down's syndrome—are born in increasing numbers. State law, including the common law, has traditionally fixed the rules to be followed in treating them—the central principle being that parents must provide the medically necessary care (Robertson 1986, 218). Nevertheless, given certain sorts of severe defects, the tendency has been for parents and medical personnel to withhold treatment and allow the infant to die.

The federal government entered the picture in 1973 when Congress enacted the Rehabilitation Act mentioned above. The act specifies that hospitals and programs in receipt of federal funds must not discriminate against handicapped persons who are "otherwise qualified" for medical care—that is, qualified apart from the handicap itself. Defective infants count as handicapped persons. Congress supplemented its rule in 1984, requiring states receiving federal money in connection with child abuse programs to prevent the withholding or withdrawal of medically indicated care from any child.

These rules call for interpretation in individual cases, and various principles are relevant. On the one hand, treatment that would be futile or that simply prolongs the process of dying is not required. On the other hand, treatment that promises to be "medically beneficial" must be provided. The "best interests" of the child must be served—determined, presumably, by the answer to the question whether such life as the child has before him is destined to be so full of pain and suffering that he is better off dead (Robertson 1986, 226).

Such principles are helpful, of course, but in many cases they do not point clearly to the course of action that ought to be pursued. Given the federal legislation, medical and hospital personnel are likely to hesitate about playing a crucial role in a decision to withhold or minimize treatment. Parents with an afflicted infant are then likely to find themselves in an excruciatingly difficult position. If they refuse consent to treatment for their infant, they are answerable to state law—though the dominant tradition is to respect their judgment; prosecutions have been rare (Elias and Annas 1987, 168-87; *Bowen v. American Hospital Assn. 1986*). If they call for treatment, they may be opening themselves and their other children to financial and other burdens that will blight their lives (Smith 1984, 725, 729).

I have put the focus here on infants, but should recognize that comparable problems arise with respect to older persons who, perhaps as a result of an accident, are left permanently unconscious and in a vegetative state, though not brain dead.

General Medical Care

The international Covenant on Social, Economic, and Cultural Rights goes to the limit in calling for equal treatment with respect to medical care, speaking of "the right of everyone to the enjoyment of the highest attainable standard of physical and mental health."

A century ago, or even 50 years ago, this principle would have raised fewer questions, for what health services could do was limited. But the advancements of recent decades, including the possibility of heart and other transplants, make the principle portentous. The possibility of keeping people alive and the costs of doing so suggest the danger of an absurd extreme, in which so high a proportion of the resources of the country are devoted to health that other values are relatively neglected.

The tendency to put health care in a special category accentuates the problem. With respect to food and shelter, the general presumption is that people will shift for themselves and accept different resulting standards. Perhaps government stands by with a "safety net," but it does not promise a "decent minimum," let alone "the highest attainable standard." The presumption of self-reliance, implying different standards, is not so generally accepted with respect to medical care, and one of the puzzles is why this should be so.

The problem about "the highest attainable standard" is reduced if we think of health care in a restricted sense, excluding, for example, cosmetic surgery and sessions with a psychiatrist. And the problem is further reduced by the fact that, in many circumstances, nothing less than "the highest attainable standard" of health care offers a promise of success. The idea of a "decent minimum" may have little relevance.

Nevertheless, the reasons for the special concern for health care remain puzzling. Daniels seeks to explain it in terms of what he calls a social "guarantee" of equality of opportunity (Daniels 1985, 38-39, 54). Although the word *guarantee* is much too strong, the explanation has merit. A Ford Foundation report on the promotion of "the common good" plays on the same thought: "We believe in giving people a fair chance to succeed." Sick people do not have that chance. And those who die in infancy do not have that chance. It is absurd to speak of equality of opportunity, or a fair chance, for black infants when their mortality rate is twice that of white infants (Ford Foundation 1989, 11). At the same time, it is odd to explain and justify health care for the elderly in terms of equality of opportunity.

Other considerations no doubt help explain the special concern for health care. The principle is already accepted that government should provide aid to persons who are incapable of supporting themselves—dependent children, the disabled, the elderly—and it is not much of an extension of that principle to put those in need of medical care in the same category, however unjustified this is in particular cases. Moreover, the view that life is precious and that death is to be resisted makes it easy to assume that money (especially other people's money?) should be no object when a life is at stake, even though the money spent could save the lives of more (unidentified) people if used in another way.

Perhaps the special concern for health care is due in part also to the assumption that the individual bears no responsibility for creating the need—that just as accidents are to be expected in the work place, with the attendant costs paid by the employer, so are medical needs to be expected as an aspect of life in society, with society paying the costs. The frailty of this view is suggested by the obvious fact that some individuals create medical needs by the choices that they make and the life style they pursue. Should a government dedicated to the principles of equal treatment and equality of opportunity have to bear the medical costs of the motorcyclist who suffers brain damage in an accident, of the smoker who gets lung cancer, or the intravenous drug user who gets AIDS from one of his needles?

Those appalled by the potential costs of assuring the universal enjoyment of the highest attainable standard of health care do not necessarily want government to wash its hands of the problem. Instead they tend to favor programs that are selective about the groups to serve or the needs to meet, arguing that selection is reasonable and thus not a denial of the equal protection of the laws.

In the United States the federal health program is of this selective sort. Medicare provides for those over 65 and the permanently disabled, and Medicaid provides for the indigent, including indigent pregnant women, the babies of indigent mothers, and those covered by the AFDC program. Interestingly enough, Congress also extended Medicare to persons under 65 in need of a kidney transplant or renal dialysis (Caplan 1981, 488-503; Kirby 1986, 7-21). The necessary equipment could be produced, and Congress decided that it should be produced, thus avoiding the problems about equal treatment that would be involved if some were selected for dialysis and others left to die.

A special measure for those needing dialysis is presumably compatible with the equal protection requirement in that Congress is free to take one step at a time; it is not obliged to refrain from acting simply because it cannot solve all problems at once. But still a question about the wisdom of the special measure, if not about its constitutionality, is legitimate. On the average, dialysis extends life for about five years, and even with it, the quality of life is impaired (Callahan 1987, 143).

No similar solution is in sight for those who need a heart transplant. Apparently thirty or more people are in line for each heart that becomes available (Merrikin and Overcast 1985, 8).

The Elderly

The problem of health care for the elderly at public expense is especially difficult, for the financial burden is great and the social returns are relatively meager. The problem leads Califano to ask rhetorically whether "it make sense to allocate 30 percent of our multibillion-dollar Medicare bill to high-tech medical services for those who have less than a year to live" (Califano 1986, 182). And it led the governor of Colorado to comment that "we're heading for the day when they can keep us alive long past when our quality of life is gone with transplants and high-technology medicine." His view was that the very ill elderly "have a duty to die and get out of the way" (Quoted by Califano 1986, 182).

In a book on *Setting Limits. Medical Goals in an Aging Society* (1987), Callahan argues that when the taxpayers' money is being spent

> medicine should be used not for the further extension of the life of the aged, but only for the full achievement of a natural and fitting life span and thereafter for the relief of suffering. . . . There will be better ways in the future to spend our money than on indefinitely extending the life of the elderly (p. 53).

Callahan defines a "natural life span" as one "in which life's possibilities have on the whole been achieved and after which death may be understood as a sad, but nonetheless relatively acceptable event" (p. 66). And he says that life's possibilities are normally achieved by the late 70s or early 80s.

Callahan does not say how to decide whether a "natural life span" has been reached. Presumably it would have to be done individually in the light of each person's prognosis, onerous as it would be to handle the problem in this way. To rely on life expectancy tables would surely be to deny the equal protection of the laws. Women tend to live longer than men; their life expectancy in 1984 was calculated at 78 years in comparison with 71 for men. Whites tend to live longer than blacks: 75 for whites in 1984 and 70 for blacks. People in some states tend to live longer than people in others: 77 for those in Hawaii, and 72 for those in Louisiana. And so on.

In connection with pension plans the Supreme Court has already ruled that equal treatment is denied if premiums and payments are adjusted to the different life expectancies of men and women; this discriminates as to sex. The corollary is that any reliance on life expectancy tables in terminating life-extending medical care would be discriminatory too. So the kind of judgment for which Callahan calls would have to be personal to the individual. Such judgments are already being made, of course. But Callahan obviously proposes an earlier cut-off point than is now the norm.

Income Support

Aid to families with dependent children (AFDC) is one of the major income support programs. Perhaps the most notorious of the issues arising in connection with this program concerns Alabama. Its practice was to calculate the needs of various categories of people on welfare, and then to decide what percentage of the needs it could meet. In the period leading up to the court judgment on the matter, it regularly met substantially all of the recognized need of the elderly but never more than 55 percent of the need of families with dependent children.

The crucial underlying fact was that most of the elderly were white, whereas most of the families with dependent children were black. The court found that this racial difference figured explicitly and purposefully in the decision about the allocation of funds, and the court therefore ruled that Alabama was denying the equal protection of the laws (*Whitfield v. Oliver 1975*).

A policy followed in Maryland once raised a different kind of issue. Maryland was willing that income support should increase with the number of children in a family, but it made the increase smaller with each additional child and fixed a maximum beyond which it would not go. Thus the income support attributable to child number one might be, say $50, and the income support attributable to child number seven might be zero. Among other things, Maryland wanted to avoid a situation in which a family living on AFDC did better than a family with a working breadwinner. The obvious question is whether such a policy should be deemed to deny the equal protection of the laws.

From one point of view discrimination was obvious: child number one got $50 and child number seven got zero. If you assume that the support was intended for the children individually, then only one conclusion is possible. Moreover, you can add the warning that Maryland's policy tended to subvert the family, encouraging parents to farm "excess" children out to relatives, who would then claim them as dependents and perhaps get aid accordingly. Two dissenting justices took this view.

From another point of view, Maryland's classification of families was not based on a "suspect" criterion and the effort to avoid making children more attractive than work as a source of income was reasonable. Since the policy was thus "rationally based" and was not invidious, it did not violate the equal protection requirement. This is the view that the Supreme Court took. It quoted a principle that it had endorsed earlier: "A statutory discrimination will not be set aside if any state of facts reasonably may be conceived to justify it" (*Dandridge v. Williams 1970*).

States differ considerably in the size of their monthly AFDC payments. The range in 1989 was from $118 in Alabama to $740 in Alaska for a mother and two children who were without other income. Illinois provided $342 and Wisconsin $517. According to the governor of Wisconsin, this induced poor people, mostly from

Chicago's inner city, to move to Wisconsin, so in 1989 he proposed a deterrent: for three months after their arrival their benefits would be reduced by 25 percent.

You be the judge whether the Supreme Court would approve this plan. The Court has already set two major precedents. One concerns Connecticut, which completely denied welfare assistance for the first year of residence. The Court saw this measure as penalizing the right to travel. Moreover, it classified the right to travel as "fundamental," which meant that measures impinging on it could be justified only by a "compelling governmental interest." And it saw no governmental interest that was sufficiently compelling to justify the year-long denial of welfare assistance (*Shapiro v. Thompson 1969*).

The other main precedent concerns Arizona, in which each county provides free medical care to indigents, but, except for emergencies, only after they have resided in the county for a year. Again the Court held that "the conservation of the taxpayers' purse is simply not a sufficient state interest to sustain a durational residence requirement which, in effect, severely penalizes exercise of the right to freely migrate and settle in another state" (*Memorial Hospital v. Maricopa County 1974*).

Wisconsin's proposed rule is less severe than either Connecticut's or Arizona's. Wisconsin would not deny welfare payments, but only reduce them; and the period of reduced payments would be limited to three months. Would this deny the equal protection of the laws?

Two other questions have a narrower reach:

May welfare benefits be given only to citizens, to the exclusion of resident aliens? The courts say no. The fourteenth amendment assures equal protection not to citizens but to persons. Moreover, aliens pay taxes, perhaps serve in the armed forces, and perhaps make other social contributions (*Graham v. Richardson 1971*).

Is it permissible to deny food stamps to persons (hippies?) simply because they live in the same house without being related to each other? Again the answer is no. And in calculating entitlements to social security, it is impermissible to impose a dependency test on widowers that does not also apply to widows.

A Note on Residence Requirements

Is it a denial of equal protection for a state university to fix a durational residence requirement in connection with tuition fees? In a sense the question is irrelevant to the present chapter. I mention it because of the analogy with residence requirements in connection with eligibility for welfare and health care.

It has long been settled that a state university may fix tuition fees at a higher level for nonresident students than for residents. The right to travel into the state is not really the issue, and education is not a fundamental right. Thus the state need only establish a rational relationship between the differentiation and a legitimate state interest. It can do this easily, for residents have borne a greater financial burden in developing and maintaining the university. It is therefore reasonable to even out the costs somewhat by charging nonresidents higher tuition fees (*Starns v. Malkerson 1970*).

A different problem arises when the person charged at the nonresident rate claims to have become a resident. Suppose, for example, that although he has been nonresident, he has married a resident and has moved into the state expecting to reside there indefinitely. He registers as a voter in the state, gets the state's license plates on a car, and obtains a driver's license in the state. But the law establishes an irrebuttable presumption that he is a nonresident for tuition purposes unless he has lived in the state for at least a year.

The courts have stricken down the rule that the presumption is irrebuttable. The university must fix criteria for judging a claim of bona fide residence, and the student who meets them may not be charged at the rate for nonresidents even if he has just moved into the state (*Vlandis v. Kline 1973*).

10   Administering Justice

Various questions concerning equal treatment arise in connection with the administration of justice. The most significant of them relate to the selection of judges, special concessions to the poor, the composition of juries, the language problem, and evenhandedness in the enforcement of law.

The Selection of Judges

In the federal judicial system, the president appoints the judges. In the states, the governor may appoint or the voters may elect.

Whatever the procedure, the tradition has been that judges would be white men. This seemed so natural that it was not thought of as discriminatory; but the tradition is being repudiated. The civil rights movement of the 1960s included a demand that minority persons and women be appointed and elected to the bench, and more and more of them are in fact serving throughout the federal and state judicial systems. President Johnson appointed a black to the Supreme Court, and President Reagan appointed a woman.

The prevailing view is that districts in which judges are elected need not conform to the equal population principle but that in other respects the election of judges must occur according to the same rules that apply to other elections. The most common complaint is that at-large elections are used in such a way as to prevent the election of black judges, and where this complaint is established the courts have been requiring change (*Chisom v. Edwards 1988a* and *1988b; Clark v. Edwards 1988; Martin v. Mabus 1988*). Georgia has been violating the

Voting Rights Act by failing to observe its pre-clearance requirement with respect to judicial elections, and a federal district court has ordered it to seek clearance for the many changes it has put into effect since 1965 (*New York Times*, 12/6/89, 15:1).

Equal Justice and the Poor

Equal justice is the general ideal, but the rich have obvious advantages over the poor. The reactions of government vary depending on whether criminal or civil law is involved.

The sixth amendment says that in all criminal prosecutions the accused shall enjoy the right to the assistance of counsel. In 1790 Congress provided that, in capital cases and on the request of the defendant, government must supply counsel, but otherwise through most of American history the provision was interpreted to mean simply that an accused person was free to obtain the assistance of counsel if he could and free to have the counsel represent him in court. With the exception indicated, no special effort was made to help the poor.

The courts have taken a series of steps away from the historic view, beginning in 1932. The culminating statement—by the Supreme Court in 1963—is that "in our adversary system of criminal justice, any person hailed into court, who is too poor to hire a lawyer, cannot be assured a fair trial unless counsel is provided for him" (*Gideon v. Wainwright 1963*). In particular, no one may be imprisoned unless ("absent a knowing and intelligent waiver") he is represented by counsel at his trial (*Argersinger v. Hamlin 1972*). The theory is that since the government takes the initiative in criminal cases, putting the accused in jeopardy, it is under a special obligation to see to it that the judicial proceedings are fair. Even so, of course, the rich may be able to hire more expensive counsel than the court provides for the poor.

The governing principles are less clear in civil suits. In some kinds of cases government makes concessions for the benefit of the poor and in other kinds it does not.

One of the leading cases concerns divorce, and more particularly Connecticut's requirement that anyone seeking divorce must pay a filing fee of $60 in order to get his case considered. Connecticut was adamant about the matter, refusing to waive the fee for indigents, but the Supreme Court overrode its position. One of the grounds that the Supreme Court cited for its action was that the monopoly position of the state with respect to divorce put it under a special obligation to see to it that the poor were not denied effective access (*Boddie v. Connecticut 1971*).

The outcome was different when a debtor seeking to be declared bankrupt was unable to pay a filing fee. The reasoning was that in this kind of case the state did not have a monopoly; bankruptcy was "not the only method available to a debtor for the adjustment of his legal relationship with his creditors." Thus the state was under no obligation to waive the filing fee—even if, as a dissenting justice pointed out, a refusal to waive it meant that a person might be too poor to go bankrupt (*United States v. Kras 1973*).

Jury Service

As in so many respects where equal treatment is concerned, the general principles relating to jury service are agreed, but issues arise concerning their implementation.

Congress stated the principles in the Jury Selection and Service Act of 1968. Both grand and petit juries are to be selected at random from a fair cross section of the community in which the court convenes; and no citizen is to be excluded on account of race, color, religion, sex, national origin, or economic status.

A judgment by a Mississippi court in 1966 suggests the reason why Congress acted. The court upheld the exclusion of women from juries, declaring that "the legislature has the right to exclude [them] so that they may continue their service as mothers, wives, and homemakers, and so to protect them from the filth, obscenity, and obnoxious atmosphere that so often pervades a courtroom during a jury trial" (*State v. Hall 1966*).

Problems concerning jury service by women continued after the adoption of the federal law. A Louisiana law, for example, provided that no woman should be selected for jury service unless she had previously filed a written declaration of her desire to serve. The result was that, as a rule, few women if any were named on the lists from which juries were selected. On this basis, the losing party in a 1972 trial appealed, and the Supreme Court upheld the appeal. The judgment was that, although defendants are not entitled to a jury of any particular composition, the list from which members are selected "must not systematically exclude distinctive groups in the community and thereby fail to be reasonably representative thereof" (*Taylor v. Louisiana 1975*).

In addition to problems concerning the list from which jurors are selected, others concern the process of selection. Those who seek to be excused from jury duty are likely to be accommodated, with the result that the representative character of the jury may be reduced. More serious are the possible results of the rule that attorneys on both sides may challenge those called up as potential jurors, seeking to bar their selection. The attorneys can challenge any number "for cause," and can challenge others—usually a limited number—peremptorily. A "for cause" challenge prevails only if the judge agrees that it is justified, but the very idea of a peremptory challenge is that it need not be justified to the judge or anyone else. It may be arbitrary.

But what if an attorney employs his peremptory challenges in such a way as to exclude blacks or Hispanics or women? This particular kind of arbitrariness was not envisaged when the idea of peremptory challenges originally developed in British history, but it clearly occurs. Thus a conflict exists. On the one side is the common law rule and tradition concerning peremptory challenges, and on the other side is the principle that no one is to be excluded from jury service simply on the basis of characteristics such as race, sex, or national origin. To permit a prosecuting attorney to use his peremptory challenges to obtain an all-white jury, for example, is to permit a result that would be unconstitutional if attempted on an open and avowed basis.

The problem is complicated by the likelihood that the prosecuting attorney will deny racism, sexism, or any other prohibited motive. If in a considerable number of successive cases he regularly ends up with few if any blacks or Hispanics or women on his juries, it becomes statistically clear that his denial is hypocritical, but how can anyone prove that prohibited motives influence what happens in any one case? In any one case it is at least possible that the attorney's peremptory challenge was made for acceptable reasons.

The Supreme Court faced the problem in 1965 (*Swain v. Alabama 1965*). Swain was black, convicted by an all-white jury of raping a white woman. Eight blacks had been on the list of potential jurors, but two of them were excused and the other six were excluded by peremptories. No black had served on a petit jury in the county involved (Talladega County, Alabama) since 1950. Nevertheless, the court refused to take the view that Swain was denied the equal protection of the laws. "A defendant in a criminal case is not constitutionally entitled to demand a proportionate number of his race on the jury which tries him . . . ."

The judgment has been much criticized, and a number of state courts have taken a different position. In 1984 a Circuit Court, hearing a comparable case, deferred to the Swain decision in so far as the equal protection clause is concerned, but went ahead to act differently on the basis of the requirement in the sixth amendment that trials occur before impartial juries. It granted that the defendant in a criminal trial "has no right to a petit jury of any particular composition," but it insisted that the state must create and maintain the possibility that the jury will be a fair cross section of the community. This possibility, it said, is blighted if "the prosecutor is allowed arbitrarily to remove entire segments of the panel . . . ."

The judgment was that when a prosecuting attorney makes peremptories in such a way as to create a presumption of a racial motivation, the state must be asked to rebut the presumption, and that if the state fails to do so a mistrial must be declared, with a new jury selected from a new panel for a second trial (*McCray v. Adams 1984*; cf., Van Dyke 1977).

The Language Problem

Theoretically it is possible to ignore race and sex in connection with most of the actions and policies of government, but it is not possible to ignore language; and where different languages are spoken, one language group is bound to be disadvantaged.

In the United States, of course, English is the dominant language, which necessarily implies disadvantage for those with a different mother tongue. Within government, English is ordinarily the language of the work place and the language in which people are served. English is thus a bona fide occupational qualification (bfoq) for most government jobs, and is the language in which federal civil service examinations are given.

For the most part, the primacy of English is accepted as natural and inevitable. To give equal status to all languages spoken in the country would be impossibly expensive; and even to put Spanish alone on a par with English would be unduly burdensome in most parts of the country—at least in the eyes of almost all of those who speak English. This is another of the many instances in which a balancing of values occurs, with the meaning of equal treatment adjusted to prevailing beliefs about the wise use of resources. Many countries with larger language minorities (Canada, for example) have chosen to interpret the requirements of equal treatment differently.

Nevertheless, although English is dominant in the United States, government uses languages other than English in some circumstances. In New Mexico, for example, the rule is that if 75 percent or more of the population served by a local government speak the same language, be it Spanish or English, certain documents are printed solely in that language; otherwise, they are printed in both. In Chapter 5 I have already noted the requirement that elections must be bilingual when the minority language group reaches a certain size.

Judicial processes are in a special category, so far as language is concerned. Court proceedings occur in English, but federal law requires that in any action initiated by the United States judicial authorities must provide the services of a translator when necessary. The rule applies to criminal proceedings and to hearings before immigration judges considering the claims of those who seek political asylum.

The law of most states includes a comparable rule. New York City has 118 full time Spanish-language court interpreters. County courts in the Los Angeles area are said to employ 400 translators, handling 80 languages and dialects (*New York Times* 8/11/87, 1:4). Wherever those who speak a minority language are numerous the usual practice is to make informal adjustments so that they can obtain the more vital governmental services in a language that they understand.

In recent years language has become more of an issue. Sixteen states now name English as their official language (Schmidt 1989; cf. Official English 1987, 1345-62). Arizona became one of the sixteen in 1988. Among other things, its new constitutional amendment specifies that "this State and all political subdivisions of this State shall act in English and in no other language."

The statement looks sweeping, but the Attorney-General of Arizona interprets it narrowly. He holds that the word *act* "applies only to official acts of government, and not to every act of every government official or employee." Thus, he says, governmental services may be extended to people in a language that they understand (Corbin 1989).

Further, the Arizona amendment includes various exceptions to the English-only rule, including a stipulation that the state shall comply with federal law. And the Attorney-General, construes federal law to require the use of a language other than English when this is "reasonably needed to provide governmental services fairly and effectively without adversely impacting an ethnic/linguistic group." He cites Title VI of the Civil Rights Act of 1964, providing that no person, on the ground of national origin, may be subjected to discrimination under any program or activity receiving Federal financial assistance; and he cites the equal protection clause of the federal and state constitutions.

The general conclusion of the Arizona Attorney-General is that, although the amendment requires that "official acts of government" be in English, "it does not prohibit the use of languages other than English that are reasonably necessary to facilitate the day-to-day operation of government." The Attorney-General did not spell out the implications for the administration of justice. Presumably, languages other than English may be used as necessary in judicial proceedings—and must be used in some cases to assure the equal protection of the laws—even though the final judgment of the court must be in English.

Having given its final judgment in English, could the court publish a Spanish translation without violating the requirement that it "act in English and in no other language?"

Evenhanded Laws and Evenhanded Law Enforcement

Where the administration of justice is concerned, the law itself is sometimes discriminatory. Thus an Oklahoma law once provided for the sterilization of "habitual criminals," but excepted (among others) those convicted of embezzlement. The law reflected class bias in favor of those guilty of white-collar crimes; and a court struck it down. Similarly, courts have stricken down laws that provided for the differential sentencing of men and women guilty of the same offense—the bias usually being against women (Babcock et al. 1975, 120, 128, 932-36).

The police are sometimes guilty of discrimination. Differentiation of a sort is of course inevitable, for the police cannot be expected to catch literally everyone who breaks the law. But discrimination is indicated if the police establish a pattern and practice of arresting only or mainly the members of one cognizable group (blacks, for example) and ignoring the infractions of others.

Prosecutors and juries are sometimes guilty of discriminating. Prosecutors must decide whether to prosecute, whether to plea bargain, and what kinds of bargains to accept. Juries must decide not only whether the accused is guilty but also, in most jurisdictions, what the sentence should be. Even within the same state many different prosecutors and many different juries make the decisions, and over the United States as a whole the numbers who make them are vastly greater. Judgments and choices are bound to differ. Of course, cases differ too, but the similarities are often great enough to leave no doubt that unjustifiable differentiation occurs. The system makes this virtually inevitable.

The Inter-American Commission on Human Rights seized on this fact in criticizing the arbitrariness with which the death sentence is imposed in the United States, resulting, it said, in inequality before the law, contrary to the American Declaration of the Rights and Duties of Man (Inter-American Commission . . ., Annual Report 1986-7, 173).

The arbitrary differences between sentences imposed at both the federal and the state level have been getting increased attention. The

United States Sentencing Commission, established by Congress, has been issuing guidelines for the federal courts to follow in sentencing those convicted of crime. So far as the states are concerned, scholars have been drawing attention to arbitrary differences between sentences imposed, and in some instances those differences have led to action in the federal courts.

A case concerning Georgia led to a Supreme Court decision in 1972. The nine justices split badly, writing nine different opinions. The theme on which five of them came closest to agreeing was that the courts of Georgia imposed the death penalty in an arbitrary and discriminatory manner. As one of the justices put it, Georgia's statutes, which left discretion to juries, "are pregnant with discrimination" (*Furman v. Georgia 1972*). And the finding was that since the sentencing procedures "created a substantial risk that [the death penalty] would be inflicted in an arbitrary and capricious manner," it must not be imposed (*Gregg v. Georgia 1976*).

Subsequently Georgia adopted guidelines for juries to follow in imposing that penalty and gave the state Supreme Court the job of overseeing adherence to the guidelines.

Nevertheless, the problem did not go away. Facing another case in 1987—the McCleskey case—the Supreme Court considered a study by David C. Baldus and others, based on over 2000 murder trials that occurred in Georgia during the 1970s. According to the court's summary of the Baldus findings,

> prosecutors sought the death penalty in 70% of the cases involving black defendants and white victims; 32% of the cases involving white defendants and white victims; 15% of the cases involving black defendants and black victims; and 19% of the cases involving white defendants and black victims. . . . The death penalty was assessed in 22% of the cases involving black defendants and white victims; 8% of the cases involving white defendants and white victims; 1% of the cases involving black defendants and black victims; and 3% of the cases involving white defendants and black victims (*McCleskey v. Kemp 1987*, 1763. Cf., Baldus, Pulaski, and Woodworth, 1986).

More generally, the finding of the study, as summarized by a dissenting justice, was that "blacks who kill whites are sentenced to death at nearly 22 times the rate of blacks who kill blacks, and more than 7 times the rate of whites who kill blacks."

In the McCleskey case, however, the Supreme Court refused to set the death sentence aside. Between the two cases it had taken the stand that "proof of racially discriminatory intent or purpose is required to show a violation of the Equal Protection Clause" (*Arlington Heights v. Metropolitan Housing Corp. 1977*), and it maintained that stand in relation to the prosecution and sentencing of those facing a possible death sentence.

But how do you prove that a prosecutor or a jury was influenced by an intent or purpose to discriminate? It may be possible to do it in rare instances, of course, but in the main the kind of bias that influences prosecutors and juries seems to stem from subconscious attitudes and inclinations, not from conscious intent (Cf., Gross and Mauro 1984, 108-9). In any event, statistics derived from a large number of cases cannot establish an intent or purpose to discriminate in any one case, especially since the composition of the jury differs for every case.

The Court acknowledged that its refusal to be guided by statistical evidence concerning the death penalty seemed inconsistent with its acceptance of such evidence with respect to peremptories, but it distinguished between the two kinds of cases. Peremptory challenges, when they are at issue, have presumably occurred openly, thus making exclusive reliance on statistical evidence unnecessary. Moreover, in the case of peremptories, the state may be asked to rebut the charge that they were based on race, which is scarcely feasible in connection with the decision of a jury. Thus the court allowed McCleskey's death penalty to stand.

> Because discretion is essential to the criminal justice process, we would demand exceptionally clear proof before we would infer that the discretion has been abused. The unique nature of the decisions at issue in this case also counsels against adopting such an inference from the disparities indicated by the Baldus study. Accordingly, we hold that the Baldus study is clearly insufficient to support an inference that any of the decisionmakers in McCleskey's case acted with discriminatory purpose.

Thus in connection with prosecuting and sentencing, the problem of systemic bias on the basis of race is unresolved.

If systemic bias operates in connection with the death penalty where race is involved—and the Baldus study shows that in Georgia it clearly does—it presumably also operates in connection with crimes that call for lesser penalties (Cf. Gordon 1984).

11   Taxing and Spending

Whenever government taxes or spends, the question is almost automatic whether it is meting out equal treatment. The object in this chapter is to identify and appraise the rules and principles that have developed in response to this question.

Earlier chapters have touched on questions that are relevant again here. The courts have stricken down the poll tax because it tended to exclude the poor—notably the blacks—from the political process, and they have stricken down features of income support programs that involved racial discrimination. Further, as noted in the preceding chapter, they have seen to it that certain concessions relating to money are made to poor persons involved in judicial processes. Nevertheless, although the subject has come up in earlier chapters, interesting questions remain.

The Irrelevance of Equal Treatment to Major Policies

Many of the policies of government are of such a nature that the requirement of equal treatment is regarded as irrelevant—whether it should be or not. Either no explicit classification occurs or the classification fails to direct attention to problems of equal treatment.

When government builds a highway, for example, or sets aside land for a park, you know that some people will derive more benefit than others; and the same is true if government operates a city bus service, or supports a university, or appropriates money to the National Institutes of Health, or involves itself in dozens of other sorts of activities. If discriminatory intent influences the choices, a violation of equal treatment occurs, but otherwise the question of equal treatment is unlikely even to be raised. The rule that government shall not deny the equal protection of the laws does not necessarily mean it must assure an equal enjoyment of benefits.

Even when government provides for classification and differentiation, the question of equal treatment, if it is raised at all, is likely to be raised only within the framework that the government itself fixes and not outside that framework. Think, for example, of the legislation that Congress has adopted to meet the needs of two sets of persons: the elderly, and children living in poverty. In each case classification occurs, but the elderly are treated in one set of actions and the children in another. The two groups do not fall within the same framework. The question might be raised whether one elderly person gets equal treatment as compared to another elderly person, or whether one child gets equal treatment as compared to another child, but prevailing principles do not lead to the question whether children get equal treatment as compared to the elderly.

To put the same thought in other words, the requirement that government shall not deny the equal protection of the laws suggests the question: equal in comparison with whom? The common answer is: equal in comparison with those similarly situated. But who count as "similarly situated?" As noted in Chapter 2, whoever answers the question usually has leeway for choice. Children and the elderly are similarly situated in some respects but not in others. On the one hand, those in both categories are ordinarily dependent for their livelihood on something other than their current earnings; and in the absence of income support, a sizable portion of those in both categories would live in poverty. On the other hand, the elderly differ in that they have working lives behind them, during which they paid into social security. And the presumption is that children have parents who can support them—although this is in fact by no means always true. Whatever you think the judgment ought to be, the elderly and children are not ordinarily classified together.

A comparable question can be asked concerning manufacturers and consumers. They may be similarly situtated in that a tariff has a financial effect on both of them, but they are differently situated in that one gains and the other loses. Again it is the second consideration that prevails—if it is consciously thought of at all. No court has ever set a tariff aside because it denies the equal protection of the laws.

The failure to make certain comparisons is sometimes difficult to explain or justify, suggesting that government might give broader application to the equal protection clause in the future.

Sometimes the explanation is simply that those with political clout get what they want; it is not their intent to discriminate against others but rather to obtain what is desirable for themselves. Thus the elderly get more attention than children, and thus manufacturers get tariffs adopted regardless of the interests of consumers. Sometimes the explanation of the failure to think in terms of equal treatment is suggested by the following statement of the Supreme Court:

> [W]e are guided by the familiar principles that "a statute is not invalid under the Constitution because it might have gone farther than it did," . . . that a legislature need not "strike at all evils at the same time," . . . and that "reform may take one step at a time, addressing itself to the phases of the problem which seems most acute to the legislative mind" (*Katzenbach v. Morgan 1966*).

In other words, a legislature does not have to do everything at once. Even if there is no visible prospect that poor children will come to be treated as well as the elderly, the possibility is there, and that is enough. Similarly, if the farmer and merchant are treated differently, or the manufacturer and consumer, you assume that the legislature may rectify the situation some time in the future. The historical record gives no basis for expecting the courts to provide a remedy. They are not asked to tot up a comprehensive score so as to judge the net effects of numerous pieces of legislation on different groups or classes.

Deference to Legislatures

The quotation appearing above is among the indications that the courts are deferential to legislatures where taxing and spending are concerned. I have not seen a comprehensive statement of the reasons, but think they are fairly obvious. One of them is surely the desire of the courts to avoid being flooded with complaints. The burdens and benefits of governmental taxing and spending are rarely the same for all. If the courts were to welcome complaints about unequal treatment, they would risk being asked to do over again a high proportion of the work that the legislature has already done. They decline to do this, sometimes expressing a faith that the legislature is more familiar with the relevant circumstances (Hartman 1981, 134). In any event, if they interfered on any extensive scale, they would be usurping functions that democracy assigns to the elected representatives of the people.

Numerous pronouncements of the courts express the principle of judicial deference or restraint. For example, the Supreme Court has said, with reference to taxation, that the presumption of constitutionality can be overcome only by the most explicit demonstration that a classification is hostile and oppressive discrimination against particular persons and classes. . . . No scheme of taxation . . . has yet been devised which is free of all discriminatory impact. In such a complex arena in which no perfect alternatives exist, the Court does well not to impose too rigorous a standard of scrutiny lest all local fiscal schemes become subjects of criticism under the Equal Protection Clause (*San Antonio School District v. Rodriguez 1973*).

And in another case the Court took a similar stand:

When local economic regulation is challenged solely as violating the Equal Protection Clause, this Court consistently defers to legislative determinations as to the desirability of particular statutory discriminations. . . . Unless a classification trammels fundamental personal rights or is drawn upon inherently suspect distinctions such as race, religion, or alienage, our decisions presume the constitutionality of the statutory discriminations and require only that the classification challenged be rationally related to a legitimate state interest (*New Orleans v. Dukes 1976*).

The court spoke of *Morey v. Doud* (1957) as "the only case in the last half century to invalidate a wholly economic regulation solely on equal protection grounds." And, declaring the *Morey* decision wrong, the Court overruled it.

The courts sometimes refer to the "purpose" that is pursued rather than to the "interest," asking whether the purpose is legitimate. In the present context these words—along with the word *values*, which I tend to use—are synonyms.

The Supreme Court has not been clear and consistent on the question whether the legislature must itself identify the allegedly legitimate purpose(s) being pursued. One extreme is expressed in the statement that "it has long been settled that classification, though discriminatory, is not arbitrary nor violative of the Equal Protection Clause of the Fourteenth Amendment if any state of facts reasonably can be conceived that would sustain it" (*Allied Stores of Ohio v. Bowers 1959*). In other words, if the court can imagine that differentiation associated with taxing or spending serves a legitimate purpose, no denial of equal protection is involved.

In contrast, a dissenting justice in a later case cited various considerations supporting the conclusion that "this Court will no longer sustain a challenged classification under the rational-basis test merely because Government attorneys can suggest a 'conceivable' basis upon which it might be thought rational." In his view, the court may consider only the "actual" purpose of the classification, that is, a purpose that the legislature itself has articulated (Brennan, in *U. S. Railroad Retirement Bd. v. Fritz 1980*).

Implicit in the above is the fact that legislative actions frequently raise questions about equal treatment in connection with taxation. Eisenstein (1961) provides illustrations (pp. 147ff). What kinds of gifts should be deductible for income tax purposes? If a person borrows money to buy a house, should the interest on his mortgage be deductible when the person who rents gets no comparable tax concession? Should all income be treated alike, whether earned abroad or at home, and whether derived from salary or from capital gains or from social security? Should the oil industry get its oil depletion allowance? What do you do about a tax exemption that is general in form but that is so narrowly drawn that only one person can qualify? Answers to such questions come from legislatures. So far, the courts have declined to rule on them, which leads some to ask whether the courts have abdicated their duty with respect to claims that taxing and spending measures are unfair.

Unacceptable Differentiations

Having emphasized the deference of the courts to legislatures, let me now swing the other way and acknowledge that judicial restraint has limits. The courts do sometimes strike down taxing and spending measures on equal protection grounds. In recent years, especially interesting illustrations concern the assessment of property for purposes of taxation, distinctions between old and new residents, and distinctions between domestic and foreign (out-of-state) business concerns.

The property assessment case arose from the practice of assessing property on the basis of its most recent sale price, with no more than minor adjustments in the case of property that had long been in the same hands. The result was that a property sold recently might be taxed at up to 35 times the rate applied to a comparable property. Not surprisingly, the Court found this to involve a denial of the equal protection of the laws (*Allegheny Pittsburgh Coal Co. v. County Commission of Webster County 1989*). The case arose in West Virginia, but more or less comparable problems are widespread in California.

Alaska provides an illustration of a proposed distinction between old and new residents. In 1969 Alaska's total budget came to $124 million. Then oil revenues began pouring in, amounting to $3.7 billion in 1981, with a prospect that the magnificent windfall would continue for many years. What should the state do with all that money?

Among other things, Alaska decided to establish a fund from

which it would make annual payments to the people of the state. It would assign a "dividend unit" to each citizen 18 or older for each year of residency subsequent to 1959—the year Alaska became a state. For 1979 the state fixed the value of a dividend unit at $50, which meant that a one-year resident would get $50 whereas a person who had resided in the state since 1959 would get $1,050.

The result was that some one-year residents went to court, claiming that they were denied the equal protection of the laws.

The courts found the case difficult. The Superior Court of Alaska agreed with the one-year residents, only to be reversed by the Supreme Court of Alaska, which in turn was reversed by the Supreme Court in Washington (*Zobel v. Williams 1982*). Thus in the end the Alaskan plan was stricken down on the ground that it denied equal protection. The issue was whether the differentiation between persons rationally served a legitimate state purpose.

Alaska named three purposes. The Supreme Court in Washington was clearly correct in holding that the differentiation did not rationally serve two of them. The more difficult question was whether the third purpose was "legitimate." This purpose was to apportion benefits so as to recognize "contributions of various kinds . . . which residents have made during their years of residency." The Supreme Court held that this purpose was not legitimate, supporting its view by conjuring up a slippery slope. If a state were permitted to give out money on the basis of the number of years of residency, it might later differentiate between old and new residents in other ways too, for example, in tuition fees at the university, in eligibility for civil service jobs, even in the taxes imposed. And the Court could not accept the possibility of the division of citizens into "expanding numbers of permanent classes." This would deny equal protection.

One of the concurring opinions focussed on the point that Alaska's proposed differentiation was inconsistent with the federal structure of the country, impinging on the right to travel. This opinion conjured up a different slippery slope: if Alaska were permitted to differentiate between old and new residents, then other states might follow its example, leading to unacceptable results. "If each State were free to reward its citizens incrementally for their years of residence, so that a citizen leaving one State would thereby forfeit his accrued seniority, only to have to begin building such seniority again in his new State of residence, then the mobility so essential to the economic progress of our Nation, and so commonly accepted as a fundamental aspect of our social order, would not long survive."

In contrast, the lone dissenting justice pointed out that "this Court has long held that state economic regulations are presumptively valid, and violate the Fourteenth Amendment only in the rarest of circumstances." He thought that Alaska's distribution scheme, far from impeding the right to travel, would encourage travel into Alaska; and he held that Alaska's plan "clearly passes equal protection muster."

I describe this case in some detail to indicate first of all how much leeway the justices find for different and even opposing judgments. And my second purpose is to illustrate the role of subjective preferences in choosing the values to consider and assigning relative importance to them. The Court's opinion put the stress on minimizing distinctions among citizens of the state. The concurring opinion put the stress on safeguarding the federal system, and more particularly on keeping interstate travel unimpeded. The dissenting justice appealed to the force of precedent (deference to state legislatures) and showed no fear of slippery slopes.

My supposition is that all the justices shared all the values cited. They disagreed, however, in choosing the ones on which to focus and in assigning weight to them. They made subjective judgments. Further, they had no choice but to make subjective judgments. As stated in Chapter 2, theoretically they might hold that treatment is equal only if it is the same, but this would lead to the destruction of other precious values, and once you acknowledge that other values should be considered you make subjective judgment inevitable.

Another case is somewhat similar. It concerns a lifetime exemption from a property tax that New Mexico offered to Vietnam veterans. The hitch was that the offer went only to those veterans who resided in the state before May 8, 1976; and a veteran who moved into the state in 1981 went to court, claiming that he was denied the equal protection of the laws (*Hooper v. Bernalillo County Assessor 1985*).

Differentiation between veterans and nonveterans was not in dispute. The view prevailing throughout the country is that it is legitimate for a state to reward veterans, despite the inequality created between them and nonveterans. But New Mexico proposed to differentiate among veterans themselves, and this raised the question whether the differentiation was rationally related to a legitimate state purpose.

One of the declared purposes was to encourage veterans to settle in the state, but the court pointed out that the denial of the exemption to veterans coming into the state after May 8, 1976, was not rationally related to this purpose. The other declared purpose was to reward veterans for their military service, but obviously the distinction between veterans did not serve this purpose either.

So the Court sided against New Mexico, quoting its ruling on Alaska: "the Constitution will not tolerate a state benefit program that 'creates fixed, permanent distinctions . . . between . . . classes of concededly bona fide residents, based on how long they have been in the state.'"

Three justices dissented. To them the exclusion of the newly arrived veterans from the favored group served a legitimate interest in that it put a limit on the costs. Moreover, it left the ineligible veterans in the same category with a majority of the people in the state, so no second class citizenship (no invidious distinction) was involved. If the state had simply awarded gold medals to its resident veterans on May 1, 1976, this would not have obligated it to give such medals to veterans who came into the state later; thus, by analogy, the state could reasonably distinguish between veterans in granting a tax exemption.

Furthermore, the dissenting justices were willing to credit New Mexico with a purpose that it apparently did not claim: to help veterans readjust to civilian life. And if this was the purpose, the dissenters said, it was reasonable to suppose that the need for the help was reduced in the case of veterans who had already had considerable time to readjust before coming to New Mexico.

So six justices took the view that New Mexico's purpose in distinguishing between the veterans was illegitimate, and three took the opposite view. Again, as I see it, it was a question of choosing the values to consider and assigning them relative weight. The justices made subjective judgments, unavoidably.

Differentiating between Domestic And "Foreign" Businesses

A "foreign" business is an out-of-state business.

The tradition is that if a state imposes a "privilege tax" on a foreign business (that is, a tax in exchange for the privilege of doing business within the state), the courts accept it. The tradition is strange in that, in addition to being questionable as a usurpation of the right of Congress to regulate interstate commerce, a privilege tax seems manifestly to deny the equal protection of the laws.

The tradition is called into question in a case decided in 1981 (*Western & Southern L. I. Co. v. Bd. of Equalization 1981;* McGuiddy 1982, 879). In it the Supreme Court considered a challenge mounted by an Ohio insurance company doing business in California against what it regarded as a discriminatory tax. The ruling of the Supreme Court, in effect, was that if California's tax was classified as a privilege tax, it would be a denial of equal protection, as the Ohio company claimed—which means that the privilege taxes of many states became unconstitutional. More broadly, the Supreme Court ruled that if the purpose of the California tax was to confer advantage on domestic as against foreign businesses, or to raise revenue at the special expense of foreign businesses, this too would deny equal protection.

But California claimed a different purpose: to induce other states in which California companies sought to do business to give them equal treatment, lest their own companies seeking to do business in California be required to pay a retaliatory tax. And the Court found this purpose legitimate: states have a legitimate interest in promoting the fortunes of companies incorporated under their laws. Moreover, the Court was unable to conclude that California was irrational or unreasonable in supposing that its retaliatory tax might actually promote the declared purpose. Therefore, the retaliatory tax withstood the strictures of the Fourteenth Amendment.

Two justices dissented. They pointed out that the foreign insurance company doing business in California was not responsible for discrimination by its home state. An innocent company was thus treated as a hostage in order to coerce another state to change its policies. This violated the Equal Protection Clause.

Note the slippage in the test employed. The dissenting justices did not say that California's declared purpose was illegitimate, and they did not deny that the retaliatory tax might serve that purpose. They objected on other grounds: that California imposed a penalty on an innocent party. It was this that they found illegitimate.

Again it seems probable that the justices all agreed on all of the values that any of them cited; but they disagreed on the relative importance to assign to them.

In 1985 the Supreme Court struck down an Alabama law that required foreign insurance companies to pay three to four times as much in taxes as its domestic competitors. Alabama cited two purposes in imposing its discriminatory tax: to encourage the formation of new insurance companies within the state, and to encourage the investment of capital in certain Alabama assets and governmental securities.

According to the Court, neither purpose was legitimate, at least when considered in the context of the Fourteenth Amendment. One justice dissented, seeking to preserve the widest latitude for the states in matters of taxation (*Metropolitan Life Ins. Co. v. Ward 1985*).

The Rich and the Poor

People differ in their economic circumstances, raising the question what it means to give them equal treatment. I have already referred to several early cases that reflected special solicitude for the poor — cases involving access to the political process and to the judicial system. In one of the cases the Court spoke of "an affirmative duty to lift the handicaps flowing from differences in economic circumstances" (Tribe 1988, 1627).

In 1974 the Supreme Court upheld a Florida law granting widows, but not widowers, a $500 property tax exemption (*Kahn v. Shevin 1974*). The paradox is that in approving a concession to those presumed to be poor the Court also approved differentiation based on sex. It described the exemption as "reasonably designed to further the state policy of cushioning the financial impact of spousal loss upon the sex for which that loss imposes a disproportionately heavy burden." Justice Brennan dissented because of the differentiation based on sex, but he nevertheless spoke of a "compelling state interest in achieving equality" for groups that had long been the victims of purposeful discrimination.

The Court also evidenced concern for the poor in *Goldberg v. Kelly 1970*. The case concerned a violation of due process in terminating welfare benefits, but the reasoning advanced is relevant to equal protection claims. According to the Court,

> From its founding the Nation's basic commitment has been to foster the dignity and well-being of all persons within its borders. We have come to recognize that forces not within the control of the poor contribute to their poverty. . . . Welfare, by meeting the basic demands of subsistence, can help bring within the reach of the poor the same opportunities that are available to others to participate meaningfully in the life of the community. At the same time, welfare guards against the societal malaise that may flow from a widespread sense of unjustified frustration and insecurity.

Neverthless, the Court limits its concern for the poor. In 1971 it faced an amendment to the constitution of California forbidding the construction of low-rent housing in any community unless the project got majority support in a referendum. The amendment put no limit on the construction of other sorts of housing. Three justices disapproved, holding that "by imposing a substantial burden solely on the poor, [the amendment] violates the Fourteenth Amendment." But six justices approved, and of course their view prevails (*James v. Valtierra 1971*).

The Court came to a similar conclusion when it faced a claim that those living in a tax-poor school district were denied equal protection. It rejected the view of a lower court that classification by wealth (or poverty) is "suspect." Although in an earlier case it had accepted the right to travel as "fundamental," it refused to put education in that category. Further, it held that "where wealth is involved, the Equal Protection Clause does not require absolute equality or precisely equal advantages." All that is required is that the state's arrangements for financing education bear "some rational relationship to a legitimate state purpose," a rule with which you are familiar. On this basis the Court refused to "intrude in an area in which it has traditionally deferred to state legislatures" (*San Antonio School District v. Rodriguez 1972*).

The United States, of course, has a progressive income tax, and its progressive feature is judged to be compatible with the requirement of equal protection. The country also has numerous other taxes, some of which are regressive. Prevailing interpretations give the equal protection clause relatively little influence on the distribution of the tax burden. If you want to know more about that subject, you might read Joseph A. Pechman, *The Rich, the Poor, and the Taxes They Pay* (1986).

3 REGULATION OF THE NONGOVERN- MENTAL

12 Public Accommodations. Civil Rights. Housing

The preceding chapters, in Part II, relate to governmental programs and activities, to which the strictures of the Fourteenth amendment are directly applicable. No *state* is to deny the equal protection of the laws. The reference is to state action, to governmental action.

The chapters of Part III relate to governmental regulation of the nongovernmental. The focus is thus on private action as contrasted to state action.

Government has extensive powers over private action. State governments and their subdivisions may impose regulations on the basis of their police power— their vaguely defined but broad power to act on behalf of the general welfare (*Nebbia v. New York 1934*). The federal government, in contrast, is a government of enumerated powers, so it has to find a basis in the constitution if it wants to regulate private behavior; but it is usually able to do so. It may adopt appropriate legislation to enforce the Thirteenth and Fourteenth amendments (prohibiting slavery, and calling for equal treatment). It may act on the basis of its power to regulate interstate commerce, or may attach conditions when it appropriates money or makes a contract. And the constitution provides other possible bases for congressional action.

In practice, government leaves wide areas of private action untouched, partly because of restrictions imposed by the Bill of Rights and partly out of a more general respect for individual liberty. You have a right, for example, to freedom of association. If you choose your friends partly on the basis of race or sex or religion, that is your business. You may guide yourself by moral rules, but in the distinctly private realm no constitutional or legal rules restrict your freedom of choice.

Although it is clear that public and private realms exist side by side, it is not always clear where the boundary line is between them. Thus the first question taken up in this chapter concerns the meaning and limits of "state action." Then the chapter focuses on governmental efforts on behalf of equal treatment in the private realm—efforts relating to common carriers, public accommodations, the enjoyment of civil rights, and housing.

Questions about equal treatment with respect to employment and pay are reserved for the following chapter.

State Action

What counts as state action is ordinarily clear, but questions arise. Think, for example, of a private club that accepts only whites as members. Government gives the club a liquor license, and the club then refuses to serve food or liquor to the black guest of a member. Is "state action" involved? Does "state action" become involved if the city provides the club with police and fire protection and with water and sewage service?

Think also of a softball team allowed to play on a diamond in the city park despite the fact that it discriminates against blacks. Is there "state action?" If a town has a volunteer fire department that rejects black volunteers, is there "state action?"

All of the above questions have come before the courts. The case most commonly cited is *Moose Lodge No. 107 v. Irvis* (1972). The Lodge was a private club, but the state of Pennsylvania had given it a liquor license. The state restricted the number of licenses it gave out, thus conferring a special advantage on those favored. One of the conditions was that the Lodge must adhere to its own constitution and by-laws, which specified that only white males could be members. A member brought a black to the Lodge as a guest, and it refused to serve him food or drink simply because he was black.

The question was whether government was sufficiently involved that "state action" occurred within the meaning of the equal protection clause. A federal district court and three members of the Supreme Court said yes, pointing to the fact that the state required adherence to a discriminatory constitution and to the fact that the state put whites in a favored position by granting the club a scarce liquor license. Six of the justices of the Supreme Court said no, and of course their view prevailed. They held that the involvement of the state was too slight to count—that no significant symbiotic relationship existed between the state and the Lodge, and that access to liquor remained relatively easy—for blacks and others—outside the Lodge.

Which side do you take? Why? I doubt that you can get a confident answer simply by looking at the facts of the case. Your answer is much more likely to be shaped by the relative weight that you choose to give to liberty and equality.

Before *Moose Lodge* was decided, the rule had already been established that the extension of police protection and other ordinary municipal services does not involve government in a private action sufficiently to transform it into state action within the meaning of the Fourteenth amendment; to hold otherwise, one court said, would emasculate the distinction between the public and the private. But the courts say that state action is involved if a baseball team that discriminates is permitted to use the diamond in the city park or if a town provides equipment to a volunteer fire department that excludes blacks. I have already noted in an earlier chapter that governmental enforcement of a restrictive covenant (a clause in a sale contract forbidding resale to a black) would be state action.

Suppose that a sheriff is ineffective in preventing members of the Ku Klux Klan from seizing and beating a prisoner in his custody and thereafter does nothing to apprehend or punish the offenders. Should his inaction count as action? The court said yes (*Lynch v. United States 1951*).

Suppose that a deputy sheriff releases three civil rights workers from jail and then joins with others to intercept the three on the highway and kill them. Is this state action? Do the private persons who join with the deputy sheriff share in the state action and become liable to trial and punishment on the same basis? Again the Court said yes (*United States v. Price 1966*).

Other cases might be cited. "State action" is sometimes clearly involved, but sometimes what you face is essentially a policy decision about the kinds of conduct that government should regulate.

Common Carriers and Public Accommodations

Although in this book I am focussing mainly on constitutional and statutory law, I should also mention the common law, for it requires equal treatment. Haar and Fessler emphasize the common law in *The Wrong Side of the Tracks* (1986). They say that "over the course of centuries Anglo-American jurists clearly and consistently articulated the principle that enterprises providing functions and services that are essential and public in character have a common law duty to serve—a positive obligation to provide all members of the public with equal, adequate, and nondiscriminatory access" (p. 15).

In other words, the rule is long-established that the private owner is not necessarily free to conduct his business as he pleases. Where the function or service that he provides is "essential and public in character," he must accord equal treatment to all customers and clients. Another way of putting it is that once a person enters the market to sell a commodity or service, he leaves the distinctly private realm and must abide by any regulations on behalf of equal treatment that government lawfully imposes.

The reason for the rule is most obvious in the case of a monopolist, for if he were free to discriminate as he pleases, he would have undue and perhaps intolerable power over others. The reason for the rule is not so strong in a competitive, open market situation, but the Jim Crow record in the United States indicates that even competitors may join in policies of discrimination if permitted to do so. It is also conceivable that divisions would appear comparable to those of the feudal period, when vassals were required to give loyal service to a lord.

If you want to couch the above in more general language, you might argue that one person should not be permitted to use his liberty so as to deprive the liberty of another person of its worth, that a society concerned about the general welfare should take at least some kinds of measures to regulate or limit policies that impair it, and that one of the functions of government is to protect the weak against the strong.

Common carriers (railways and ferries, for example) are among those to whom the rule of equal treatment applies. Railways in the United States violated the rule in dealing with John D. Rockefeller and thus helped him build his fortune; and of course they violated it in relation to the blacks during the period of Jim Crow. But the rule exists nevertheless.

Those offering public accommodations (that is, businesses offering goods or services to the public) are also subject to the rule. One of the leading historic cases in the United States concerned a warehouse for the storage of grain. Considering its practices, the Supreme Court cited a ruling by a British court in the 17th century that when private property is "affected by a public interest," it ceases to be purely private. The Supreme Court held that "property becomes clothed with a public interest when used in a manner to make it of public consequence and affect the community at large." Bringing these principles to bear on the case before it, the Court held that warehousemen "exercise a sort of public office and have public duties to perform." They could not pick and choose among potential customers or differentiate arbitrarily in the rates that they charged (*Munn v. Illinois 1876*).

The common law is not sacrosanct. Through legislative action government may override it, substituting rules of its choice. Some of the states did this in times past, wanting to permit the differential treatment of blacks. But government may also reinforce, clarify, and extend the common law.

In effect, Congress attempted to reinforce, clarify, and extend the common law in 1875 when it enacted a civil rights bill saying that all persons in the United States "shall be entitled to the full and equal enjoyment of the accommodations, advantages, facilities and privileges of inns, public conveyances on land or water, theaters, and other places of public amusement." But the Supreme Court of that time ruled that neither the Thirteenth nor the Fourteenth amendment, nor any other provision of the constitution, authorized Congress to enact the law. The result was that for a number of decades blacks suffered egregious discrimination, discrimination to which the Supreme Court turned a blind eye later in *Plessy v. Ferguson* (1896), when it adopted the "separate but equal" rule.

The civil rights movement of the 1960s led to revolutionary change. Among other things it produced the Civil Rights Act of 1964. Title II is the portion of the act that is relevant at the moment. It prohibits discrimination or segregation on the ground of race, color, religion, or national origin in places of public accommodation; and it lists as places of public accommodation: retail stores; restaurants and other establishments that sell food for consumption on the premises; theaters, sports arenas and other places of exhibition or entertainment; and hotels and other places that provide lodging for transient guests. Title II says nothing about possible discrimination based on sex.

This time the Supreme Court found that, in the kinds of places named, the treatment of persons is related to interstate commerce (*Heart of Atlanta Motel v. United States 1964*), bringing about a revolution in race relations, blacks gaining freedoms that they had long been denied.

Title II makes an exception for Mrs. Murphy, who rents out no more than five rooms and who lives on the premises; she is free to pick and choose her renters.

Many states and municipalities have laws of their own concerning public accommodations, and many of these laws ban discrimination based on sex. The most interesting current issue is whether certain clubs count as private and whether they are therefore free to exclude women. One of the first cases concerned the Jaycees. The bylaws of the national Jaycees organization specified that only men could be regular members, though women could be associate members. The chapters in St. Paul and Minneapolis rejected this distinction and made women regular members along with men, only to be informed that they would therefore lose their charters. The national organization sought to justify its position by citing the constitutional right to freedom of association.

Minnesota, however, has a Human Rights Act, which prohibits discrimination as to sex and various other traits in places of public accommodation, including "public business facilit[ies]." So the issue was whether the local Jaycees clubs count as places of public accommodation or "public business facilit[ies]." Minnesota said yes, and the question then went to the Supreme Court.

The Supreme Court pointed to the fact that the local Jaycees chapters are "large and basically unselective groups." The St. Paul and Minneapolis chapters had over 400 members each. Both gave membership (either regular or associate) to virtually anyone of proper age who applied. Women, as associate members, participated in many projects and functions. These characteristics and practices persuaded the Court that the chapters were more like public business facilities than like private clubs exercising their right to intimate or expressive association. Thus the decision went in favor of the state human rights law. Government had a "compelling interest in eradicating discrimination against its female citizens . . . in the distribution of publicly available goods, services, and other advantages" (*Roberts v. United States Jaycees 1984*).

Later the Supreme Court made a similar judgment in the case of a Rotary club. It held that "the relationship among Rotary Club members is not the kind of intimate or private relation that warrants constitutional protection," and that, though the obligation to admit women infringes slightly on the right of expressive association, "that infringement is justified because it serves the State's compelling interest in eliminating discrimination against women" (*Board of Dirs. of Rotary Intern. v. Rotary Club 1987*).

Sally Frank brought a more difficult case to the Division on Civil Rights in New Jersey. She was a student at Princeton University, and held that just as the university itself had shifted from an all-male policy to the admission of women, so should three social and eating clubs of the students. The clubs were nonresidential. They were selective, including approximately 70 members each. They had no formal connection with the university, but obviously had a "symbiotic relationship" with it. Thus the question was whether the "symbiotic relationship" made them places of public accommodation under New Jersey law, or whether, as they claimed, they remained private, with a right to freedom of association.

You can argue this issue yourself. It offers one of the many illustrations of the fact that the law often fails to provide decisive guidance. Technically, you must decide the question as stated above—whether the clubs should count as places of public accommodation. But, as in the Moose Lodge case, you are likely to make this judgment by first deciding on the relative weight to assign to the values at stake: the right to freedom of intimate association v. the right of women to equal treatment. In other words, it is theoretically possible to define the idea of a public accommodation so as to support your preferred values.

The ruling in the Sally Frank case was that the eating clubs provide a vital service to the university by helping to feed students and that they therefore classify as places of public accommodation.

Many other clubs that traditionally have been for men only are being obliged to admit women. A number of cities have enacted relevant ordinances. New York City, for example, forbids discrimination because of race, creed, color, national origin, or sex in clubs that are not "distinctly private." And a club is not "distinctly private" if it has more than 400 members, provides regular meal service, and regularly receives money from nonmembers for the furtherance of business. Money might come from nonmembers for a variety of possible reasons—for example, to pay the dues of an employee or to rent space for a party.

A consortium of clubs in New York—some of them for men only, some for an ethnic group only—challenged the law, only to be rebuffed. The court spoke of the "compelling interest" of the city in assuring to women and minorities equal access to advantages and privileges such as leadership skills and business contacts, and held that the city's law is a valid exercise of the police power (*N.Y.S. Club Ass'n v. City of New York 1987*). The Supreme Court affirmed (1988). Los Angeles has a comparable law, and a number of other cities do too.

It is implicit in what is said above that public utilities are "affected by a public interest." In offering goods and services, therefore, they must follow the rule of equal treatment. They are not free to pick and choose among potential customers or to discriminate arbitrarily in their charges. The gas company, for example, must get service to the potential customer who is inconveniently located as well as to the customer who is close by.

The Enjoyment of Civil Rights

The civil rights campaign of the 1960s involved numerous offenses against the civil rights of those conducting the campaign. White supremacists and racists did not look kindly on those, often outsiders, who wanted to bring white supremacy and racism to an end, and they resorted to a variety of tactics, ranging from harassment to murder, to maintain a racist order. Offenses were occurring on a much larger scale against the civil rights of blacks themselves, whether or not they took any part in the campaign. And a combination of political circumstances sometimes made the local and state governments unreliable in enforcing respect for the law.

The situation was such that the federal government decided to involve itself, and the equal protection clause of the Fourteenth amendment gave it a basis for doing so as against state action. But many of the hostile actions were the work of private parties, and the basis for federal action against them was not so clear.

What the federal government did was to revive civil rights laws that Congress had enacted in the years following the Civil War. In the Civil Rights Cases of 1883 the Supreme Court had put a narrow construction on these laws, rendering them nearly useless, but they were still on the statute books, open to new interpretations.

The laws in question included the one already quoted concerning equal access to public accommodations. They also provided that all citizens should have the same right as white citizens to make contracts and to buy or rent property. They made it a civil offense to "conspire or go in disguise on the highway" for the purpose of depriving any person of the equal protection of the laws or the equal enjoyment of the rights, privileges and immunities of citizens. And they made it a criminal offense to conspire to injure or intimidate any citizen in exercising or enjoying rights or privileges secured by the constitution or laws.

Jones v. Mayer (1968) was one of the first major cases coming to the Supreme Court under one of these revived laws. Jones was black, and he claimed that Mayer had not conceded him the same right as a white person to buy a home—that Mayer had refused to sell to him solely because he was black. And he won his case. The Supreme Court—rejecting the view of 1883—held that the law prohibits "*all* discrimination against Negroes in the sale or rental of property— discrimination by private owners as well as discrimination by public authorities."

A later case involved a group of men who had stopped a car on the public highway and clubbed its occupants, thinking that they were civil rights workers. The charge was that those who committed the assault were guilty of conspiracy for the purpose of depriving others of the enjoyment of the rights, privileges, and immunities of citizens, and the Supreme Court upheld the law on which the charge was based (*Griffin v. Breckenridge 1971*).

Still another case arose out of the refusal of a private school to admit a black as a student. The claim was that the school denied to a black the same right to make a contract that whites enjoyed. And again the Supreme Court accepted the argument, concluding that the law of almost a century earlier "prohibits private schools from excluding qualified children solely because they are Negroes" (*Runyon v. McCrary 1976*).

These and other like cases suggest a clear triumph for the equal protection of the laws. But the words that the Court interpreted led to a problem, for they are ambiguous. They say that all citizens shall have the same right as white citizens to make contracts and to rent or buy, but precisely what does this mean? Who or what must accord the rights in question? Is an obligation imposed on private persons or on government or on both? If a private person stands ready to do business with a white person, must he then stand ready to do business with anyone on the same terms, or do the words simply mean that government must assure the same legal rights to all citizens that it assures to whites?

The two interpretations have vastly different implications. If the law means only that government must concede to blacks the right to make a contract or to rent or buy, that might not do them much good, for they might be left standing there, unable to find whites who are willing to do business with them.

As indicated above, the Court construed the words to apply to private conduct. The skepticism of some of the justices about this interpretation led the Court to reconsider the issue in 1989, but it decided to let the earlier decision stand (*Patterson v. McLean Credit Union 1989*).

I might note that in connection with the above judgments the Supreme Court conceded Congress virtually unlimited constitutional authority to adopt legislation designed to eliminate the "badges and incidents" of slavery and to punish all conspiracies to interfere with Fourteenth amendment rights (Tribe 1988, 332; Brennan, in *United States v. Guest 1966*; Estreicher 1974, 497-98).

Housing

A Federal Housing Authority came into existence in 1936. For many years it went along with and even reinforced local discriminatory measures relating to housing. For example, it refused to guarantee mortgages when blacks sought to buy property in a white area; and it went along with local efforts to select sites for public housing in such a way as to preserve the racial character of different communities.

Such policies were obviously inconsistent with a series of measures: the post Civil War legislation mentioned above, providing that all citizens should have the same right as white citizens to make contracts and to buy or rent property; the requirements of the Fourteenth amendment; the principles reflected in *Brown* in 1954; and the Civil Rights Act of 1964.

Finally in 1968 Congress adopted a Fair Housing Act (Title VIII of the Civil Rights Act of 1968). The Act makes it unlawful "to refuse to sell or rent . . . or otherwise make unavailable or deny, any dwelling to any person because of race, color, religion, or national origin." In 1974 Congress added sex to the "because of" list, and in 1988 it added handicap and the presence of children in the family.

The courts have given a broad construction to the legislation. Race is the most common issue, so I will focus on it. According to the courts, the law prohibits not only outright refusals to sell or rent based on race, but also a variety of other practices that have the purpose or effect of maintaining segregation. Racial steering is outlawed. So is the giving of false or misleading information about the availability of dwellings. So is redlining—that is, special measures based on racial considerations relating to the mortgages and other financial aspects of purchases and sales. So is discrimination with respect to insurance. And so is exclusionary zoning (Lind 1982, 617; Metcalf 1988, 86).

The principal problem concerns enforcement. Racial discrimination by those who have property to sell or rent is rarely open and blatant, so the gathering of proof sufficient for judicial action usually calls for organized effort. Violations are not uncommon (Newburger 1984). The 1988 amendments to the Fair Housing Act, however, strengthened the provisions for enforcement.

Several sorts of questions about the interpretation of the law have attracted special attention—concerning the building of low-cost public housing, concerning its location, and concerning the use of racial quotas to promote integration.

Philadelphia illustrates a question concerning the building of low-cost housing. In the late 1950s its Public Housing Authority condemned properties in the Whitman area and cleared the site for the purpose of constructing low-income public housing. The clearing of the site forced the removal of a number of black families, which in effect changed a previously integrated area into an all-white area. Then the city changed its mind, the mayor equating public housing with black housing, and holding that black housing should not be constructed in white neighborhoods. On this basis, the city delayed and ultimately cancelled the project.

What would you say about the legality and constitutionality of the city's behavior? The courts held that the cancellation had an adverse impact primarily on the black community, and that this alone indicated a violation of the Fair Housing Act. Moreover, they held that racial motivation was clear; and, since the city's action was "state action," this meant that the equal protection clause was violated as well (*Resident Advisory Bd. v. Rizzo 1977*).

Yonkers illustrates a question concerning the location of low-cost housing. Again, as in Philadelphia, the assumption was that the low-cost housing would be occupied mainly by blacks; and the question was whether Yonkers was free to restrict such housing to the Southwest section of the city. Since Yonkers was following a neighborhood school policy, continued segregation in the schools was implied.

The court said no. To confine low-cost housing to one section of the city for racial reasons was to violate both the Fair Housing Act and the equal protection clause of the constitution; and the neighborhood school policy added another violation (*United States v. Yonkers Bd. of Educ. 1985*, 1542). The decision reinforced earlier decisions to the same effect (Dimond 1985, 205; Farrell 1985, 560-61).

Yonkers, however, was obdurate. It simply refused to go ahead with housing projects located outside its Southwest section—which finally led the federal district judge to declare the members of the council in contempt of court, and to impose fines that doubled every day, threatening the city with bankruptcy in short order. Only then did the council finally give in.

Starrett City, a housing project in the New York metropolitan area, illustrates the question whether racial quotas are permissible in order to assure racial integration. The City was originally developed on the basis of a promise to establish and maintain integration, and for a number of years it rented out its apartments on a quota basis. When its practices became an issue, it was reserving 21 percent of the apartments for blacks, 14 percent for other minorities, and the remainder for whites. Over the years, both the city and the federal government were partners in these arrangements, the city making tax concessions and HUD making subventions.

The assumption in Starrett City was that 35 percent minority occupation was the tipping point, and that if a higher proportion of the apartments went to minorities, white flight would occur. Minorities regularly applied for apartments disproportionately to their quota, so were ordinarily on waiting lists longer than whites, if they ever got an apartment at all.

These policies and assumptions raise a number of issues and suggest even more arguments. The first question is probably whether the plain words of the law were controlling, for those words explicitly prohibit any refusal to rent because of race. If you could establish the view that the law must be applied literally, that would be decisive. But someone else may point out that the courts are authorized to sit in equity and that this enables them to approve policies designed to undo the effects of prior illegal or unconstitutional actions.

In any event, a number of precedents indicate that the "plain words" of a law are not always to be followed literally—that the spirit and purpose of the law are also to be considered, with the law applied accordingly. The trouble is that discussion of the issue in Congress was too meager to permit a reliable conclusion as to congressional intent. Apparently Congress did not even consider the possibility of benign quotas (Benign Steering 1980). The act calls on all executive departments and agencies to administer their programs and activities relating to housing and urban development in a manner affirmatively to further the purposes of the act, but what this means is not entirely certain. The purposes of the act include an end to segregation, but whether they include affirmative action to achieve and maintain integration is less sure.

A second issue is whether racial quotas are morally justified. In considering this question, you may want to differentiate between kinds of quotas, for some are like floors and others are like ceilings. The quota system that the University of California at Davis used in selecting medical students was a floor, fixing a minimum; it reserved 16 places for minority applicants but permitted them to get more. In contrast, Starrett City's quotas were ceilings; they fixed maximums. No more than 35 percent of the dwelling units were to go to minorities. An apartment earmarked for a white would go vacant rather than be rented to a black. Furthermore, since minorities applied disproportionately to their allotment, the burden of the system fell especially on them, that is, on the politically and economically weak.

A third issue concerns the question of pandering to prejudice. In a sense, this is what the quota system did. The system was an adjustment to white prejudice against blacks. From this point on you can go either way. You can say that the law must not give effect to private prejudice, and that government must not adopt or condone policies that reflect a belief that blacks are unacceptable as neighbors. Or you can say that since government is itself partly responsible for the prejudice, it should be willing to follow policies reasonably designed to overcome it.

A fourth issue concerns the idea of a tipping point. Although evidence that tipping occurs in some cases is impressive, it does not necessarily occur in all cases, nor is the tipping point always predictable. Those who assume that such a point exists are likely to differ in locating it. Starrett City offered low-cost housing, meaning that lower income whites found it financially advantageous to live there even if it meant living next door to blacks. Thus, short of the test that experience provides, you cannot be entirely sure whether a tipping point existed or precisely where it was. All that you can be sure of is that tipping did not occur when 35 percent of the apartments were occupied by minorities.

Reagan's Department of Justice, with William Bradford Reynolds as its principal spokesman, took the initiative in bringing Starrett City into court. I have already spoken of Reynolds in Chapter 6 in connection with his objections to Tennessee's efforts to promote graduate and professional training for blacks. Just as he objected to that arrangement as denying equal treatment to whites, so he objected to the quota system for maintaining integration in Starrett City and comparable housing developments.

This time Reynolds relied on the literal words of the law, which prohibit racial discrimination in housing and make no exception in favor of discrimination aimed at integration. Reynolds's stand was clearly influenced by his view that "no amount of 'residential integration' is worth attaining if discrimination is the price that must be paid." A possible alternative view is suggested above: that since government is partially responsible for racial bigotry, it should approve reasonable measures to undo the evil it has helped to promote.

The court decision on the matter did not turn on the "plain words" of the law, nor did the court endorse Reynolds's colorblind stand. Nevertheless, the court ruled against Starrett City, citing three considerations. First, it held that "a plan employing racial distinctions must be temporary in nature with a defined goal as its termination point." Second, it held that "the use of quotas generally should be based on some history of racial discrimination . . . within the entity seeking to employ them." And third, though apparently willing to accept quotas designed to increase or assure minority participation, it was skeptical of quotas that impose a ceiling, for reasons given above. The conclusion was that the Fair Housing Act does not permit the use of rigid racial quotas of indefinite duration to maintain integration (*United States v. Starrett City Associates 1988*).

The court did not say where the line is between the temporary and the permanent, permitting one to wonder what would happen if Starrett City would put, say, a 35-year limit on the application of its quota system. The second point is in a way more formidable in that it seems absolutely to prevent the use of a new housing development to undo racial discriminations of the past, for by definition a new development cannot itself be guilty of prior discrimination. If, however, government is named as at least an accomplice in the discrimination of the past, then the question is whether government should not be permitted to reverse its role and approve efforts to undo the evil that it has previously supported. (See Smolla 1985.)

13 Employment and Pay

This chapter deals with federal policies relating to employment and pay. It takes up equal employment opportunity for minorities, and equal treatment regardless of age, handicap, or language. It then focuses on "gender justice": hiring and promoting women, equal pay and comparable worth, the protection of women from unsuitable work, pregnancy, pensions, sexual harassment, pornography, and child care. The final section asks about employment policies relating to homosexual persons.

EEO: Minorities

EEO stands for Equal Employment Opportunity. Title VII of the Civil Rights Act of 1964 calls for EEO, making it unlawful to select or discharge employees or otherwise discriminate between them on grounds of race, color, religion, sex, or national origin. It applies to employers with fifteen or more employees (including state and local governments) and to trade unions and employment agencies (Player 1988, Chapter 5; Combs and Gruhl 1986, 128).

The title names possible exceptions. Differentiation may occur on the basis of any of the traits named if it is "reasonably necessary" to the operation of the business or enterprise. In that case the trait classifies as a bona fide occupational qualification (bfoq).

The criteria for judging when a characteristic is "reasonably necessary" in a given enterprise are not spelled out, and disagreement is not unusual. The desire for authenticity is one of the criteria, making it acceptable, for example, to take sex into account in casting a play or in selecting a person to model clothes. But not all decisions are that easy. How about making it a bfoq that members of a police force shall be under 50 (or 55, or 60)? How about the airline that classifies sex as a bfoq in hiring flight attendants on the ground that passengers find women more comforting and caring? Can a rejected man properly claim that the airline has violated Title VII?

The title does not include race among the possible bfoqs, though surely it is a bfoq in some instances.

The title makes an exception permitting religious associations to distinguish as to religion in their employment policies. And it does not cover Indian tribes. Federal law permits the Bureau of Indian Affairs, the Indian Health Service, and organizations of the Indians themselves to hire Indians preferentially, and the Bureau requires that private employers do the same when it makes a contract with them for work on or near a reservation (Van Dyke 1985, 92).

An Executive Order supplements Title VII. With minor exceptions, it requires companies working under federal contract to mount affirmative action programs designed to promote EEO. Contractors pledge a good faith effort to achieve the "prompt and full utilization of minorities and women" at all levels of their work force. Broadly, this is taken to mean that the proportion of minorities and women in the work force should be approximately the same as in the relevant labor market.

Of the many Title VII cases that have come before the courts relating to minorities, I will describe two for purposes of illustration, one concerning the Duke Power Company and the other concerning the Detroit Edison Company.

Prior to the adoption of the Civil Rights Act, the Duke Power Company openly discriminated by race in its employment policies. Then it switched to standards that were ostensibly neutral: to be eligible for employment, an applicant had to have a high school diploma and to pass two aptitude tests. As it turned out, however, these standards disproportionately excluded minority applicants, leading to the claim that their use violated Title VII.

According to the Supreme Court, the crucial question was whether the new standards were demonstrably related to success on the job. It was all right for Duke Power to try to make sure that the people it hired were qualified, but not all right to use screening devices that had a disparate racial impact for irrelevant reasons. Moreover, the Court took the view that the fact of a disparate impact put the burden on the company to show that the new standards were valid indicators of prospective performance.

Duke Power was unable to show that they were. In truth, the

evidence showed that persons who had not graduated from high school or passed the tests were performing satisfactorily on the job. This was decisive.

The Court conceded that Duke Power had no intent to discriminate, but held that in this kind of case it was violating the law anyway. Effects were decisive, regardless of intent. "Good intent or the absence of discriminatory intent does not redeem employment procedures or testing mechanisms that operate as 'built-in headwinds' for minority groups and are unrelated to measuring job capability" (*Griggs v. Duke Power Co. 1971*).

In the second case, the Detroit Edison case, the court found "overwhelming evidence that invidious racial discrimination" permeated the company's employment practices (*Stamps v. Detroit Edison 1973*). Moreover, trade unions with which the company dealt were party to these practices. Discrimination was "deliberate and by design" in identifying the kinds of jobs for which blacks would be considered, in restricting their employment and promotion, and in calculating seniority. Nevertheless, the company denied that it engaged in discrimination, refusing "to acknowledge the obvious."

According to the court, Title VII gave it the "authority and duty to enter a decree which not only prevents future discrimination but which also corrects insofar as feasible the effects of past discrimination."

Thus the court ordered several sorts of remedies and penalties. Its general requirement was that

> subject to the availability of qualified applicants, the Company shall recruit and endeavor to hire black applicants for all positions within the Company on an accelerated basis with the goal of having a number of blacks employed by the Company at 30% of its total work force.

The court considered 30% a reasonable proportion in light of the fact that blacks comprised 44% of the available labor force in Detroit.

At a more specific level, the court ordered that vacancies occurring in certain employment categories be filled by blacks and whites at a ratio of two to one until blacks held 25 percent of the jobs. It ordered that every other promotion to the level of supervisor go to a black. It ordered back pay for persons who had suffered discrimination, restoring them to the economic position in which they would have been but for the discrimination. It ordered that those previously rebuffed for racial reasons should have "first opportunity" to apply for vacancies in high opportunity jobs. And it ordered changes in the rules pertaining to seniority.

The court thus ordered "ratio-hiring," just as the court did in the case involving Alabama's state troopers, described in Chapter 8. This goes counter to the ideal reflected in the law, which is that all decisions relating to employment should be color blind. In principle, the court might have adhered to this standard by adopting the theory of "victim specificity" described in Chapter 7 and then by saying that people were entitled to redress not because of race but because they had suffered discrimination. But the court did not do this. It accepted statistical evidence of discrimination and ordered ratio-hiring by race.

In a later case that went to the Supreme Court the Solicitor General, speaking for the Reagan administration, asked the Supreme Court to espouse the "victim specificity" rule, only to be rebuffed. Instead the Court endorsed the principles underlying the judgment in the Detroit Edison case (*Local 28, Sheet Metal Workers v. EEOC 1986*).

You can put varying interpretations on the order to engage in ratio-hiring. You can say that what the court did, in effect, was to order the company to reduce or eliminate its preferential treatment of whites. Or you can say that what the court did, in effect, was to order the company to start giving preferential treatment to qualified blacks until they held their assigned proportion of the jobs. Or you can say that the court ordered a mixture of the two.

If you accept the first interpretation, you presumably assume that the object was to obtain what the court envisaged as the likely result if fair color blind criteria of selection could have been counted on. If you accept the second, you face the question whether preferential treatment is compatible with the principle of equal treatment— a subject that I will examine in Chapter 15.

In 1989 the Supreme Court made two decisions that add to the difficulties of those seeking remedial action with respect to discriminatory employment policies. It held that imbalance in the work force is not alone sufficient to prove that racial discrimination has occurred; in addition, the aggrieved party must demonstrate that one or more specific employment practices of an illegitimate sort have caused the disparity. Further, contrary to the rule laid down in *Griggs*, the employer does not have to prove his innocence. All he needs to do is to produce evidence that seems to justify his practices, and the burden remains on the aggrieved party to demonstrate that the justification is inadequate (*Wards Cove Packing Co. v. Antonio 1989*).

The second 1989 decision concerned the city of Birmingham, Alabama, which had hired and promoted black firefighters in accordance with a consent decree approved by a federal court. White firefighters protested, claiming that the city was violating their rights by making promotions on a racially discriminatory basis. The question was whether the whites had a right to sue for injunctive relief or whether the so-called reverse discrimination was legally protected because it occurred in accordance with a consent decree.

By a five to four vote, the Court said that the aggrieved could sue. The vote reflected change in the composition of the Court, for ten years earlier the decision would surely have gone the other way. Of the five who comprised the majority, three were Reagan appointees. Their view was that, although a judgment or consent decree resolves issues between the parties before a court, it does not deprive third parties of their rights. Third parties may thus challenge what is done.

The four dissenting justices agreed in principle that third parties could sue, but only on narrow grounds—grounds that no one had invoked. Their more significant view was that, given a need for race-conscious remedies, no legal bar exists to "affirmative action plans that benefit non-victims and have some adverse effect on non-wrongdoers. . . . [C]ompliance with the terms of a valid decree remedying violations of Title VII cannot itself violate that statute or the Equal Protection Clause" (*Martin v. Wilks 1989*).

The decision of the Court creates a serious problem. The white-dominated International Association of Fire Fighters has instituted suits in a number of cities challenging judicially-ordered ratio-hiring (Rockwell 1989, 714-16). It is not yet sure how such suits will turn out, but, among other things, they impose high litigation costs on employers who comply with court orders—with the possible alternative of judicially-imposed penalties if they fail to comply. The future of ratio-hiring is thus in doubt.

EEO: Age

With respect to persons over 40, the law prohibits employment discrimination based on age. This means, among other things, that older employees are not to be fired simply because they are older (and perhaps paid more), and that mandatory retirement is outlawed. The assumption is that the effects of age differ, and that it is therefore arbitrary to assume that all employees over a certain age have the same undesirable characteristics. Instead, they are to be treated individually according to merit.

Where state action is concerned, the courts might themselves have brought about the elimination of age discrimination by holding that it denied the equal protection of the laws. But in fact they left the initiative and the responsibility to Congress.

The principle of the bfoq modifies the prohibition of age discrimination, but the exception that it provides is "extremely narrow" (*Western Air Lines, Inc. v. Criswell 1985*). An employer can treat age as a bfoq only if all or substantially all those over the age limit lack the appropriate qualification(s) for the job or only if it is impractical to deal with older employees on an individualized basis.

EEO: Handicap

Federal limitations pertaining to the handicapped apply to agencies of the federal government itself, to those under contract with the federal government, and to programs and activities supported by federal funds. They thus do not apply as extensively as limitations concerning discrimination based on race, age, or sex. At the same time, the law requires those covered not only to refrain from discriminating against handicapped persons who are "otherwise qualified," but also to take affirmative action to bring about their employment and advancement. Congress is considering, and seems likely to adopt, a bill extending obligations with respect to the handicapped to enterprises affected with a public interest. Many states have their own laws on the subject.

The expression "otherwise qualified" is a potential source of misunderstanding, but the law is taken to mean that no discrimination shall occur because of a handicap if, despite it, the person is able to do the job about as well as others could. A qualifier is added that the actual or prospective employer or institution facing the problem must be willing to make "reasonable accommodation" to the handicap.

The courts in effect add another qualifier in connection with contagious diseases, which count as handicaps. The leading case concerns a person with TB, but questions are also arising about the treatment of persons with AIDS, who also count as handicapped. The general principle is that no concession is to be made to unfounded fears or prejudices, which are so widespread especially concerning AIDS. Thus, as a rule, the law protects the victim of AIDS as long as he or she is capable of meeting all job requirements. At the same time, differentiation is permissible when and if it is necessary to protect the health or safety of the handicapped person or of others.

EEO: Language

Discrimination based on language is discrimination based on national origin, which Title VII bans.

Of course, differentiation based on language is often necessary. If the customers who come into a store speak English, then English becomes a bfoq for the clerks. And if reliable communication is of vital importance on a job, then the use of one prescribed language is also likely to be a bfoq.

But what if a person who wants to be a clerk in a store and who speaks English correctly is denied employment because of her accent? What if a test for a carpenter's job is given only in English? What if a trade union authorized to represent all employees in collective bargaining fails to provide Spanish-speaking employees with information in their own language? What if an employee is discharged because, despite the company's English-only rule, he used two words of Spanish in a situation where a misunderstanding would have little or no consequence?

Cases involving all of the above issues have come before the courts, and in each of them the ruling has been that illegal discrimination based on language occurred.

"Gender Justice"

As noted above, Title VII makes it illegal for an employer to discriminate on the basis of sex; and at least 40 states have similar laws (Getman 1972, 164). The equal protection clause supplements the various statutes where "state action" is involved. Problems arise in a number of areas.

Hiring and Promoting

As a general rule, employers must hold out equal employment opportunities without distinction as to sex. They are not free to reserve some jobs for men and others for women.

The principle is clear, but as is so commonly the case, its application in specific circumstances may not be. Think, for example, of the company that refused to hire women with preschool-age children. It denied that it was differentiating on the basis of sex, pointing to the fact that it was willing to employ women without preschool-age children. The lower courts agreed, but the Supreme Court reversed. The crucial point to the Supreme Court was that the company's rule applied only to women and not to men with preschool-age children (*Phillips v. Martin Marietta Corp. 1971*).

I raised the question above whether an airline, responding to alleged preferences of passengers, may properly treat sex as a bfoq for the job of flight attendant. A Circuit Court said no. It acknowledged that the law permits a bfoq that is a business necessity, but denied that necessity was involved. It refused to take the view that the preferences and prejudices of customers give validity to discrimination otherwise outlawed (*Diaz v. Pan Am. World Airways 1971*).

Another kind of case is worth mentioning. It concerns a nationwide accounting firm, Price Waterhouse, that employed Ann Hopkins. By almost all the usual tests, she did well, and in due course the partners in her office proposed that she be promoted into a partnership. At that time, 7 of 662 partners in the firm were women.

The vote in the firm was to put the promotion on hold, and the next year the partners in her office refused to renew their recommendation, so she sued. It turned out that a number of the negative reactions to her stemmed from the fact that she was a woman. One of her associates described her as "unladylike." Another said that she needed to take a course at charm school. Another advised her "to walk more femininely, talk more femininely, dress more femininely, wear make-up, have her hair styled, and wear jewelry." Another was more sweeping: he could not consider any woman seriously as a candidate, for he did not believe that women were capable of functioning as senior managers. In other words, some judgments were based at least in part on stereotypes concerning the proper appearance and behavior, and the abilities, of women. In addition she was said to be deficient in interpersonal skills, abrasive in her relationships with others.

The law forbids employment discrimination "because of" sex, so the first issue was what "because of" means. You can imagine a range of possibilities. At the one extreme, an employer might discriminate solely because of sex, and at the other extreme he might make his decision solely because of other considerations. Between the extremes, considerations might be mixed. You can also imagine an action that is over-caused: two or more factors operate, each of them sufficient by itself to produce the result.

In the Price Waterhouse case, the considerations were clearly mixed, so the question concerned the relative importance of those that were legitimate and those that were illegitimate. The "but-for" principle gives the clearest guidance on this issue—the principle that if the decision would have gone the other way "but for" considerations based on sex, then it was made "because of" sex. In a concurring opinion Justice O'Connor endorsed this as the guiding principle, but the opinion of the Court used vaguer language, obliging Hopkins simply to prove that gender had played "a motivating part" in the Price Waterhouse decision. The Court agreed that once evidence is adduced to show that gender played a motivating part, it is then up to the employer to prove that he would have come to the same decision even if he had not taken gender into account.

A question also arose about the standard of proof that the employer must meet. The Circuit Court had called for "clear and convincing" evidence, but the Supreme Court considered this too rigorous and called simply for a "preponderance of evidence." It remanded the case to the lower court for decision on this basis (*Price Waterhouse v. Hopkins 1989*).

Equal Pay/Comparative Worth

In 1963, asked by the Kennedy administration to adopt a law calling for equal pay for work of comparable worth, Congress instead adopted one calling for equal pay for equal work—the Equal Pay Act (Weiler 1986, 1732. Player 1988, Chapter 4).

The act is limited in scope. It becomes operative only when the treatment of men and women can be compared, being irrelevant when all of the employees are women. The men and women must be within the same establishment, which rules out comparisons between establishments. The reference to "equal" work opens the way to an argument that work is equal only if it is identical, but the courts are more permissive, saying that it is enough if the work is "substantially equal." At the same time, even the requirement of "substantial equality" is limiting, providing no basis, say, for a comparison of the treatment of nurses and doctors in the same hospital.

Although the Equal Pay Act (EPA) is narrow, it is significant. One of the illustrations concerns a company which, in its warehouse, established a beauty aids division and a dry grocery division, hiring women in one and men in the other and paying women 30 percent less than men. Since the work in the two divisions was substantially equal, violation of the EPA was clear (Weiler 1986, 1748). In this and a great many other cases the EPA has led to a substantial improvement in the treatment of women (Hutner 1986, 29).

A year after Congress adopted the EPA it adopted the Civil Rights Act of 1964, including Title VII with its broad prohibition of discrimination in employment on the basis of sex; and questions immediately arose about relationships between the two measures. Could the prohibition of sex discrimination in Title VII be a basis for a claim of equal pay for work of comparable worth?

In a series of decisions, the courts have said no. The usual plea of employers is that they are not discriminating against women; they are simply paying what they need to pay to get their jobs filled, differences being a function not of sex but of supply and demand. And they may add that it is in the interest of everyone concerned to accept this reliance on the market, lest a business dedicated to equality incur high costs that render it uncompetitive.

The courts are sympathetic to this plea. They tend to point out first of all that Congress rejected the comparative worth principle when it adopted the equal pay for equal work principle in 1963. They see no reason to think that Congress changed its mind the next year in adopting Title VII. And they are reluctant to make judgments about comparative worth. How do you know what a bookkeeper should be paid in comparison with a sign painter or a tree trimmer, or what a secretary should be paid in comparison with an electrician? Various employers concerned about the problem have retained consultants who make studies and recommendations, but the courts have so far refused to take the view that consultants can determine comparative worth with sufficient reliability to justify a judicial order that their findings be implemented.

One of the notable cases involved a suit against the state of Washington by a union of its employees, referred to as AFSCME (*Am. Fed. of S., C., & Mun. Emp. v. State of Washington 1985*). The state government claimed that the salaries it paid reflected prevailing market rates. Nevertheless, a consultant employed by the state found that, considering jobs of comparable worth, women were in general paid about twenty percent less than men. So one of the issues before the court was whether a violation of Title VII occurs if the payment of prevailing market rates results in lower salaries for women than for men in jobs of comparable worth.

The court refused to order Washington to change its practices. It spoke of the complex market forces that influence the fixing of wages and salaries, and it assumed that these forces are neutral as to sex. If these complex and neutral forces had a disparate impact on the sexes, this was not evidence of discrimination. You might want to dispute the court on these points. Implicitly the court rejected the idea that Title VII requires equal pay for work of comparable worth.

This did not end the matter, at least not in principle, for the court accepted the view that, independently of any judgments about comparative worth, Title VII is violated if direct evidence or legitimate inference justifies the conclusion that an employer has intentionally discriminated by sex. But discriminatory intent is sometimes difficult to prove, and the court held that AFSCME failed to do it. So the court refused to hold that the challenged employment policies violated the requirements of Title VII. Nevertheless, the state of Washington entered into negotiations with AFSCME that led to comparable worth increases for women ranging from 2.5 to 20 percent (Werwie 1987, 20).

Subsequent cases have had similar outcomes in court. Courts

are reluctant to try to implement the rule of equal pay for work of comparable worth, but most of the states have addressed the problem in other ways (Werwie 1987, 130; Hutner 1986, 197-99; Weiler 1986, 1754-5; *California State Employees Assn. v. State of California 1989*).

One of the questions is how much difference it would make if the comparable worth principle were accepted. The common statement is that women get about 60 percent as much as men, and the usual innuendo is that the rule of equal pay for work of comparable worth would lead to parity. But that is surely an illusion, for a number of factors in addition to discrimination help produce the discrepancy.

The number of hours worked and the amount of overtime account for part of the discrepancy. Differences in "human capital," that is, in such matters as education, experience, and tenure with the present employer account for nearly half of it. Marriage and its implications account for a substantial portion, women who have never married earning approximately as much as comparable men. For whatever reason, women tend to be employed disproportionately in types of enterprises in which wages and salaries for both men and women are relatively low. And finally, women are not organized into unions on the same scale as men (Weiler 1986, 1785-93; cf. Fuchs 1988).

The adoption of the principle of equal pay for work of comparable worth would have no effect on these sources of inequality in pay. Weiler's conclusion is that "the maximum level of wage gap to be explained by sex discrimination, and which might thereby be closed by a comparable worth strategy, is on the order of ten to fifteen percent" (Weiler 1986, 1784). Fuchs cites an extensive study leading to the conclusion that the "implementation of comparable worth by every employer might reduce the existing overall wage differential of 34 percent by 3 to 8 percentage points . . . ." (Fuchs 1988, 124).

Weiler's judgment is that the prospective payoff for women is greater through unionization and collective bargaining than through an effort to make equal pay for work of comparable worth legally mandatory. At the same time, he speaks of the Executive Order mentioned above, requiring federal contractors to avoid sex discrimination in employment, and suggests the addition to it of a comparable worth dimension.

Protection for Women

In times past, considerable legislation has ostensibly been designed to protect women. They were not to be employed in certain kinds of jobs or to work during certain hours. Moreover, when challenged in the courts, such laws tended to be upheld as reasonable in that they reflected and reinforced cherished values. Paternalism was acceptable. And in some cases men got protection against competition from women.

Paternalistic laws are gone, but some employers are posing similar issues when they refuse to hire pregnant women, claiming that something about the job is hazardous to them or to the fetus that they carry.

Pregnancy

I noted a case above that stemmed from a refusal to employ women with preschool-age children. The argument was that the refusal did not involve sex discrimination in that it was based simply on the presence of the children. The company was willing to hire, and did hire, women without preschool-age children.

In the light of that case, think of another stemming from a refusal to include pregnancy in a medical insurance program that covered virtually every other imaginable disability. The argument was that the refusal did not involve sex discrimination in that it was based simply on the fact of pregnancy. The company was willing to hire, and did hire, women who were not pregnant.

The Supreme Court rejected the argument in the first case but accepted it in the second. It said that sex discrimination occurred in the first case in that the rule did not apply to fathers. And it said that sex discrimination did not occur in the second case, for the refusal to insure applied to pregnant men as well as to pregnant women (*Geduldig v. Aiello 1974; Gilbert v. General Electric 1976*).

The judgment concerning women with preschool-age children is understandable in that the company's rule reflected a stereotypical assumption about the proper role of the sexes, which government should not support. But the judgment concerning pregnant women is in a different category: that women alone become pregnant is more than a stereotypical assumption. To stand innocently willing to apply the same rule to pregnant men is to ignore the fact that men never become pregnant while, at some time in their lives, a high proportion of women do. Discrimination based on pregnancy is inevitably directed against women, with no counterpart for men.

The fact that justices of the Supreme Court could put the two cases in the same category suggests a problem with a focus on the idea of equal treatment as to sex. Catharine A. MacKinnon proposes a drastic solution. It is that instead of focusing on discrimination or even on equality of opportunity, we should focus on the subordination of women and the domination of men: the evil to be overcome is not simply unequal treatment but subordination. Surely no one who regards subordination as the problem would find it tolerable to exclude pregnancy from the disabilities that insurance covers. According to this view, pregnant women, far from being penalized for the social function that they perform, should be the beneficiaries of special compensatory measures (MacKinnon 1979, 106-27).

Congress did not go quite as far as MacKinnon suggests, but it overrode the Supreme Court—which it could do since the Court was interpreting a statute (Title VII) and not the constitution. Through the Pregnancy Discrimination Act (PDA), Congress amended the statute, specifying that its ban on sex discrimination extends to discrimination based on pregnancy, childbirth, and related medical conditions.

In adopting the PDA, Congress used words that led to another dispute. It said that pregnant women are to be treated "the same for all employment-related purposes" as other persons with disabilities. But it happens that California has a law that operates in some cases to give pregnant women especially favorable treatment. They must not only be given leave for childbirth but must be reinstated afterward in the same or a comparable job, a rule that does not necessarily apply to those with other disabilities. A California company objected, and went to court claiming that the federal law supersedes the state law, with the result that "the same" treatment is all that is required.

The reasoning that the Supreme Court applied to this case is too complicated to describe in detail. The plain words of the law seem to support the company's position. But the Supreme Court emphasized the purpose of the law: to promote equal employment opportunity and to remove barriers to it. The Court quoted and approved the statement of the Circuit Court that the intent of Congress was "'to construct a floor beneath which pregnancy disability benefits may not drop—not a ceiling above which they may not rise.'" It also quoted approvingly the statement of a senator that "'the entire thrust . . . behind this legislation is to guarantee women the basic right to participate fully and equally in the workforce, without denying them the fundamental right to full participation in family life.'" California's requirement that employers reinstate women in their jobs, or in comparable jobs, following leave for childbirth goes beyond the requirement of the PDA, but, according to the Court, is compatible with its spirit and is not superseded by it (*California Federal S. and L. Assn v. Guerra 1987*).

I might add that the rule of equal treatment for pregnant women prohibits any flat requirement that they take leave from their jobs at a certain point, and prohibits making pregnancy leave an occasion for the loss of seniority rights (Siegel 1985, 932). It also requires that rules concerning unemployment benefits be neutral as to pregnancy, but this does not necessarily safeguard the pregnant woman's interests. The law of Missouri, for example, denies unemployment benefits to those who leave work "voluntarily and without good cause attributable to [their] work or to [their] employer." Since the "good cause" that leads a pregnant woman to give up her job is not so attributable, she is ineligible for unemployment insurance. And the Supreme Court holds that she is not a victim of discrimination in that Missouri's reasons are neutral as to sex (*Wimberly v. Labor and Indus. Relations Com'n. 1987*).

I might also add a query about the classification of pregnancy as a disability. I speak of it as a disability above in conformity with widespread usage, but I do it with hesitation. The classification of pregnancy as a disability suggests a procrustean effort to apply the same standards to women as to men, and in the case of pregnancy this tends to be demeaning. I wonder whether pregnancy and childbirth should not be recognized as unique phenomena, leading to special treatment designed to minimize disadvantages for women who want both a family and a career. Measures to compensate women for nature's discrimination against them may be in order (cf. Williams 1984-85; Scales 1986).

A query concerning the following case: A girls club with members ranging from eight to eighteen seeks to help them maximize life's opportunities. It wants its staff members to be role models, and it dismisses an unmarried staff member who becomes obviously pregnant. She claims sex discrimination. The club contends that she no longer meets a bfoq. Whose side do you take? Why? (The court sided with the club.)

Pensions

You have a choice between respectable arguments in connection with pension plans. One argument is that since women tend to live longer than men, it is reasonable and desirable either that they should contribute more to pension funds or receive less per month once they retire. Otherwise, men will be subsidizing women. You can argue that the distinction would not be invidious or involve stigma, but would respond to a concern for fairness and would therefore be compatible with the rule of equal treatment.

Of course, if you accept this argument, you must also accept a logical extension of it. As I noted in Chapter 9, whites tend to live longer than blacks; so if you want to differentiate between men and women you should also be willing to break down each category by race. And probably you will want to treat Hispanics and perhaps other minorities on a differential basis. Moreover, as I pointed out earlier, people in some states tend to live longer than people in others. Once you begin to classify people according to sex, race, and so on, the stopping point is uncertain. You can argue that in every case those in classes with longer life expectancies should either pay more into pension funds or receive less per month once they retire, but you may decide that it is better to minimize all such distinctions and accept arrangements under which those who die at an early age subsidize those who live longer.

Although saying nothing about distinctions based on geography, Title VII of the Civil Rights Act of 1964 takes the second of the above positions so far as distinction by race, religion, sex, or national origin is concerned. The court construed the title to "focus on fairness to individuals rather than fairness to classes," but whether unisex tables are in truth fair to individuals is a question (*Los Angeles Dept. of Water & Power v. Manhart 1978*).

Sexual Harassment

My concern here is with cases where sex is not in any reasonable sense job-related but where it nevertheless comes to figure in the atmosphere of the work place or the conditions of employment. The assumption is that the workplace is hierarchical, some having power over others, which ordinarily means that men have power over women. If a man with power and status brings sex into a workplace relationship in ways that are unwelcome to a female subordinate or in ways that reduce her opportunities for job-related achievement, he is engaging in sexual harassment. Of course, harassment might occur too at the hands of a woman or a homosexual in a position of power, or at the hands of a professor in relations with a student. Here I will assume that a heterosexual man harasses one or more women who are subordinate to him.

His harassment may take various specific forms, ranging from unwanted and unwelcome comments to a requirement that a woman engage in sexual intercourse if she wants to get or keep a job or secure a pay raise or promotion. Or it might take the form of a requirement that she do a sexual favor for a third party, perhaps a customer or client (MacKinnon 1979, 1-2, 237-39). Potentially it affects not only the woman who is the direct target but others in the workplace as well, for they confront unfair competition.

For long sexual harassment did not figure in questions about

EEO. The assumption was that if a supervisor took unfair advantage of his power position, it was simply a personal matter between him and the woman imposed upon. But increased sensitivity to questions about equal treatment brought change.

After all, sexual harassment entails sex discrimination. Members of one sex—usually women—face different conditions of work than members of the other sex. Some women may of course take the special conditions in stride, and even derive advantage from them, but others face strains and anxieties from which male colleagues are free. Women may lose self-respect, or fail to gain it, if they are given reason to think that they are wanted and valued not for their abilities on the job but for other reasons. They may find it demeaning and degrading to have to submit. As one writer says, it is as if a black were required to shuffle or to dance a jig in order to get or keep a job.

Courts have come to treat sexual harassment as discrimination, similar to racial discrimination, forbidden by Title VII. Thus the Supreme Court quotes a Circuit Court as follows:

> Sexual harassment which creates a hostile or offensive environment for members of one sex is every bit the arbitrary barrier to sexual equality at the workplace that racial harassment is to racial equality. Surely a requirement that a man or woman run a gauntlet of sexual abuse in return for the privilege of being allowed to work and make a living can be as demeaning and disconcerting as the harshest of racial epithets (*Meritor Savings Bank v. Vinson 1986*).

A district court has held that "even a woman who has never been the object of harassment might have a Title VII claim if she were forced to work in an atmosphere in which such harassment was pervasive," the theory being that such an atmosphere implies a hostile work environment (*Broderick v. Rudder 1988*).

I have referred here only to Title VII. I should note too that, if state action is involved, sexual harassment denies the equal protection of the laws (*Woerner v. Brzeczek 1981*).

The remaining question is where responsibility for sexual harassment lies. The person who engages in it is of course at fault, but the prevailing view imputes ultimate responsibility to the company or institution that tolerates his behavior (Berger 1986, 428-29).

Pornography

If pornography suffuses a workplace, it may create an environment hostile to women and thus count as sexual harassment. Otherwise, pornography provides another illustration of a weakness of the rule of equal treatment in handling certain problems.

I take it for granted that pornography tends to demean and degrade women. As MacKinnon emphasizes, it is evidence of their subordination and of the dominance of men. In some of its forms, it encourages the mistreatment of women and even violence against them. West German courts take the view that it is "inconsistent with constitutionally guaranteed human dignity" (Sunstein 1987, 835, 841).

But though pornography discriminates against women as a class, it is rarely personal; and therefore, with the exception noted above, you cannot do much about it if you rely on rules calling for the equal treatment of persons. It is this consideration that leads MacKinnon to urge that those seeking equality for women should focus not simply on the relatively narrow rule of equal treatment at the personal level but on a broader principle that what needs to be eliminated is the general socially-contrived relationship of subordination and domination that prevails between the sexes.

Child Care Centers

The same point applies to child care centers. Given the tradition that mothers have primary responsibility for the care of children, the absence of such centers makes it difficult for women to develop careers outside the home. And this accentuates their dependence on men. The goal of equal treatment, calling for the protection of individual persons, provides little help in connection with the problem. The more relevant goal is the one that MacKinnon urges: bringing the subordination of women to an end.

EEO for Homosexual Persons

Federal statutory law does not attempt to assure EEO to homosexual persons. The courts have specifically held that Title VII, prohibiting discrimination in employment based on various characteristics including sex, does not prohibit discrimination based on "affectional or sexual preference."

Given that 24 states still make sodomy a crime, it is scarcely to be expected that they would attempt to assure EEO to those who presumably practice it. The problem is illustrated by the case of an avowedly homosexual person, Steven Childers, who sought a position in the police department of Dallas, Texas. Chapter 8 refers briefly to this case. Childers was told that he would not be hired "because he would be a security risk and because his sexual practices violated state law" (*Childers v. Dallas Police Dept. 1981*). A federal district court upheld the rejection. Since Childers "actively publicized his life style," the department was justifiably concerned "to protect its public image and to avoid ridicule and embarrassment. . . . There is legitimate concern about tension between known and active homosexuals and others who detest homosexuals. There are also legitimate doubts about a homosexual's ability to gain the trust and respect of the personnel with whom he works." To refuse to hire him, the court said, was neither arbitrary nor capricious.

Every aspect of the above decision is open to question. The most nearly respectable point is that Childers's sexual practices violated state law, and in a questionable judgment the Supreme Court has upheld the right of the states to adopt such a law. But every one of the other reasons cited by the federal district judge to justify his decision suggests pandering to prejudice more than a determination to assure the equal protection of the laws.

The case in which the Supreme Court upheld the constitutionality of anti-sodomy laws is described in Chapter 8 (*Bowers v. Hardwick 1986*). The decision is of course authoritative, but the vote was five to four, and the dissenting opinions strengthen doubt whether the five were on good ground.

In the eyes of the five, the central issue was whether the constitution confers a "fundamental right" to practice sodomy, whereas in the eyes of the dissenting four, the central issue concerned "the right to be let alone." The five also asked whether the law rationally served a legitimate state purpose, and answered that it did: it reinforced a widely held conception of morality. But the five gave no explicit attention to the question of the equal protection of the laws; the four protested the fact but did not themselves express a relevant judgment, treating the "right to be let alone" as conclusive.

With respect to the Childers case, it is difficult to argue that the persistent and avowed violation of law should not count against a person who applies for a position in a police department. But a strong case can be made for the repeal of anti-sodomy laws. The argument is that such a law is not justified by any legitimate public interest and so encroaches unjustifiably on individual liberty; that it is unreasonable and arbitrary to classify persons according to their sexual orientation and then to differentiate between them, with prejudice playing a powerful role; that the even-handed enforcement of anti-sodomy laws (against heterosexual and homosexual persons alike) is so improbable that a denial of equal protection is to be assumed; and that even if the law were enforced in an even-handed way it would be far more burdensome to homosexual than to heterosexual persons, denying them a major form of physical intimacy.

The twenty-six states that have repealed anti-sodomy laws have not, as a rule, gone on to try to assure EEO to homosexual persons. Wisconsin and Pennsylvania are exceptions—Wisconsin by law and Pennsylvania by an Executive Order that forbids discrimination in state offices and agencies. In addition, some thirty cities forbid it through municipal ordinances (Notes 1985, 1286; Rivera 1979, 826).

A few intimations of further change are on the horizon. As indicated in Chapter 8, the Supreme Court of California holds that "both the state and federal equal protection clauses clearly prohibit the state or any governmental entity from arbitrarily discriminating against any class of individuals in employment decisions . . . . [T]his general constitutional principle applies to homosexuals . . ." (*Gay Law Students Ass'n v. Pacific Tel. & Tel. 1979*). In 1988 a U. S. Circuit Court confirmed this position, calling in effect for the elimination of discrimination against homosexual persons wherever "state action" is involved, including action by the armed forces (*Watkins v. U.S. Army 1988*).

The California court went on to hold that "in California a public utility is in many respects more akin to a governmental entity than to a purely private employer," and it thus concluded that "in this state a public utility bears a constitutional obligation to avoid arbitrary employment discrimination."

Even more, the California court invoked "the broad common law principle which place[s] numerous obligations, including an obligation to avoid discriminatory conduct, upon enterprises said to be 'affected with a public interest.'" It held that this doctrine is dynamic and that it has "developed to encompass discrimination in employment as well as in rates and service." The court made no effort to give an exhaustive list of enterprises "affected with a public interest," but it explicitly included public utilities, trade unions, and professional and business associations. All of them, it said, "are bound, under common law principles, to refrain from arbitrary exclusion of individuals from employment opportunities." The rule, according to the court, protects homosexual persons as well as others.

A dissenting justice raises questions about the court's position. He concedes that enterprises that are in anything like a monopoly position are affected with a public interest and must therefore follow nondiscriminatory policies, but held that the monopoly or quasi-monopoly relates to the goods or service provided and not to the labor market; thus the common law rule of equal treatment relates to customers and clients, not to actual or potential employees.

14 Interpersonal Relations: The Sexes

Government adopts various measures having to do with sexual activity, marriage, the married, divorce, and children. In so doing it raises questions concerning equal treatment that this chapter seeks to explore. The chapter also describes and appraises the Equal Rights Amendment (ERA), designed to assure that government does not deny equal rights on the basis of sex.

As the above suggests, the chapter concerns the treatment of individuals by the government in the private, familial realm. It thus supplements what has already been said concerning policies relating to the sexes in chapters 8 and 13.

Sexual Activity

Governmental efforts to regulate sexual activity concern miscegenation, sexual orientation, rape, contraception, and abortion.

Miscegenation

Legal issues concerning miscegenation (interracial sex) seem to be resolved. To differentiate by race with respect to sexual activity or marriage would be to deny equal protection.

One of the cases establishing the rule concerns a Florida law that made it a criminal offense for a white person and a Negro of opposite sexes, not married to each other, to habitually live in and occupy the same room in the nighttime. If both persons were white, or if both were black, the law left them undisturbed.

The question that the Supreme Court asked was whether an overriding public purpose justified the racial differentiation, and its answer was no. Its judgment therefore was that the law denied equal protection (*McLaughlin v. Florida* 1964).

Another case concerns interracial marriage. Sixteen states still forbade it when Virginia's law came before the Supreme Court in 1967. Virginia claimed in effect that its law served an overriding public purpose. In other words, it claimed that cherished public values justified a requirement that married couples should be of the same race. Allegedly, this was God's will. It prevented "the corruption of the blood" and "the obliteration of racial pride." Further, Virginia claimed that the law met the equal protection requirement in that it applied to both races equally.

The Supreme Court decided otherwise. It made no specific comment about God's will, but pointed out that to endorse the values cited was to endorse the doctrine of White Supremacy. It rejected the claim that the application of the law to both races brought it within the requirements of the constitution—and I leave it to you to decide why. The Court's conclusion was that Virginia's law violated "the central meaning of the Equal Protection Clause" (*Loving v. Virginia* 1967).

Sexual Orientation

In chapters 8 and 13 I have already described public policies concerning sexual orientation. The most relevant point here is that twenty-four states still make sodomy a crime, and the Supreme Court has upheld their right to do so. These laws are rarely enforced. They serve several functions: to express, and presumably to reinforce, a conception of morality and/or a prejudice; and to provide a reason or an excuse to refuse to hire, or perhaps to fire, those whose orientation or conduct is homosexual.

Rape

Rape raises several kinds of questions about equal protection. One concerns the very definition of the offense. Some states define it in such a way that only males can be guilty, thus ignoring the possibility that the female may be the one who uses coercion and thus also offending those who believe that whenever at all possible laws should be sex-neutral. A number of states have revised their laws to eliminate the problem.

Another question concerns laws making a man automatically guilty of statutory rape if he has sexual intercourse with a woman under a certain age. Such laws are clearly open to question in that they differentiate (discriminate?) by sex. A number of states have either repealed their law or revised it so as to make it applicable only when the two parties differ considerably in age.

Still other questions concern marital rape. The historic inclination has been to reject the very idea, the assumption being that when a woman marries she makes herself available to her husband for sexual purposes. Many police officers are still influenced by this view, and are reluctant either to go to the defense of a wife who calls for help or to arrest the offending husband. Wives themselves may be reluctant to press charges. Similar problems arise about the battered wife. Nevertheless, the applicable principle is clear:

> A man is not allowed to physically abuse or endanger a woman merely because he is her husband. Concomitantly, a police officer may not knowingly refrain from interference in such violence, and may not automatically decline to make an arrest, simply because the assaulter and his victim are married to each other. Such inaction on the part of the officer is a denial of the equal protection of the laws (*Thurman v. Torrington 1984*).

The principle holds not only for wives but also for any female companion.

Contraceptives

Laws on the distribution of contraceptives sometimes raise a question—for example, a Massachusetts law that came before the Supreme Court in 1972. The law was odd in that it permitted anyone to obtain contraceptives for the purpose of preventing disease, but permitted only the married to obtain them for the purpose of preventing pregnancy.

The government of Massachusetts gave no clear reason for the differentiation. Various considerations led the Court to the view that the prevention of premarital sex was not the aim, and the court saw no other aim that was permissible. Its holding therefore was that that law violated the rights of single persons under the equal protection clause: "whatever the rights of the individual to access to contraceptives may be, the rights must be the same for the unmarried and the married alike" (*Eisenstadt v. Baird 1972*).

Abortion

I have already dealt in Chapter 9 with equal treatment and abortion. Given the decision in *Roe v. Wade*, abortion is a private matter in the first trimester of pregnancy, and no one associated with it—the woman, the doctor and medical staff, the hospital, if any—is guilty of an offense against the law. This statement needs to be qualified to recognize that federal and state law may forbid the use of governmental funds or facilities in connection with abortion—raising a question about equal treatment. *Roe v. Wade* permits the states to regulate abortion for certain purposes during the second and third trimesters even if governmental funds and facilities are not involved.

Marriage

Questions about equal treatment relating to marriage concern the age and the sexual orientation of the parties.

The main question concerning age is whether the minimum can be lower for the bride than for the groom. The laws of a number of states say yes, fixing a differential of from one to three years (Avner 1984, 154).

The question of marriage between homosexual persons is difficult. And it is not an entirely academic question, for the recognition of a marriage has significant implications of both a practical and a psychological sort. For example, if one partner should ever need to be placed under a guardian, marriage gives the other partner a claim to the role. Marriage ordinarily brings tax advantages, and may bring advantages to spouses relating to insurance and pensions. Married persons in the armed forces, and veterans, get benefits for certain dependents, but the unmarried do not. A married person has rights of inheritance even in the absence of a will. Married persons automatically count as a family, and in some cities this assures them the benefits of ordinances relating to housing. Further, marriage formalizes and confers dignity on a relationship, undercutting prejudice that might otherwise operate and reducing the basis for discrimination.

Nothing prevents homosexual couples from going through a marriage ceremony, but no state gives the ceremony legal significance. Some cities, however, have "domestic partnership" laws that allow gay and lesbian couples to register and thus to qualify for benefits otherwise reserved for heterosexual married couples (Sullivan 1989, 20). And in some instances gay and lesbian couples have been legally recognized as constituting a family. This happened in 1989 in New York when a homosexual man died who was the legal tenant of an apartment under rent control. The landlord gave the surviving male partner an eviction notice, but the partner claimed the protection of a law that gave "family" members rights of continued occupancy. And he won his case. The highest court in New York found that the homosexual couple had had a relationship that was "long term and characterized by an emotional and financial commitment and interdependence." They had conducted their everyday lives, had presented themselves to society, and had relied on each other for daily family services in about the same way as a legally married couple. "They regarded one another, and were regarded by friends and family, as spouses." Therefore, in the eyes of the court, they comprised a "family" within the meaning of New York City's rent control law (*Braschi v. Stahl Associates 1989*).

Such instances are exceptional. For the most part homosexual partners are legally regarded as single persons, unrelated.

The reasoning behind policies concerning marriage is open to question. It is that society has an interest in promoting stable relationships for the sake of the bearing and rearing of children. But many persons of opposite sex marry even if they are incapable of having children, and persons living as homosexuals are denied the benefits of marriage even if they have children or want to create a family that includes children. They may have children through an earlier heterosexual marriage. Lesbian women may bear children, and gay men may get them through a surrogate mother. Either a gay couple or a lesbian couple might adopt children.

The argument that the rule of equal treatment calls for a recognition of same-sex marriage appeals to the same logic that the Court adopted with respect to interracial marriage. The argument there was that if a black man can marry a black woman but a white man cannot, the white man is denied equal treatment. No compelling public interest justified the racial classification and differentiation.

The analogous argument is that if a man is permitted to marry a woman but a woman is not, the woman is denied equal treatment. Or, to turn the statement around, government is not treating persons equally if it refuses to permit a man to do what a woman is free to do: marry a man (Friedman 1987-88, 144-46).

The issue, of course, is whether differentiation by race and differentiation by homosexual orientation should be treated according to the same standard. Differentiation by race is made acceptable only by a compelling public interest or an overriding governmental purpose. A few courts have taken the view that the same standard should apply to differentiation by sexual orientation, but no consensus on the point exists. Tradition goes against homosexual marriage, and so does prejudice, along with an unwillingness to confer status and dignity on a homosexual life style. But, especially in the light of the AIDS epidemic, it is arguable that a compelling public interest dictates an opposite course, encouraging homosexual persons to establish and maintain stable, monogamous relationships.

The question of equal treatment becomes poignantly acute when a court denies a lesbian custody of her own child simply because she is a lesbian or unless she breaks up a home that she maintains with another lesbian (Rivera 1979, 883-904).

Rights, Duties, and Obligations of the Married

Marriage has implications for the status, rights, and obligations of the parties, and problems of equal treatment are suggested by the fact that the implications have been especially extensive for women.

The rules of common law, as recorded by Blackstone (d. 1780), indicate what some of those implications have been. The American states took these rules over from Britain. According to them, a woman, once she married, had no legal existence separate from her husband. Any property of a bride passed forthwith to the groom, and so did any earnings of a wife. Furnishings that the couple bought for their home belonged to him. She took on his name. If she refused to live where he chose and to move where he moved, she was guilty of desertion. She could not sue or be sued, or make a will or a contract. All this meant, among other things, that she was not a good credit risk, so she was likely to be unable to borrow money in her own name. "She could not even protect her own physical integrity—her husband had the right to chastise her (although only with a switch no bigger than his thumb), restrain her freedom, and impose sexual intercourse against her will" (Williams 1982, 176-77).

The husband had obligations too, mainly to support his wife and family.

Legislation deliberately adopted through the years added to the differentiation provided for in the common law. For example, a number of the states adopted legislation ostensibly designed to protect women, limiting them, for example, in the kinds of employment they could accept and the hours during which they could work. And, as indicated in earlier chapters, women were denied the suffrage, were exempted from compulsory military service, were treated differentially with respect to jury service, and were patronized and rendered subordinate in other ways.

Eventually many of the differentiating and discriminatory measures came under attack in much the same way as discrimination based on race. At first the attacks occurred mainly in the political and

legislative realm. States adopted one law after another that superseded the common law, and they modified their own legislation so as
to reduce the differentiation between men and women. Similarly, the
federal government took various actions providing for a greater
degree of equality between the sexes. The constitution itself was
eventually amended to eliminate discrimination based on sex with
respect to the suffrage.

Those seeking aid from the courts in eliminating discrimination
based on sex were slow to take advantage of the equal protection
clause, and even then they found the courts reluctant. Once cases
began coming into the courts, a major issue concerned the standard
of judgment to be employed. As indicated in Chapter 2, the Supreme
Court has never been willing to classify differentiation by sex along
with differentiation by race as "suspect," calling for "strict scrutiny."
Instead, the court developed an intermediate standard, according to
which the appropriate test is whether the differentiation serves an
"important governmental objective" and is "substantially related" to
its achievement.

Not until 1971—more than a hundred years after the Fourteenth
amendment was adopted—did the Supreme Court find a denial of
equal protection based on sex. At issue was an Idaho law saying that
when a man and a woman were equally entitled to be the administrator of an estate, the man was to be preferred (*Reed v. Reed 1971*).
The Court set an important precedent in reaching what now seems to
be the obvious conclusion that the preference was arbitrary and thus
unconstitutional.

Whether through legislative or judicial action, much (but not
nearly all) of the legal differentiation based on sex has been eliminated. Nowhere does marriage now deprive women of their separate
legal status. In almost all states wives can retain their maiden name.
Laws obliging the wife to accept the husband's choice of residence are
on the way out, as are laws that fix the obligation of support solely on
him. Wives retain title to their property and their earnings, and may
share in the ownership and management of property held jointly.
They are legally free to make contracts just like men, and federal law
rules out credit restrictions aimed at them. Legislation barring women
from certain kinds of work and certain hours of work has been
repealed. Women are now legally free to get whatever training and
education they can, and to enter the various professions on the same
basis as men.

Nevertheless, in many states and in many contexts, differentiation between the sexes persists, and agitation on the subject
continues.

Divorce

In general, theoretically, husbands and wives enjoy equal treatment so far as divorce itself is concerned, but surrounding conditions tend to be unfavorable to women.

The common law rule that imposed an obligation to pay alimony only on husbands and not on wives is now superseded by rule that alimony, if required, shall be assessed not on the basis of sex but on the basis of the financial circumstances of the parties. Nevertheless, on the average, the woman's standard of living, and that of children in her custody, drops sharply in the year following divorce, while the standard of living of the ex-husband tends to go up (Weitzman 1985, 362).

Several considerations account for the discrepancy. Even if the assets of the family are divided equally between husband and wife, the odds are that the wife will need to support children out of her half. Further, the odds are that the wife will have subordinated her own career to marriage in some degree, perhaps entirely, and thus may not be able to qualify promptly for a job that permits her to maintain her standard of living. Alimony, if any, may be based on the judge's conception of her need, and may be limited to a few years—the judge assuming that she should become self-supporting (Becker 1987, 220-22). It is no longer automatic that custody of children should go to the mother—the best interests of the child being the governing rule. Although this appears to eliminate discrimination based on sex, it also gives the husband leverage for bargaining: he will not claim custody if she will make concessions concerning alimony and child support.

Weitzman's conclusion is that ostensibly equal treatment at the time of divorce is a trap for women.

> One clear implication of the present allocation of family resources at divorce is that women had better not forgo any of their own education, training, and career development to devote themselves fully or even partially to their families. . . . Divorce may send her into poverty if she invests in her family ahead of—or even alongside of—her career (Weitzman 1985, 372).

Children

State laws have sometimes differentiated between girls and boys, and between legitimate and illegitimate children. And they have differentiated between parents with respect to custody over children.

Until 1975 Utah differentiated between girls and boys with respect to the age of majority. The law freed parents of an obligation to support girls once they were 18 but required support for boys until they were 21. The Utah Supreme Court considered the differentiation reasonable and thus compatible with the requirement of equal treatment, asserting that boys needed more parental support for education than girls if they were to fulfill their traditional role as breadwinners. Given its new outlook (new as of 1971), the Supreme Court reversed this judgment. "No longer is the female destined solely for the home and the rearing of the family, and only the male for the marketplace and the world of ideas" (*Stanton v. Stanton 1975*; Freedman 1983, 922).

Similarly, the Supreme Court struck down an Oklahoma law permitting the sale of beer to women after their eighteenth birthday but requiring men to be 21 (*Craig v. Boren 1976*).

Differentiation of several sorts occurs between legitimate and illegitimate children, and it occurs for fairly clear reasons. In the case of legitimate children, the identity of the parents is officially established, and it is reasonable to presume that the children are dependent. In contrast, the identity of the father of an illegitimate child may not be clear, and the illegitimate child who lives outside the father's home may not be dependent on him.

The fact that questions arise about the illegitimate that do not arise about the legitimate makes differential treatment highly probable. If paternity is in doubt, the question must be resolved; and so must the question whether the illegitimate child classifies as a dependent. The possibility of spurious claims suggests caution. The illegitimate must have the opportunity to establish their entitlement, but special checking in their case does not necessarily indicate a denial of equal protection.

More difficult is the question of the equal treatment of unacknowledged illegitimate children in sharing their father's estate. The law of Louisiana excludes them, and a Louisiana court has upheld the law. The question is whether in this kind of case too the illegitimate child should not be allowed to establish a claim and have it treated equally with the claims of legitimate children (*Weber v. Aetna Casualty & Surety Co. 1972*).

The Equal Rights Amendment

Since change making for a greater degree of equality between the sexes has come so slowly and remains incomplete, some have sought to speed it up and extend it through an amendment to the federal constitution—an Equal Rights Amendment (ERA): "Equality of rights under the law shall not be denied or abridged by the United States or by any state on account of sex." Congress endorsed this amendment and proposed it to the states in 1972, but it failed to get the support of enough states to bring it into effect.

Uncertainty about the precise import of the ERA was among the considerations working against it. Advocates of the amendment illustrated the problem unwittingly by endorsing the idea that the right of privacy would continue to justify differentiation after ratification (Brown et al. 1971, 901). Government would still be free to separate the sexes, out of respect for their privacy, in public rest rooms and in the sleeping quarters of prisoners and members of the armed forces; and when the police needed to conduct a body search, the person conducting the search would still need to be of the same sex as the person searched. And the advocates of the amendment add, "It is impossible to spell out in advance the precise boundaries that the courts will eventually fix in accommodating the Equal Rights Amendment and the right of privacy."

Further, the same advocates of the amendment took the view that the ERA would leave the way open for measures designed to undo the effects of past discrimination based on sex, just as the equal protection clause leaves the way open for measures designed to undo the effects of past discrimination based on race.

In other words, advocates of the amendment did not want it applied literally and unconditionally. They granted that it did not quite mean what it seemed to say, acknowledging other values that would in some circumstances take priority. And in doing this, they implicitly granted that they could not reliably predict what the effects of the adoption of the amendment might turn out to be.

One of the central issues was whether the ERA, if adopted, would preclude differentiation between men and women with respect to service in the armed forces. A strict and literal reading of the amendment suggests that it would, but not all of its advocates favored such a reading. Senator Bye, for example, argued that after the adoption of the amendment "'compelling reasons' of public policy" would still permit Congress to exempt women from compulsory military service (Brown et al. 1971, 888), which again raises the question what the ERA would really end up prohibiting and permitting.

Senator Erwin was so fearful that the ERA would be given an absolute interpretation that he wanted to add the statement that "this article shall not impair . . . the validity of any law of the United States which exempts women from compulsory military service." In the 91st Congress the Senate endorsed the addition, but the House did not, and no solution to the impasse was then reached. As later adopted, the amendment did not include the Ervin addition, but no one could be sure what interpretation would come to prevail

Many factors combined to bring about the eventual defeat of the ERA. Uncertainty about its consequences, and associated fears, were clearly among them. To be sure, no one could predict the meaning that would eventually be given to many of the provisions of the original constitution and its various amendments when they were adopted, but the fact that other provisions have had unexpected consequences did little to reassure doubters about the ERA. Many people clearly want some kinds of differentiation based on sex; and they chose caution rather than take the risks that the proposed amendment entailed. In any event, the fact that the Supreme Court began to strike sex differentiation down as a violation of the equal protection clause made adoption of the ERA seem less urgent (Mansbridge 1986, 45-59).

A number of states—at least sixteen of them— have adopted ERAs of their own, most of them doing so after Congress adopted the federal ERA. Both the political and the judicial branches of government in these states have become more sensitized to the issue of "gender justice," and the courts seem more inclined to require a strong case before they will uphold differentiating measures, but the consequences of the state ERAs have not been extreme (Avner, 1984). The ERA states have been among those that have repealed or otherwise abandoned most of the discriminatory rules described earlier—for example, rules having to do with the age of marriage, domicile, divorce, alimony and the division of property, child support and child custody, and payment of the costs of abortion. And as I noted in Chapter 7, some of the ERA states have put a stop to the segregation of the sexes in public schools.

SPECIAL
PROBLEMS

15 Affirmative Action

The term *affirmative action* has come to denote efforts to promote fair and unprejudiced treatment, if not preferential treatment, for persons belonging to groups that have been the victims of discrimination or that are otherwise disadvantaged. The principal concern has so far been with victims of discrimination based on race or sex.

Affirmative action is usually backward-looking, with a remedial purpose: to compensate for past discrimination, or to undo its effects, or to reduce the extent to which they are carried into the future. Forward-looking affirmative action is also possible, designed to shape the future in a certain way, regardless of what has happened in the past. For example, it might be designed to promote the incorporation of a disadvantaged group into mainstream society. Goldman is worth reading on these kinds of affirmative action (Goldman 1979, Chapters 3 and 4).

I will focus here on affirmative action in race relations, leaving it to you to apply the analysis in other areas.

The chapter begins by asking about the realms in which affirmative action occurs and about the kinds of action taken. Then it asks about moral issues—whether various kinds of affirmative action are right or wrong. And finally it asks about legal issues—whether various kinds of affirmative action are permitted by the terms of the constitution and of the Civil Rights Act of 1964. An addendum describes the stand of other countries on affirmative action.

The chapter pays special attention to issues relating to preferential treatment, which means that it pays special attention to the Bakke, Weber, Fullilove, Wygant, Croson, Wilks, and related cases.

The Realms and Kinds of Affirmative Action

Affirmative action occurs in different realms. Chapter 5 describes its use in the political realm. A court engages in affirmative action when it acts against racial gerrymandering, that is, when it requires that the boundary lines of electoral districts be redrawn if they were first drawn so as to minimize the voting strength of the black community; and a court engages in affirmative action when it orders a shift away from at-large elections to an electoral system that gives minorities a fairer chance.

Chapter 6 describes affirmative action in the realm of education. Recall that the Supreme Court spoke years ago of the "affirmative duty" of school boards to convert to a unitary system, that is, to integrate the schools. The repeal of rules requiring segregation was not enough. Neither was freedom of choice or the neighborhood school principle. The court required that school boards act affirmatively to bring integration about, perhaps by assigning students and staff to schools on a race-conscious basis and perhaps by busing. Integration can also be promoted affirmatively by appropriate decisions concerning the sites for new schools and new housing projects.

In higher education, affirmative action by traditionally white or black institutions may take the form of recruiting and other activities designed to attract qualified persons of the other race to the student body, faculty, and staff. It may take the form of preferential admissions, the issue in *Bakke*. And it may take the form of merging two or more institutions or coordinating their programs.

Further, Congress takes affirmative action in making grants to various organizations and institutions for the benefit of blacks. For example, it subsidizes CLEO (the Council on Legal Educational Opportunity), which helps minority students, mainly blacks, to get into and through law school. And as noted in Chapter 6, it subsidizes the traditionally black colleges, explaining that it seeks to make up for earlier discriminatory actions of the states and the federal government.

Affirmative action gets major attention in connection with employment policies, both governmental and private. According to an Executive Order issued in 1965 and still in effect, it is the policy of the federal government "to provide equal opportunity in Federal employment for all qualified persons, [and] to prohibit discrimination in employment because of race, creed, color, or national origin." Sex was added to the list later. Each executive department and agency must establish and maintain "a positive program of equal employment opportunity for all civilian employees and applicants for employment . . . ."

Further, the order requires firms under contract with the federal government not only to be equal opportunity employers but also to take affirmative action accordingly. An affirmative action program is acceptable only if based on a study of the utilization of minority groups and women in the work force, with contractors obliged to make a good faith effort to remove deficiencies by meeting goals and timetables that are themselves included in the program (Player 1988, 310, 461, 623).

Later, universities with federal contracts were also required to become equal opportunity employers.

In 1977 Congress provided for another kind of affirmative action. In offering grants to state and local governments for local public works, it stipulated that at least 10 percent of the money granted should be set aside and used to procure services or supplies from businesses owned by members of minority groups ("Negroes, Spanish-speaking, Orientals, Indians, Eskimos, and Aleuts"). A later act adds businesses owned by women to the list. A number of municipalities also have such set-aside programs. In principle, these programs might be either backward- or forward-looking.

Federal courts have ordered affirmative action with respect to employment in case after case. Recall the orders described in Chapter 8 obliging the Department of Personnel in Alabama to hire and promote blacks as state troopers on a ratio basis. A considerable number of municipalities have been put under comparable orders, especially with respect to their police and fire departments. And a number of state and local governments have themselves voluntarily adopted laws and ordinances calling for the same kinds of equal employment policies as those described above.

Finally, some private firms have adopted affirmative action programs even though not required to do so. A Kaiser Aluminum plant in Louisiana illustrates the point. It acted on the basis of a finding that blacks comprised 39 percent of the work force in the area from which it recruited, but held less than 2 percent of its skilled craft jobs. On the basis of a collective bargaining agreement, it therefore initiated an affirmative action program in selecting workers for in-plant training: blacks were to get half of the appointments until they held 39 percent of the craft jobs in question. To accomplish this, the company established two lists of applicants, white and black, ranking those on each list on the basis of seniority and alternating between the lists in making its appointments.

Brian Weber, a white worker, challenged this plan in court after being rejected for the training program despite the fact that he had seniority over black applicants who were appointed. His case is somewhat analogous to Bakke's, described in Chapter 6. In both cases a white was rejected even though, in terms of the standards considered relevant, he outranked a black who was appointed. In neither case was the question taken up whether any of the parties was guilty of or the victim of discrimination in the past. Thus moral issues arise in these cases, as they do in relation to affirmative action in general.

Moral Issues

In order to facilitate the consideration of the moral issues, I will use a classification scheme in this section that differs from the one used in the preceding section.

The new scheme treats discrimination as either active or passive, and as either governmental or societal. The various kinds of discrimination described in the preceding section all fit in these new categories. I will take up the categories in turn, and then will take up the question of the innocent and the undeserving.

As noted in Chapter 2, active discrimination involves specific, concrete action. The acting party may be a person or firm or any kind of unit capable of action, and the victim may be a person, group, or community. Both the acting party and the victim are in principle identifiable, whether or not they are in fact identified.

Passive discrimination does not involve action but arises out of conditions and attitudes, reflecting custom and social pressures. Suppose, for example, that as a matter of common knowledge certain jobs in a plant or community are held by whites and others by blacks. A black believes that he is qualified for one of the "white" jobs, but refrains from applying in order to avoid the scorn and contempt, perhaps the hostility, that he thinks an application would evoke. You could say that in the absence of an application and a rejection, no discrimination occurs, but surely this would be a misleading if not a false assessment. You would do better to speak of passive discrimination.

One of the features of passive discrimination is that, since no concrete action occurs, it is difficult if not impossible to identify a sinner or his victim.

Active Discrimination

Given an instance of active discrimination, the moral problem is minimal if the sinner admits his guilt, for that implies an obligation to provide redress. Any issues that develop are likely to concern the kind or amount.

For example, the firm that rejects a black applicant for a job simply because he is black is surely obliged morally to place him at the head of the list for any similar job that becomes available. But should the firm give him back pay—and start counting his seniority—from the time he was rejected? Should it fire the white who was wrongly hired and put the black in his place, thus giving the black the job that he should have gotten earlier? Is the white who was wrongly hired in about the same position as a person who receives stolen goods?

Usually the problem is more complex. The accused party is unlikely to admit guilt, raising the problem of proof. Statistics provide one of the possibilities—showing, for example, that although qualified blacks comprised, say, 25 percent of those in the relevant labor pool, whites got 99 percent of the jobs. Statistical proof may establish passive as well as active discrimination, but it obviously does not identify specific victims.

Proof at the personal level may also be possible; that is, the identity of the sinner and of the victim may be established, in which case "victim specificity" becomes possible in the remedy. Proof at the personal level may be difficult or impossible if the discrimination occurred months or years or decades ago. It may be difficult to locate the accused party together with the relevant witnesses and documents. The process of establishing the truth is likely to be slow, and the costs high; and success is likely to be uneven, more and more so as the cases go back in time. Moreover, the process is likely to have morally troubling aspects: many instances of discrimination, especially the more remote instances, may go unredressed; redress for a black may involve some kind of cost for an innocent white; and questions arise whether those alive today are responsible for the sins of their fathers and grandfathers or whether something like a statute of limitations should operate.

Passive Discrimination

The problems about passive discrimination are fairly clear. One is that the tests of its occurrence are imprecise. And another is that since the sinners and the victims are not explicitly identified, moral and legal responsibility are hard to assign and "victim specificity" is impossible.

Passive discrimination occurs in other realms in addition to admissions and employment. Suppose, for example, that one or more black persons who are experienced in the construction industry would like to establish their own firm. But they know that they would have more trouble than white competitors if they had to borrow money or provide for bonding, and they believe that both public agencies and private concerns with construction projects would be prejudiced against them and inclined to give contracts to white competitors. They therefore give up, and do not make the gamble. Nobody actively discriminates against them, but they end up continuing to work for others rather than having a business of their own.

Governmental and "Societal" Discrimination

Active discrimination is "governmental" whenever state action is involved. Passive discrimination is "governmental" to the extent that government shares or reinforces the relevant attitudes and customs. Active and passive discrimination that is not governmental is "societal" (Justice O'Connor, in *Wygant v. Jackson Board of Education 1986*, 298).

In a moral sense government is surely responsible for its own discriminatory policies, just as a person or firm is. And the role of government in the system of discrimination has been significant, more so in some parts of the country than in others. Government adopted and enforced laws concerning slavery. It adopted and enforced laws requiring segregation in education and in other activities, and the education that government provided for blacks was frequently inferior; at the higher levels it was sometimes not available at all. Informally if not formally government assisted and encouraged segregation in housing. It discriminated in its own civil and military services, and in its law enforcement policies. By current standards it was grossly negligent and therefore legally as well as morally liable in failing to protect black citizens from various kinds of harassment, including lynching. Through its example, it put a stamp of approval on discrimination in the private realm.

The generally accepted view is that a democratic government speaks and acts for the people under its jurisdiction, for the collectivity; and the people are collectively responsible for what government does or fails to do. Moreover, government is an enduring if not an immortal person, with rights and obligations that are passed on from one administration to the next. Thus government today continues to be responsible for its discriminatory policies of the past, and people today continue to share that responsibility collectively. The principle is illustrated by the fact that the federal government has promised token reparation to Japanese-Americans for denying them equal protection during World War II. And the federal government is still making amends to Indian tribes.

As suggested above, moral responsibility for "societal" discrimination may be clear if the discrimination was active and if it occurred in the not too distant past. Moral responsibility is likely to be unclear if the discrimination was passive or occurred in the more remote past.

The "Innocent" and the "Undeserving"

In some eyes, the moral problem relating to the "innocent" and the "undeserving" is acute. The "innocent" are the whites who are guilty of no personal fault in race relations. Either they have had little or nothing to do with blacks, or they have conducted themselves fairly in the relationships that they have had. In addition, they may not have benefited from discrimination against blacks in any clear and direct way. A moral issue thus arises if they are required to sacrifice for the benefit of blacks. As Justice Powell put it in *Bakke*, "there is a measure of inequity in forcing innocent persons . . . to bear the burdens of redressing grievances not of their making."

The "undeserving" are the blacks who have suffered least from discrimination, perhaps believing that they have not suffered from it at all. Usually they are middle class blacks with a good education. And it is such blacks who tend to be the beneficiaries of programs of preferential treatment, for ordinarily they are better qualified than other blacks with whom they compete.

Given the above, the obvious possibility is that, when preferential treatment occurs, the undeserving may benefit at the expense of the innocent. And the claim is that this is immoral. (See Cohen 1979.)

Note that the claim does not necessarily apply to all kinds of affirmative action. It may not even apply to all instances of ratio-hiring, for such hiring may simply indicate that whites are no longer being hired preferentially. Theoretically a comparable statement might apply to what is called the preferential admission of minority students. Moreover, so far as I am aware, racial "balance" in employment is never sought by firing persons already on the job, even if they themselves got the job originally through preferential discrimination. The problem of seniority rights is more difficult, but I will postpone it for the moment.

Nevertheless, affirmative action does sometimes call for preferential treatment and therefore raises a moral issue, and the issue becomes excruciating in cases like *Bakke* and *Weber*, leading reasonable and moral people to take opposite sides. One way of appraising the issue follows.

Start with questions about other matters. What stand do you take on conscripting people into the armed forces in time of war or the serious threat of war? If you grant that conscription may be justifiable, are you not accepting the principle that "innocent" persons may be required to accept burdens or make sacrifices when a public need is sufficiently urgent? Suppose that American sailors by mistake shoot down an Iranian passenger plane over the Persian Gulf. In case reparations are paid, do you think it justifiable to ask American taxpayers to foot the bill? Do you accept the principle that even taxpayers who are childless should pay taxes to support the schools? Do you accept the principle that the children and grandchildren of Ronald Reagan can be expected to pay taxes in order to repay the public debt contracted while he was president?

Whatever your personal answer to questions such as these, is it not true that in many connections we ask "innocent" persons to take on burdens for the public good? To put the same question in other words, when we face a conflict between values relating to the person and values relating to society, do we not sometimes decide that those relating to society are overriding?

Of course, just as we try to make the punishment fit the crime, so do we seek proportionality in imposing costs on the innocent. We say, in effect, that only an extremely urgent situation justifies conscripting a person into the armed forces; and we assume that the taxes imposed should bear a reasonable relationship to the need of the government and the ability of the person to pay. As to the childless, we say in effect that taxes to support the schools are moderate enough to be tolerable and that, in any event, the general public interest in having an educated citizenry is great enough to justify asking people to support schools whether they have children or not. Further, we sometimes manage things so that both the costs and the benefits of action in the public good are so diffused that questions about the treatment of specific individuals scarcely arise.

The above line of thought does not lead ineluctably to any one judgment. The question is what relative importance you should assign to conflicting values. You can take the view that Bakke and Weber were innocents who had a moral claim to equal consideration without regard to race and that this claim is overriding. And you can reinforce this view by appealing to the ideal of a colorblind society in which individuals are treated according to their merit.

Alternatively, you can take the view that the public interest in providing redress, eradicating the effects of discrimination, and getting the blacks integrated into mainstream society is sufficiently compelling to justify affirmative action, including some measure of preferential treatment. If you accept this view you must also accept the need to impose burdens on the innocent, although you presumably will strive to keep them within tolerable limits; and you must also accept the likelihood that blacks who cannot prove that they personally have suffered discrimination will enjoy benefits.

Morris B. Abrams—a participant in the civil rights movement through most of his life and a presidential appointee to the Commission on Civil Rights—makes the first of these choices. His emphasis is on what he calls "equality of opportunity and a fair shake for individuals." Thus he pictures himself as a "fair shaker." The alternative that he sees is an emphasis not on opportunity for individuals but on results for groups, with the goal of assuring each group proportional representation in the various human pursuits. Those making the second choice he calls "social engineers" (Abrams 1986).

Abrams's choice is respectable, but it is also vulnerable. It is vulnerable first of all because it virtually ignores the question of redress. Abrams surely deplores the fact that so many people in the past, including virtually all blacks, did not get a fair shake, but he says little about the problem.

The first vulnerability suggests a second. It is that "social engineering" is inevitable, going hand in hand with government and law. Did not the slave system reflect social engineering? Was not the whole system of Jim Crow and racial discrimination a system of social engineering? Is not Abrams himself suggesting a covert sort of social engineering when he recommends principles that are ostensibly neutral but that will in practice safeguard the advantages that whites have gained from the social engineering of the past? Can Abrams achieve equality of opportunity if the blacks at the starting line are already handicapped?

Abrams's charge that those favoring preferential treatment seek the proportionate representation of different groups in the various human pursuits has a grain of truth in it, as indicated by the fact that, when ratio-hiring occurs, it is ordinarily on the assumption that blacks should be represented according to their numbers in the relevant labor pool. Moreover, schools that provide professional training, and the employers of the professionally trained, are under pressure to go in the direction of proportional representation by considering race as well as merit in the appointments that they make. Blacks who are clearly meritorious are thus in great demand and are likely to command salaries accordingly.

But the grain of truth needs to be put in context. First, when racial proportionality is sought, it is in terms of the racial composition of the pool of persons whom it is reasonable to consider, not in terms of the total size of the racial communities. For example, proportionality in employment is sought in terms of the composition of the relevant labor pool. Second, so far as I am aware, no advocate of preferential action wants proportional representation regardless of merit. In ordering ratio-hiring, the courts are respectful of merit at least to a degree: they call only for the hiring of the qualified—though to be sure not necessarily for the hiring of the most highly qualified; and a similar rule attends governmental pressures for the appointment or employment of minority persons.

Third, jobs vary in the kinds of qualities required to do them properly. Sometimes large numbers of people have the necessary qualities—the necessary merit—and differences in their merit may be difficult to determine or of little consequence. In such cases the choices can be influenced by racial considerations at a minimal social cost and with a minimum of injustice. In contrast, where relatively small numbers of people have the necessary qualities, and especially where the development of scarce qualifications reflects a major investment of time and effort, the social cost of a racial preference that neglects merit may be high, and the personal injustice extreme. Preferential action may be justified only where the differences among candidates are small, perhaps so small that the criteria for determining relative merit become unreliable.

To illustrate, large numbers may be qualified to pick up trash, and preferential hiring can occur without seriously undermining respect for merit; but a much smaller number are qualified to do a heart transplant, and strict concern for merit may be vital.

You have a choice. You can join Abrams in saying that concern for merit must be absolute and preferential treatment must be avoided. Or you can say that the case for preferential treatment is so strong, especially where large numbers of candidates have the necessary merit, that you will accept it within reasonable limits. Putting Abrams's terminology in reverse, you might say that your choice is between protecting the whites in their enjoyment of the advantages of the social engineering of the past and giving a fair shake to its victims.

The above suggests a principle that has cropped up repeatedly in this book: that in interpreting the rule of equal treatment, you are likely to have to balance values against each other. You are unlikely to be able to uphold all your values simultaneously. With respect to Bakke and Webber, you can say that they got equal consideration, but that it was and had to be equal consideration in the light of the values that were at stake, not all of which could be fully upheld.

Two additional considerations are relevant to the charge that preferential treatment may confer benefit on the undeserving. The first assumes that blacks have a sense of community, a sense of racial solidarity—that what is done for an individual black, deserving or not, may have symbolic significance for other blacks and perhaps for the whole black community. This has surely been a historic assumption; lynchings, for example, were no doubt directed at the person lynched, but they were also warnings to other blacks. In the same sense, action that enhances the pride of a single black may serve to uplift the whole community.

The second consideration sticks to the level of the individual. It is that the system of discrimination in the past was so extensive and pervasive that few if any blacks could fully escape its effects, and that the effects have been passed on from one generation to the next. Further, a careful effort to identify specific individuals who have suffered most would be so difficult, so time-consuming, and so expensive that it would unduly obstruct an effort at redress. And it is better to engage in visible efforts at redress—at least as a symbol and gesture to the black community—than to seem to look for excuses for delaying action and perhaps for not acting at all.

In saying the above, I do not mean to intimate that all of the difficulties that blacks face can justly be attributed to discrimination. I am impressed by Lawrence Mead's argument that the plight of many blacks is traceable to attitudes and behavior for which they are themselves entirely responsible (Mead 1986). Nonetheless, discrimination has obviously played a significant role in the fate and fortunes of many if not all members of the black community.

In the above paragraphs, I speak of government generally, but should perhaps be more precise. Surely the federal government and the various state governments are responsible for their own past behavior. Whether the states are responsible for what their subdivisions have done, or whether responsibility lies solely with these subdivisions themselves, is more open to question.

Legal Issues

Legal issues concerning some kinds of affirmative action—notably ratio hiring and preferential treatment—are at least as difficult as the moral issues. One important difference is that in connection with legal issues the courts give judgments that are authoritative for governmental officials (though not necessarily for you).

The Words of the Constitution and the Law

The words of the equal protection clause and of various statutes are the source of the legal problem. The equal protection clause does not mention race. Its words do not suggest a special concern for blacks or other minority persons. The statement is that no state is to deny to *any person* the equal protection of the laws, which seems to require the equal protection of Bakke and Weber and everyone else, regardless of color. The statement leads some to claim that the constitution is color blind.

The Civil Rights Act of 1964 seems to require color blind policies too. Title VI says that "no person . . . shall on the ground of race, color, or national origin, be excluded from participation in, be denied the benefits of, or be subjected to discrimination under any program or activity receiving Federal financial assistance." And Title VII makes it an unlawful employment practice for any employer refuse to hire or to discharge any individual, or otherwise discriminate against any individual, or to segregate or classify employees, because of race, color, religion, sex, or national origin.

Now Bakke and Weber were denied appointments because of race, seemingly in obvious violation of these prohibitions. Some of the justices of the Supreme Court join many others in treating the words of the law as decisive. In *Bakke*, four of the justices based their position solely on Title VI. To them, its words are so plain that no room exists for doubt. The Title is "explicit," "crystal clear," "unmistakable" in calling for a "colorblind standard." The justices who supported Weber took a similar position. "Quite simply, Kaiser's racially discriminatory admission quota is flatly prohibited by the plain language of Title VII. . . . Congress meant precisely what it said."

But other justices disagreed. We can get an understanding of their position best by taking an indirect route. Focus first on the equal protection clause of the constitution, and think of the problem that the courts faced from *Brown* on concerning the public schools. Theoretically, the courts might have said simply that laws requiring segregation denied equal protection and had to be repealed. The judges reasoned, however, that if they only did this, the effects of the earlier violations of the constitution would continue into the future indefinitely; and in effect they said that this was unacceptable. So they called for remedial action based on race. As Justice Blackmun said in *Bakke*, "In order to get beyond racism, we must first take account of race. There is no other way. And in order to treat some persons equally, we must treat them differently. We cannot—we dare not—let the Equal Protection Clause perpetuate racial supremacy."

But how could Blackmun or anyone else justify differentiating by race in the face of the plain words of the equal protection clause? Two kinds of answers are possible. One answer has been developed all through this book: that it would be preposterous to interpret the words to mean that government must treat everyone in the same way, for this would lead to one absurdity after another. As indicated in Chapter 2, such an interpretation of the equal protection clause would require that if anyone is drafted into the armed forces then everyone would have to be, and if anyone is required to attend school then everyone would have to attend. Regardless of the precise words of the amendment, a concern for values in addition to equal (the same) treatment requires that government be permitted to classify people and differentiate among them in many ways. Differentiation by race is "suspect" but not absolutely prohibited. It can be justified by a "compelling public purpose," just as the drafting of young men but not grandmothers can be justified.

A second and supplementary answer is that the courts sit in part as courts of equity, and as courts of equity they may order remedial action, whether to undo the effects of earlier violations or to prevent those effects from being carried into the future. The Supreme Court made this clear in *Swann v. Board of Education* (1971). It spoke of the broad and flexible power of the courts as courts of equity and of the use of this power in framing remedies for violations of the constitution. "The task is to correct, by a balancing of individual and collective interests, the condition that offends the constitution."

From this point of view, the order that the schools be integrated was an effort to remedy prior violations of the constitution, and just as race had been taken into account when the violations occurred, it had to be taken into account also when the remedy was ordered. Thus in effect the plain words of the equal protection clause are not quite as absolute as they seem.

But how about the Civil Rights Act, which seems even more explicit than the equal protection clause? As I note above, four of the justices in *Bakke* found this language conclusive. But five others disagreed. Both sets of justices studied congressional proceedings leading to the adoption of the act, attempting to determine the intent of Congress, and came out with contrary conclusions. As against the four who held that Congress had spoken clearly and meant precisely what it said, the other five took the uncomfortable position that Congress intended something different from what the words seem to say. I am not going to try to resolve the dispute here, but want to clarify the line of thought that prevailed.

The five justices—a majority—noted that prior to the adoption of the Civil Rights Act, government was caught in an inconsistency. It was subsidizing or otherwise supplying money to institutions and firms that were doing what government itself was prohibited from doing; that is, they were engaging in racial discrimination. And according to the five, the purpose of Congress was simply to eliminate this inconsistency: all kinds of agencies receiving money from the federal government were to be put under the same restrictions that the rule of equal protection imposes on the federal government itself. This was the intent of Congress in enacting Titles VI and VII.

As Justice Powell put it, "In view of the clear legislative intent, Title VI [and inferentially Title VII] must be held to proscribe only those racial classifications that would violate the Equal Protection Clause or the [equal protection component of the] Fifth Amendment" (*University of California Regents v. Bakke 1978*, 287). This being the view, and it being agreed that the equal protection clause does not prohibit racially conscious affirmative action of a remedial sort, it followed that Titles VI and VII do not prohibit it either.

In *Weber*, Justice Brennan, speaking for the court in interpreting Title VII, used a variation on the above theme. He quoted and obviously approved a "familiar rule" advanced in an earlier opinion that "a thing may be within the letter of the statute and yet not within the statute, because not within its spirit, nor within the intention of its makers" (*Steelworkers of America v. Weber 1979*). This seems to be a cryptic way of saying that "plain language" is not necessarily to be taken literally. The words of a law are to be interpreted in the light of the purpose for which the law was enacted. Thus the federal and state governments, state institutions such as the College of Medicine to which Bakke applied, and private firms such as Kaiser Aluminum may all take race-conscious affirmative action, the literal terms of the constitution and of the Civil Rights Act notwithstanding.

As the justices taking the above line point out, Congress could overrule them with respect to the interpretation of Titles VI and VII, but has made no move to do so. Even more, they point out that Congress seems to approve. Recall that, in appropriating money for local public works programs, Congress specified that 10 percent must be set aside for the purchase of services and supplies from minority business enterprises. Although again this can be interpreted as a requirement that the preferential treatment of white contractors should cease, it has also in some circumstances required the preferential treatment of minority contractors. And if Congress meant to require the preferential treatment of minority contractors, it seems unlikely that it would have meant to prohibit preferential treatment in connection with appointments and employment.

In *Fullilove*, the court accepted the race-conscious set-aside program of Congress, just as it had accepted race-conscious action in *Bakke* and *Weber*. There was dissent. Two of the justices held that "under our constitution, the government may never act to the detriment of a person solely because of that person's race." In their eyes, the claim that the action was remedial provided no excuse. The law calling for the preferential treatment of minority business enterprises was "precisely the kind of law that the guarantee of equal protection forbids." One other justice thought that Congress had acted in a "slapdash" manner, not being sufficiently specific in justifying the racial classification that it prescribed. But a majority accepted the view that the constitution authorizes Congress to take race-conscious remedial action (*Fullilove v. Klutznick 1980*).

The Innocent and the Undeserving Again

As you would expect from the discussion of moral issues, questions about the innocent and the undeserving come up in the legal realm too. The general answer is the same in the two realms. Given prior discrimination and a compelling (or at least an important) public interest in providing a remedy, and given a remedy that is "limited and properly tailored," the courts say that a "'sharing of the burden' by innocent parties is not impermissible" (*Fullilove v. Klutznick 1980*).

Nevertheless, concern for the innocent is real. The issue came up in *Wygant v. Jackson Board of Education* (1986). At issue was a provision of a collective bargaining agreement concerning the possibility that public school teachers would have to be laid off. If the last-hired first-fired rule were followed, the effects of affirmative action would be undone, for in general the blacks were the last-hired. So the agreement included race-conscious rules governing layoffs. The agreement was that whites and blacks would be placed on separate seniority lists, and that when and if teachers had to be fired, those fired would come proportionately from the two lists.

As it turned out, however, the School Board was unwilling to fire a tenured white teacher in order to retain a minority teacher still on probation, and the case went into the courts. Whether or not the black teacher was undeserving, the white teacher was innocent.

The court upheld the Board. It saw a difference between ratio-hiring and ratio-firing. It held that "though hiring goals may burden some innocent individuals, they simply do not impose the same kind of injury that layoffs impose. Denial of future employment is not as intrusive as loss of an existing job. . . . While hiring goals impose a diffuse burden, often foreclosing only one of several opportunities, layoffs impose the entire burden of achieving racial equality on particular individuals, often resulting in serious disruption of their lives. That burden is too intrusive" (*Wygant v. Jackson Board of Education 1986*).

What this amounts to is an appeal to the rule of proportionality mentioned in the discussion of the moral issue. When no one can identify the specific party guilty of discriminating, the burdens of remedial action should ideally be diffused among the population, no one person being especially harmed. If that is impossible, burdens may be imposed on innocent persons, provided the sacrifice is not too great in the light of the values at stake. Beyond that point, the imposition of burdens becomes a denial of the equal protection of the laws.

Locating the point beyond which the imposition of burdens is unacceptable is obviously a matter of judgment. So, I might add, is the question whether the loss of a job is more serious than the failure to get one. The requirement of equal treatment does not always point unerringly to the one correct line of action.

Rewards for the undeserving are less of a problem. After all, those who get more than they deserve are not likely to complain in court about it. It is worth noting, however, that in effect the Supreme Court has dismissed the question as irrelevant. Its view is that the purpose of affirmative action is not so much to benefit particular individuals as "to dismantle prior patterns of employment discrimination and to prevent discrimination in the future. Such relief is provided to the class [that is, to the racial community] as a whole rather than to individual members; no individual is entitled to relief, and beneficiaries need not show that they were themselves victims of discrimination" (*Sheet Metal Workers v. EEOC 1986*).

Societal Discrimination

The most explicit statements concerning societal discrimination as a basis for race-conscious remedies are those of Justice Powell. He says that "societal discrimination, without more, is too amorphous a basis" for imposing such remedies. Without more of a basis, the burdens on innocent people might become too great, and remedies might be adopted that are "ageless in their reach into the past, and timeless in their ability to affect the future." In his view, for racial differentiation to be justified, there must be "some showing of prior discrimination by the governmental unit involved" (*Wygant v. Jackson Board of Education 1986*).

The Supreme Court went farther when it considered the set-aside program of Richmond, Virginia (*City of Richmond v. J. A. Croson 1989*). The program focused on construction contracts made by the city, and required prime contractors to subcontract at least 30 percent of the dollar amount to minority business enterprises. The Court accepted the possibility that such programs might be constitutional.

> Nothing we say today precludes a state or local entity from taking action to rectify the effects of identified discrimination within its jurisdiction. If the city of Richmond had evidence before it that nonminority contractors were systematically excluding minority businesses from subcontracting opportunities it could take action to end the discriminatory exclusion.

Even Justice Scalia, the member of the Court most hostile to race-conscious measures, held that "nothing prevents Richmond from according a contracting preference to identified victims of discrimination."

But in *Croson* the Court was much more insistent than in *Fullilove* that set-aside programs be based on specific evidence of governmental discrimination. *Fullilove* focused on remedial action by the federal government, and could be based on Section 5 of the Fourteenth amendment conferring on Congress the power to enforce the article by appropriate legislation. In contrast, the Fourteenth amendment gave no similar authority to the states, but instead restricted their powers through the equal protection clause. The Court did not speak of the police power as a possible basis for remedial state action.

In any event, the Court held that to justify its set-aside program Richmond must demonstrate that it itself had engaged in active discrimination or that it had participated passively in the active discrimination of others. "Findings of societal discrimination [active or passive] will not suffice. . . . [A] generalized assertion that there has been past discrimination in an entire industry provides no guidance for a legislative body to determine the precise scope of the injury it seeks to remedy." As the Court saw it, "none of the evidence presented by the city points to any identified discrimination in the Richmond construction industry," and the city had therefore "failed to demonstrate a compelling interest in apportioning public contracting opportunities on the basis of race."

Although the Court was not asked to consider, and did not explicitly consider, the question whether forward-looking affirmative action is permissible, the opinion seems to rule it out by implication. Only remedial action is permissible, and then only if the entity taking it can demonstrate that it has itself committed or been somehow involved in specific, concrete discriminatory acts. (See Sullivan 1986.)

Croson makes it more difficult for government to justify set-aside programs, though it does not rule them out. *Wilks* (1989), described in Chapter 13, imposes a limitation on preferential treatment that is potentially even more serious. It concerns a consent decree under which Birmingham, Alabama, was promoting black firefighters on a preferential basis, and more particularly it concerns white firefighters who believed that the preferential promotions violated their rights. It permits them to sue for relief. If they can win such suits, preferential hiring and promotions will presumably become impractical as methods of affirmative action.

What Other Countries Say

In principle, at least, the United States has more of a problem about affirmative action than other countries. Most of them agree in permitting it, if not requiring it.

The International Convention for the Elimination of All Forms of Racial Discrimination reflects the prevailing view. It has been ratified by more than half of the states of the world, though not by the United States. It fixes the equal enjoyment of human rights as the goal, and says that if circumstances are such as to deny equal enjoyment to a racial or ethnic group, special measures may be taken, either for the group as a whole or for individual members. And the special measures are not to count as discrimination. This permits backward-looking affirmative action that responds to either active or passive discrimination; and it permits forward-looking affirmative action that is ameliorative rather than remedial.

The constitution or laws of a number of countries reflect similar principles. Canada provides an illustration. Its constitution act of 1982 says that every individual is equal before and under the law, entitled to equal protection without discrimination based on race, national or ethnic origin, colour, religion, sex, age or mental or physical disability. But then the act goes on to say that this provision "does not preclude any law, program, or activity that has as its object the amelioration of conditions of disadvantaged individuals or groups," including those disadvantaged because of any of the traits just listed (Brudner 1986, 470).

16 Equality v. Inequality

When Jefferson said that all men are created equal, he was surely aware that they are also unequal. It is a prominent feature of the American tradition that equality and inequality go along side by side. The two words apply primarily in different realms, equality being called for where the protection of the law is concerned and inequality being assumed in other realms, most notably in command over income and wealth. The very idea of equality of opportunity suggests inequality, for the natural expectation is that different persons will take advantage of opportunities with different degrees of success.

The simultaneous endorsement of both equality and inequality involves an obvious problem. Anatole France called attention to it ironically when he said that the law has an aura of "majestic equality" about it in that it "forbids the rich as well as the poor to sleep under bridges, to beg in the streets, and to steal bread." From the opposite vantage point, the statement might be that the law in its majestic equality permits the poor as well as the rich to get a higher education, to own newspapers, to hire skilled lawyers, and to devote millions to winning an election.

The question of the relationship between the equal protection of the laws and inequalities of wealth has come up in earlier chapters. Now the purpose is threefold: first, to state the theoretical basis for concern about the question; second, to give a brief survey of arrangements and rules designed to remove certain specific equalities from the pressures and the auction of the market; and third, to inquire into relationships between our insistence on equality in voting and our acceptance of inequality in wealth. The third purpose suggests the question whether we allow government by the people to become government by the rich.

The Problem

Inequality in income and wealth poses a problem in that it makes for inequality in other spheres too. The biblical statement tends to apply—that to him who hath shall be given, and from him who hath not shall be taken away. Given their money, the rich can do better than the poor with respect to nutrition, housing, health and medical care, education, cultural development, travel, and so on. They have greater opportunity to develop and use their talents, and greater reason for hope in the future. As Arthur Okun puts it,

> The marketplace transgresses on virtually every right. Money buys legal services that can obtain preferred treatment before the law; it buys platforms that give extra weight to the owner's freedom of speech; it buys influence with elected officials and thus compromises the principle of one person, one vote. The market is permitted to legislate life and death, as evidenced, for example, by infant mortality rates for the poor that are more than one and one-half times those for middle-income Americans (Okun 1975, 22).

Michael Walzer also focuses on the implications of economic inequality. He wants to reduce the extent to which money is convertible into goods or privileges that ought not to be up for sale. Given such convertibility, he points out, money tends to become dominant; that is, " . . . the individuals who have it, because they have it, can command a wide range of other goods," and this, to him, creates one of the central problems of justice. He does not say clearly what he considers the proper sphere of money to be, but he wants to make the sphere smaller (Walzer 1973, 405; Walzer 1983, 10). He argues for "complex equality," a system in which "no citizen's standing in one sphere or with regard to one social good can be undercut by his standing in some other sphere, with regard to some other good" (Walzer 1983, 19). In other words, he argues that justice calls for autonomous spheres of life, with success or dominance in one having little or nothing to do with a person's fate or fortune in another.

One step toward the application of these ideas is to remove certain interests from the marketplace, to classify certain rights as inalienable, and to have government follow policies that confer benefit on persons without regard to their financial standing.

Inalienable Rights and the General Welfare

As just suggested, one of the functions of rights is to render an interest secure against subversion or destruction through the use of money. The idea is to limit the sphere of the marketplace.

Your freedom to sell yourself into slavery is in point. Some libertarians take the view that you should have that freedom (Nozick 1974, 331). And those who believe this presumably also believe that all rights should be in a class with merchandise that is up for sale: that the rich should be free to pay the poor to give up their rights, thus extending and formalizing inequality.

The consensus, however, goes in the other direction. It is that civil rights should be inalienable, and so in fact the law makes them inalienable. The constitution prohibits slavery and involuntary servitude; a person who paid you to be his slave could not expect a court to enforce the bargain. Nor would a court enforce a pledge on your part to refrain from exercising your right of free speech or freedom of religion, or to refrain from voting, or to vote in a prescribed way.

The poor are protected from economic pressures and the auction of the market in other ways too. Government follows a number of policies designed to promote the general welfare. Those at every income level are entitled to a free public education at least through high school, and to a subsidized higher education. They are entitled to access to the streets and highways, to public parks, and to the public domain. They all enjoy police protection, and the protection of the country from foreign enemies. Those who are employed, at whatever income level, are all included in the social security program.

When military conscription occurs, wealth does not provide a basis for exemption. During the Civil War the federal government followed a different policy, permitting those drafted to hire a substitute or to gain exemption by paying a fee; but no comparable policy has been followed since that time and today such a policy is virtually unthinkable.

Public policies are mixed with respect to equality and inequality in the field of health care. Public health measures benefit the rich and poor alike. Those over 65 get Medicare on the basis of need, regardless of their personal financial circumstances. The indigent are entitled to care at public expense on the basis of need, and so are children in households that are on welfare. But the emphasis is not on protecting people from the implications of unequal income and wealth but rather on making health care a function of the market. In practice, it is still acceptable if the infants of the poor die at a higher rate than the infants of the rich, and still acceptable if the children of the poor are malnourished.

Political Action and Influence

The relationship between money and equal rights has probably received more attention in the field of politics than in any other field. The law gives one vote to almost every adult, and the equal population principle and the prohibition of gerrymandering are designed to assure that all votes have equal weight.

But it is easy to argue that money undermines political egalitarianism. The money and the votes that are needed to win elections do not necessarily come from the same set of people. The money may even come from outside the electoral district. So if your concern is with democracy, you can ask whom the winner really represents. Alternatively, if your concern is primarily with equality, you can ask whether those who give the money exercise influence over and above the influence of those who simply provide votes. In either case, you can ask whether government by the people tends to become government by the rich. Or, to put it in other terms, you can ask about the role of "special interests"—those with a special stake in what government does and with the money to try to influence the decision.

Reasons for suspicion about the role of money are obvious. When hundreds of thousands of people contribute relatively small sums of money to a political campaign, they cannot all expect special favors in return, but that does not necessarily hold true of a few who give large sums. They may have a fortune at stake in a vote or decision of a member of Congress, especially in the vote or decision of the chairman of a committee considering a vital piece of legislation, so they are automatically under temptation to use money for their private advantage. And members of Congress, who ordinarily need money in order to get reelected if not also for purely private purposes, are thus under temptation to solicit or accept it from special interests whose fortunes they can affect.

How can equality be protected against the inequalities to which the use of money may lead? The problem is difficult—made difficult by a contradiction inherent in democracy. You cannot expect that people will have equal influence on government, regardless of the one person one vote rule. It is natural that those who organize for action will influence decisions more than others. This does not raise a serious question as long as influence flows simply from skill in persuasion and argument, but the person who wants to persuade needs more and more money as the number of people to be reached increases; and in today's politics most of those who want to persuade need more money than they can provide out of their own pockets.

Except for the secret ballot and prohibitions of bribery, the law has done little about the problem of money through most of American history. In 1907 Congress made it illegal for corporations to dip into their treasuries for contributions to candidates for Congress or the presidency, but evasions of that rule have been easy. Later Congress placed trade unions under a comparable restriction, which led some of them to do indirectly what they were forbidden to do directly: they set up Political Action Committees (PACs), which collected and spent money for political purposes. Other organizations began following labor's example, and now PACs play a central role both in financing electoral campaigns and in lobbying.

In 1971 Congress enacted the Federal Election Campaign Act (FECA), amending it on several later occasions, especially in 1974. The act focuses on contributions to candidates in federal elections and on expenditures by them; at the same time, it in effect puts a stamp of approval on PACs, authorizing both corporations and unions to pay the administrative costs of any PACs that they establish.

As was to be expected, FECA has been challenged several times in the courts, principally in *Buckley v. Valeo* (1976). The central issues in that case were whether the act violates first amendment freedoms (of speech and association) and whether it discriminates against nonincumbent candidates and minor parties.

Basic to these issues is the question whether money counts as speech, and the Court said yes. It costs money to exercise the right of free speech on any scale, and it costs money to take advantage of the right of freedom of association. Thus, the constitutional presumption in favor of these freedoms carries over to the raising and spending of money.

But the right of free speech is no more absolute than other rights. It has to be interpreted in the light of other cherished values or interests. In this case, according to the Court, the other cherished interest is the prevention of corruption and the appearance of corruption—that is, the use of money in order to obtain special and unequal influence or favor.

To balance the interests that the Court deemed to be at stake, it distinguished between contributions to candidates and expenditures by them. It saw more danger in contributions than in expenditures, the assumption being that contributions might entail, or be suspected of entailing, quid pro quos. Therefore, the Court upheld limitations that FECA imposes on contributions: no individual is to give more than $1000 to a candidate in a federal election, and no PAC is to give more than $5000 (Sorauf 1988, 38).

In doing the balancing with respect to expenditures, the Court took a different view. It did not see enough danger of corruption in the spending of money by a candidate to justify the imposition of limits. The money would presumably come from large numbers of people, and they should not be prevented from pooling their resources to make their voices heard. The court accepted the prospect that some parties and candidates will spend more than others, denying that the government has a compelling interest in equalizing the relative ability of individuals and groups to influence the outcome of elections: "the concept that government may restrict the speech of some elements of our society in order to enhance the relative voice of others is wholly foreign to the first amendment."

Similarly, the Court took the view that a limit on what a candidate may spend out of his own pocket is an unjustified restriction on his freedom of speech. A candidate who finances himself has obviously not promised anyone else a quid pro quo. If Jay Rockefeller spends $10 million of his own money to get elected to the Senate, he is amplifying his voice impressively, but he does not make himself beholden to others in so doing (Sorauf 1988, 68).

Dissenting members of the Court did not find this consideration conclusive. It is also important, they said, that "equal access to the political arena" be maintained. They thought it dangerous to democratic values if candidacy "becomes the exclusive province of the wealthy." They might have pointed more sharply to a dilemma: when we interpret the right to free speech to protect free spending in electoral campaigns, we tend to undermine the significance of equality in voting, which we try so hard to safeguard against malapportionment and gerrymandering (Rawls 1982, 76-77). Differences in political influence are to be expected, but ideally they should stem from differences in personal qualities and interests rather than from differences in the amount of money spent.

FECA employs a special strategy with respect to presidential campaigns, offering a choice to the candidates of the major parties. Within the limitations concerning contributions, these candidates may raise and spend money as they please. Or, alternatively, they may accept public funding, promising not to accept any private contributions or to incur expenses above the amount given to them. Faced with these options, all of the candidates have chosen public funding; and since this is a free choice the courts take the view that no abridgment of freedom of speech is involved (*Republican Nat. Committee v. Fed. Elec. Com'n 1980*).

The other issues in *Buckley v. Valeo* were whether FECA discriminates against nonincumbent candidates and against minor parties, and in slightly different form these issues came up in later cases too. The argument concerning nonincumbent candidates is that they may need more money than incumbents to make up for the special advantages that incumbents usually have, but the court pointed out that nonincumbents sometimes raise large sums of money and that, in any event, it is not the function of the law to try to equalize differences between incumbents and their challengers (*Buckley v. Valeo 1976; Republican Nat. Committee v. Fed. Elec. Com'n 1980*).

Whether minor parties suffer discrimination is a more difficult question. Their presidential candidates may spend as much as they are able, but they are not eligible for public funding. The judgment of the Court was that the record provides no basis for concluding that this puts them under an invidious disadvantage, and that the constitution does not require the government to "finance the efforts of every nascent political group."

The references above are to the raising and spending of money by candidates in federal elections. Thought and experience suggest problems. One is that the limitations do not cover "independent" spending. If you yourself, acting entirely on your own, decide to put an ad in the paper endorsing your favorite party or candidate, you are perfectly free to do so. What you spend independently does not count as a contribution to him. Michael Goland provides the extreme illustration of what this may entail: when Senator Percy ran for reelection in 1984, Goland, acting independently, spent more than $1 million of his own money to bring about the election of Percy's opponent (Sorauf 1988, 65).

Not only may you spend your own money as you please for political purposes, but if you wish you may set up your own PAC, and you or your PAC are free to give money not only to candidates in your own district but to candidates anywhere. In a way, you can evade the $5000 limit on contributions to a candidate by "bundling," that is, by soliciting and forwarding contributions from others. And you can do an unlimited amount of volunteer work for a party or candidate.

A second problem is that the restrictions that FECA imposes on contributions apply only to the campaigns of candidates in federal elections. This means that contributions may be made without limit for a number of purposes: to help a party maintain its national office and to engage a number of activities not specifically related to a given campaign or candidate; to help in state and local campaigns; to support drives to register potential voters and to get out the vote on election day; and so on. If money contributed for a state or local campaign also helps a candidate for a federal office, an appropriate portion is supposed to be counted as a contribution to him, but the Federal Election Commission (FEC) has been slow to give effect to this rule (*Common Cause v. Federal Election Com'n 1987*).

Further, the law does not prevent a PAC or a person who has made the maximum contribution to one candidate from making subsequent contributions to others; nor does it prevent a wife who has given the maximum from persuading her husband—and perhaps relatives and employees—from doing likewise.

Practices concerning honoraria have been and are even more questionable. Special interest groups—for that matter, anyone—can make a generous payment to a member of Congress for giving a speech, or even for simply showing up at a meeting. Until 1989 members of the House were not to supplement their official salaries by more than 30 percent in this way, and members of the Senate by more than 40 percent. Legislation adopted in 1989 modifies this arrangement. Members of the House are to get a substantial salary increase, but are to pass on to charity any honoraria that they receive. Senators, getting a smaller, cost-of-living increase in their salaries, are to reduce their income from honoraria by a like amount.

Students of the subject react differently to the problem of money. Three books published in 1988 (before the House renounced honoraria) illustrate contrasting views. Two of them voice alarm, their titles reflecting the authors' attitudes: *The Best Congress Money Can Buy*, by Philip M. Stern; and *Honest Graft*, by Brooks Jackson. Both create the impression that PACs and special interests use money in ways difficult to distinguish from bribery and that candidates for election or reelection seek money in ways difficult to distinguish from blackmail.

In contrast, in *Money in American Elections* (1988), Frank J. Sorauf hesitates to condemn or show alarm. He calls "the best Congress money can buy" a cliché (it originated with Will Rogers), and he is skeptical of it (pp. 307-8).

Sorauf emphasizes the lack of reliable knowledge concerning the role of money: many factors influence both voters and legislators, and money may have little to do with their decisions. A large proportion of the voters are committed to one side or the other before a dollar is spent. Members of Congress have ideological and party commitments, and must please their constituents (p. 160). They usually need money, of course, but may get it from those who approve their record and simply want them to go on doing the same.

In Sorauf's view, the "key question—and a very difficult one it is—is not whether legislators vote in ways that please their contributors, but whether they would have done so in the absence of the contribution" (p. 310). He points out that in recent years "some of the heaviest spenders in the PAC movement have been among the biggest losers in Congress" (p. 311), and that "the graveyards of political ambition are . . . filled with bodies of losing candidates who outspent their opponents" (p. 299).

Larry Sabato is also skeptical of the view reflected in references to "the best Congress money can buy." He says that "the 'vote-buying' allegation is generally not supported by a careful examination of the facts. . . . [M]ost congressmen are not unduly influenced by PAC money on most votes. . . . Other considerations—foremost among them a congressman's party affiliation, ideology, and constituents' needs and desires—are overriding factors in determining a legislator's votes" (Sabato 1987, 160).

Nevertheless, the statement about what "most" congressmen do on "most" votes permits you to wonder what those other congressmen do and what happens on those other votes.

17 Equality and Collective Entities

So far, the focus of this book has been on individual persons, with no attention paid to collective entities. The focus reflects the fact, emphasized by the Supreme Court, that the rights created by the Fourteenth amendment are for the individual. "The rights established are personal rights" (*Shelley v. Kraemer 1948*).

A focus on the individual suffices for most purposes, but it ignores exceptions, and it ignores the fact that we mix a concern for certain collective entities into our individualism. If I were to omit this chapter you would sooner or later become puzzled about various practices in this country and abroad that do not fit with individualism.

I can make the problem clearest by taking a roundabout route, starting at the international and comparative level and then switching to domestic American policies and issues.

Collective Entities: The International and Comparative Level

When you turn away from an exclusively domestic perspective, it immediately becomes obvious that individual persons are not the only ones who claim status and rights, perhaps equal rights. The Charter of the United Nations, for example, says that the organization is based upon the principle of the sovereign equality of its members; and the one member one vote rule holds in the UN and most other international organizations, just as the one person one vote rule holds in domestic politics. In a few instances—in the Security Council, for example—an exception is made to the principle that all votes have equal weight or value, but even that principle is generally accepted.

Moreover, the state is by its nature a collectivity. It speaks and acts for the whole people, and they are collectively responsible for what it does, no matter how much or how little they have to do with the decisions it makes. They take on burdens not of their own making, and share benefits that they may have done nothing to deserve. In significant measure, the fate of the individual depends on the fate of the state to which he belongs.

When you turn away from an exclusively domestic perspective, it also becomes obvious that people identify themselves with the state and base their behavior on the assumption that their fate and fortunes are tied up with it. Or, if the state is multinational or multiethnic, as most states are, they may identify themselves with a nation that has not achieved independence, or with an ethnic community. In any of these cases, the people who identify themselves with the same collective entity ordinarily have a sense of solidarity, including a belief that they must promote and uphold the collective interest as against external rivals or enemies. They take pride in collective achievements and feel shamed by collective humiliation. It is not uncommon for patriotic feelings to be so strong that individuals voluntarily sacrifice their own well-being and even risk their lives on behalf of what they regard as the collective good—usually the national good. Nationalism is the most powerful ideology extant— much more powerful than egalitarianism at the personal level.

A sovereign state that is multinational or multiethnic faces a problem when peoples within it identify themselves more with their own nation or ethnic group than with the country as a whole. Yugoslavia, for example, is currently facing demands from the nations into which its population divides; that is, it is facing demands from the Serbs, Croats, Slovenes, and others, because they are not satisfied with their relative status and power. And the Soviet Union faces comparable demands from some of its peoples—for example, the Armenians, and the Estonians, Latvians, and Lithuanians.

Central governments have little chance of handling such problems by providing equal treatment to individual persons, for in an individualistic system (if it is democratic) the most numerous people are likely to dominate, subordinating and perhaps oppressing the others. Against this possibility, minority peoples often want an arrangement that focuses not on individuals but on the group. For example, they may demand autonomy, implying political decentralization. Or they may demand a guarantee that their leaders and members will have a specified share in government.

A few illustrations of such guarantees may be helpful, focusing on collective entities distinguished by language, religion, indigenous character, and race. I treat these illustrations more fully in a book on *Human Rights, Ethnicity, and Discrimination* (Van Dyke 1985).

Belgium gives legal recognition to groups identified by language. Its constitution starts out by asserting that "Belgium comprises three cultural communities: French, Dutch, and German." And the constitution proceeds to invest rights and powers in these communities. It specifies, for example, that cabinet ministers (not counting the prime minister) are to come half and half from the two main communities— French and Dutch. (The German community is small.) Civil servants likewise come half and half from the two communities. The political system thus rests on an agreement concerning preferential appointments and preferential hiring.

Belgium's purpose in making exceptions to the rule of equal treatment for individual persons is to assure each ethnic community that its interests will not be neglected. Government is not to be an instrument in the hands of one community for the domination or oppression of the other. Even if 95 percent of the best candidates come from one of the language communities, they are not to get more than 50 percent of the government jobs. And note that the representation of the two communities is to be equal, not proportionate to their population.

The Federal Republic of Germany provides an illustration focusing on religion. It stresses confessional parity—that is, the equal representation of Catholics and Protestants. As a matter of informal rule, if the minister at the head of a government department is a Catholic, his deputy is a Protestant, and vice versa; and parity also prevails with respect to posts in the judicial system and in the civil service.

Malaysia provides an illustration focusing on differences between the indigenous population and the others. The Malays are indigenous, and comprise not quite half the population. People of Chinese ancestry comprise about a third of the population, people of Indian or Pakistani ancestry about a tenth, and various other groups make up the remainder. Each group cherishes and seeks to preserve its own culture, and little intermarriage occurs. The Malays tend toward the view that the country really belongs to them, the others being intruders. At the same time, the Malays historically have been an agricultural people who did not place as much emphasis on education as the Chinese and Indians and who tended to put more emphasis on leisure. The Chinese and Indians thus tend to be more highly educated and more zealous about getting ahead.

Although all of the communities on the Malay peninsula wanted the country to gain independence from Britain, the Malays also feared what might follow, some of them pointing to the fate of the American Indians as a warning of what might happen to them. And they insisted on a bargain that assured them the leading role in politics and government in return for which they would respect the "legitimate interests of the other communities." The requirements of the rule of equal treatment are adjusted accordingly. Far from seeking to ignore ethnic divisions, Malaysia thus gives them explicit recognition. So far the system has worked tolerably well, though the ingredients for an explosion are there. The fate of similar arrangements in Lebanon and Cyprus gives warning.

South Africa is the only country that organizes its political system explicitly on the basis of race. More importantly, the whites, though comprising only about 16 percent of the population, have historically exercised complete political control, maintaining a racist system more extreme than the one associated with Jim Crow in the American South. The party in power, the National Party, has taken a number of small steps toward dismantling this system, but resists any simple transfer of political domination from the whites to the blacks. The great question is whether a nonracial system of individual rights is a workable solution to the South African problem or whether modifications along lines suggested by Belgium, West Germany, and Malaysia will be necessary.

My central point in offering these illustrations is that many countries with heterogeneous populations have not found it possible to operate simply on the basis of equal personal rights, for this opens the way to political control by the most numerous, or perhaps the most advanced and aggressive, group.

To put the point in a different perspective, alarm bells tend to sound when, in a heterogeneous population, any one ethnic or national group is allowed to become or to remain dominant. The interests of the other groups, including their culture and their special identity, are then threatened, and equal treatment for their members is at best placed in doubt. Thus measures are taken to prevent any one national or ethnic group from gaining or retaining domination; and protection for the individual is sought, in part, through protection of the group to which he belongs.

American Individualism and Its Modification

The practices just described are clearly alien to the American tradition, or at least to the American myth. The United States perforce accepts the division of the world, including the divisions that go along national or ethnic lines, but its doctrine holds that the process of division stops at the water's edge (except, of course, for purely geographic divisions that have nothing to do with race or ethnicity). Within the boundaries of the United States, we claim to be one nation, indivisible. If people choose to locate so as to create Italian or Greek or Jewish communities, they are free to do so, but government must not assist them or give their communities legal recognition. It is even unacceptable to give legal recognition to the ghettos that racism has created. Legal rights are for individuals, not for national or ethnic or racial communities.

At least that is the myth. When you inquire into it, however, you encounter anomalies and exceptions. The constitutional convention provided for an exception when it assigned two seats in the Senate to each state. Although not based on racial or ethnic considerations, the arrangement gives equality to collectivities that differ in size, abandoning the principle of equality for persons.

The constitutional convention also endorsed the slave system, and even after the abolition of slavery and the adoption of the Fourteenth amendment, the white community in a number of states established its hegemony through Jim Crow arrangements. While proclaiming liberty and equality for persons, the whites in fact established a communal system in which the effective rights of a person depended on the community to which he belonged.

Arrangements for the American Indians are also in part communal. Chief Justice Marshall made the classic statement on the subject a century and a half ago when he pointed out that "the Indian nations had always been considered as distinct, independent political communities retaining their original natural rights." They were "domestic dependent nations."

In the main, that view still holds. Although policies toward the Indians have varied at different times, the current dominant theme is respect for the desire of Indian tribes to maintain their separate identity. The tribes as such are recognized as having rights. Moreover, even the right of non-Indians to equal protection is modified out of respect for the needs and desires of Indians. Both the Bureau of Indian Affairs and the Indian Health Service give preference to Indians in recruiting their personnel, and the Bureau requires private contractors to do the same in connection with work on or near a reservation.

The United States also explicitly abandons its individualistic stance and goes in a communal direction in dealing with various Pacific dependencies. For example, the constitution conferred on

American Samoa requires the protection of "persons of Samoan ancestry against alienation of their lands and the destruction of the Samoan way of life . . . ." And it goes on to provide: "Such legislation as may be necessary may be enacted to protect the lands, customs, culture, and traditional family organization of persons of Samoan ancestry, and to encourage business enterprises by such persons." A native Samoan may buy land from another native Samoan, but you cannot.

Nor is American concern for collective entities limited to Indians and Samoans. Recall the discussion of gerrymandering and at-large elections in Chapter 5, particularly the view that these devices may involve a "dilution" or "debasement" of the black vote. These terms are unfortunate and misleading. They are taken over from another context and are not apt. The other context concerns the malapportionment of electoral districts. If one district includes only 10,000 persons and another 100,000, and if each elects one representative, votes in the larger district are "diluted" or "debased" in comparison with votes in the smaller.

Nothing quite like this happens, however, in connection with gerrymandering and at-large elections. These devices do not literally dilute or debase any individual vote. They leave the principle of one person one vote and one vote one value untouched. But they do affect the voting strength of collectivities. Their deliberate purpose is to maximize the political strength of the majority community and to minimize the political strength of the minority. Under either scheme a minority community with something like half the votes may end up without any representation at all. So it is the political power of the minority community as a whole that is diluted or debased, not the votes of individual members.

An individualistic approach offers no solution to this problem. The courts have found a solution only by adopting the idea "identifiable" minorities or "cognizable" groups. They have never said precisely what makes a group "identifiable" or "cognizable," but they have put black, Mexican-American, and Navajo communities into the category while refusing to do the same for a community of Hasidic Jews. In any event, given an "identifiable" or "cognizable" community, the courts stand ready to defend it against deliberate attempts to minimize its collective voting strength (Van Dyke 1985, 137-148). They deny that their purpose is to enable a group to gain political power proportionate to its size, but that is roughly what they in fact make possible.

You might ask yourself why white presidents have tended to appoint white persons to office, why they are under pressure to give more appointments to blacks and Hispanics, and why the strong tendency exists toward racially polarized voting. In this land of individualism, do not all of these practices reflect a consciousness of and an emphasis upon the existence of distinct ethnic and racial communities?

Whether other policies of affirmative action are based on communalism is more debatable. Perhaps what is recognized is simply an aggregation of persons rather than a self-conscious community. For example, when an employer is directed to hire qualified blacks until the proportion of blacks in his work force reflects their proportion in the relevant labor pool, the reference may be simply to two sets of persons and not to a black community. At the same time, the two sets of persons get their significance from the fact that they belong to separate self-conscious communities.

The same question arises in connection with the integration of the schools. Officials need to know what proportion of the population of the school district is black, and then they assign students so that the proportion of blacks in each school is about the same. Again we are dealing with aggregations of persons, but aggregations that are significant because of the communities of which they are a part.

We are more surely dealing simply with aggregations of persons in connection with the problem of terminating discrimination against women in sports. Recall from the treatment of the subject in Chapter 7 that differentiation sometimes occurs in the name of nondiscrimination: an outstanding girl basketball player who wants to try out for the boys' team may be told that she cannot do so. And if she says that she is a person with individual rights, she may be told that it is important to girls as a class that they have their own separate team.

How about remedial action, designed to compensate for prior discrimination or to undo its effects? No question of communalism may arise if it is a question of redress to a specific person for discrimination that he personally suffered. But, as you already know, the courts have not been insisting that those benefiting from affirmative action must be able to prove that they personally have suffered discrimination. Proof that one set of blacks suffered discrimination in the past is an adequate basis for requiring the preferential treatment of another set of blacks today.

The official justification, as noted earlier, is that, where redress for specific victims is not involved, the action is directed against the system of racial discrimination as such. The fact that some individuals are burdened and others benefited is incidental and not the main purpose. But another interpretation is also possible: that a black community exists with a continuing identity. Just as a sovereign state goes on existing even though its government and population change, so does the black community. And a wrong done to that community through one set of blacks in the past can be redressed by action benefiting a different set of blacks today. It is like Japan providing aid to a country that it wronged in an earlier time through its military aggression.

I am not saying that race relations are inevitably communal rather than individualistic; nor am I saying that race relations ought to be communal. I see no reliable basis for anticipating the probable consequences of a choice between communal and individualistic approaches. In a sense, a progressive and stable order is made more likely if government deals simply with individual persons rather than with self-conscious groups to which members give their loyalty. But when people identify themselves passionately and permanently to a national or racial or ethnic community, it becomes difficult if not impossible to ignore the fact in the political arrangements that are made and in the public policies that are followed.

In any event, the whites of the United States long ago chose to take a communal approach to race relations, and at least in some connections it may be necessary to continue that approach if only to set things right. A shift to a strictly individualistic approach looks too much like a strategy for defending the advantages of the whites.

Owen Fiss suggests a group approach to the problem of equal protection. He is critical of the antidiscrimination principle, and in its place he proposes what he calls the group disadvantaging principle. He defines a group (a social group) as follows:

> (1) It is an *entity* (though not one that has a physical body). This means that the group has a distinct existence apart from its members, and also that it has an identity. It makes sense to talk about the group (at various points in time) and know that you are talking about the same group. You can talk about the group without reference to the particular individuals who happen to be its members at any one moment. (2) There is also a condition of *interdependence*. The identity and well-being of the members of the group and the identity and well-being of the group are linked. Members of the group identify themselves—explain who they are—by reference to their membership in the group; and their well-being or status is in part determined by the well-being of the group (Fiss 1976, 148).

Fiss's theme is that the equal protection clause should be interpreted to protect "specially disadvantaged groups," most notably the blacks. He points out that "blacks are very badly off, probably our worst-off class (in terms of material well-being second only to the American Indians), and in addition they have occupied the lowest rung for several centuries." "Blacks as a group," he says, "were put in that position by others," and he holds that "redistributive measures are owed to the group as a form of compensation" (p. 150). Further, he would justify a redistributive strategy out of concern for the future, too, regardless of any question of righting past wrongs.

"The concern," says Fiss, "should be with those laws or practices that particularly hurt a disadvantaged group." What the equal protection clause prohibits, he says, is any state law or practice that "aggravates (or perpetuates?) the subordinate position of a specially disadvantaged group."

The principal merit of Fiss's suggestion is that it simplifies the problem of interpreting the equal protection clause. To apply the suggestion, you must of course decide what sets of persons count as groups and what groups to count as "specially disadvantaged," and this is sure to involve controversy. For example, should women count as a group in Fiss's sense? Should Mexican-Americans (or all Latinos) count as specially disadvantaged? Once such decisions are made, other problems become easier.

The principal flaw in Fiss's suggestion is a counterpart of its principal merit. It offers no protection to persons who do not belong to specially disadvantaged groups, and those concerned with equality and equal treatment may not be inclined to accept this limitation.

The group disadvantaging principle would be more attractive if it were the only way of meeting the problems that the equal protection clause creates for affirmative action, but it is not. The international convention on racial discrimination, quoted at the end of Chapter 15, suggests a different option, specifying that special measures taken to promote the advancement of certain racial or ethnic groups or persons toward the equal enjoyment of human rights shall not be regarded as discriminatory. As noted before, Canada has incorporated this principle into its constitution. So has New Zealand. And so have a number of other countries. Note that the principle permits action on behalf of collective entities as well as on behalf of persons.

PART

5 CONCLUSION

18 Conclusion

This chapter presents a brief summary description of the guiding principles that the Supreme Court has developed for the interpretation of the equal protection clause, asks what is wrong with those principles, and makes a suggestion.

Principles of Interpretation

The equal protection clause is enigmatic. As Lawrence Tribe says, it is in the nature of a delphic edict, without providing an "intelligible rule of decision" (Tribe 1988, 1514). It suggests that everyone should get the same treatment, but that would prevent government from operating.

To cope with this problem, the Supreme Court has developed a set of clarifying principles. The first is that differentiation is acceptable when it is reasonable and not arbitrary or invidious and when its purpose is to serve the public good. This principle permits government to function despite the equal protection clause. Agencies of government proceed with a wide variety of measures that classify and differentiate, and relatively few such measures are ever challenged on the ground that they violate the rule of equal treatment, which suggests substantial consensus on what that rule (and common sense) requires.

The second clarifying principle permits selective intervention. It is that some differentiating measures are suspect, calling for strict scrutiny, and others are quasi-suspect, calling for heightened scrutiny. They are suspect when based on race and a few other characteristics, and when they impinge on a fundamental interest. And they are quasi-suspect when based on any of an indeterminate set of characteristics, sex being the principal illustration.

Differentiation that is suspect is cleared only if it is not arbitrary or invidious and only if it serves a "compelling" public interest. In the case of quasi-suspect differentiation, the public interest served must be "important." It turns out that virtually the only "compelling" public interest is remedial; that is, differentiation that is suspect and therefore subjected to "strict scrutiny" is cleared only if it provides redress for earlier violations of the rule of equal treatment. When differentiation is remedial, a supplementary set of principles apply.

Note that the Supreme Court and not the constitution is the source of these principles. The Court has developed them in the last fifty years. It selects the criteria for differentiation that are to be considered suspect or quasi-suspect, and decides what interests are fundamental. Although the lists are reasonably stable, it would not be safe to assume that they are definitive. Changes occur now and then as new cases come before the Court, as the composition of the Court changes, and as justices change their minds.

The supplementary principles, applying to remedial measures (measures designed to redress prior discrimination), are also the work of the Court and are also open to change. The pronounced tendency is to insist on rules of a restrictive sort. In general, a given governmental unit or agency is to provide redress only for its own specific discriminatory acts. Government is not to assume responsibility for societal discrimination. Passive discrimination is not even acknowledged, and any attempt to provide redress for it would presumably be barred—except that it is automatically taken into account when statistical tests of discrimination are employed.

Such, in sketchy outline, are the principles that the Court has developed. What is wrong with them?

Criticisms of the Principles

I do not have wholesale criticisms. In many ways the equal protection clause and the related principles of interpretation work well and produce significant results. They have contributed to the well-being of multitudes of persons and to the development of a better society. Nevertheless, it is possible to think of shortcomings.

I will focus on differentiation based on race in speaking of the shortcomings.

The worst feature of the principles, as I see it, is that they tend to block differentiating measures that are forward-looking; in other words, they tend to block affirmative action unless it is backward-looking (remedial). And they tend to limit even backward-looking affirmative action unduly.

Croson provides the most recent illustration of this point. Precedents were such that the City of Richmond could not hope to get through the judicial gauntlet if it described its set-aside program as a forward-looking means of bringing blacks into fuller and more nearly equal participation in mainstream society. It had to seek justification by claiming that its program was remedial.

Even when the city described its action as remedial, it ran into trouble. The history of race relations in the city and the state makes it obvious that discrimination had occurred on an extensive scale for decades, but the Supreme Court declared this to be an inadequate basis for the set-aside program. Instead, it called for proof of specific acts of discrimination by the city against identified construction firms. Thus its principles of interpretation not only ruled out a forward-looking basis for racial differentiation but led to an extremely narrow interpretation of the backward-looking possibilities.

Similarly, when Congress decided to make grants to the traditionally black colleges, and when Tennessee decided to adopt a special program to help black students get advanced training so as to qualify for various professions, they could not say that they were acting to enable blacks to enjoy human rights more fully. Rather, they had to claim that their purposes were remedial.

I should add two qualifications. First, in *Bakke* the Supreme Court approved a preferential admission program, the crucial point being that, given the importance of academic freedom, the university was free to seek diversity in its student body. This is a forward-looking consideration, and the point is significant where university admissions are concerned, but its ramifications are obviously limited. The justices who held that preferential admissions are permissible despite Title VI based their argument not on the need for diversity but on the need for remedial action. The second qualification is that even remedial action, though backward-looking, is likely to have implications for the future. These considerations mitigate my criticism.

You may applaud the judicial restrictions on differential, forward-looking action, but I do not. Even if a government never actually adopts a forward-looking measure based on race, I think it ought to be free to do so. And I would go on to argue that it should actually do so at least in the case of the American blacks and probably in a few other cases as well. The Tennessee program, congressional subsidies for the black colleges, and set-asides for minority business enterprises all look justifiable to me not simply as remedial but also as forward-looking measures.

Sharp contrasts between the racial groups in the population seem to me to be unhealthy, foreboding for the future. Too many blacks believe, with too much reason, that the cards are stacked against them and that their future is bleak. Too large a proportion is in poverty and is culturally deprived. Too small a proportion is in the middle and upper classes and the cultural elite. On too wide a scale, proclamations of support for the ideal of equality of opportunity seem to be a mockery. It would be bad enough if this were simply a matter of the treatment of individual persons, but in fact it is a matter of the treatment of one racial community by another racial community, both being race-conscious. And when the circumstances in which the races live differ so much, it is not surprising that racial antagonism exists. I fear that it will increase.

If you appeal to the Fourteenth amendment and say that it forbids special measures to help one racial community, I say that this is simply your choice among the possibilities. You are quite willing, I assume, to differentiate between people by age in connection with compulsory school attendance, and you may be willing to differentiate between them by sex so far as combat assignments in the armed forces are concerned. If you accept these differentiating measures— and perhaps dozens of others like them—why can't you also accept socially desirable differentiations based on race?

You may recall that the idea that some criteria for classification are suspect began not with a reference to race, but with a reference to "discrete and insular minorities." But then, quite unnecessarily, concern for minorities turned into concern for differentiation based on race, and so the idea of protecting the white majority came into the picture. It is ironic and paradoxical that a clause inserted in the constitution to prevent discrimination against blacks is now employed to block action that is for their benefit.

I speak above only of race, but similar problems, though perhaps less acute, attend the principle that differentiation based on sex shall not occur. The prime purpose obviously is to protect women, just as the prime purpose behind the equal protection clause was originally to protect blacks. But the concern for women got over-generalized too, and is expressed as concern for differentiation based on sex. This leads to the current situation in which pregnancy and childbirth are demeaned as disabilities.

My second criticism is that the interpretative principles that the Court has developed tend to give a false impression. They tend to suggest that the basic problem is to decide which differentiating measures to classify as suspect or quasi-suspect and that the judgment can be objective. Actually, choices among values, and decisions about the relative weight of different values, lie somewhere behind the answers to such questions, but the terminology of the Court does not call attention to this fact.

The result is a tendency to minimize the role of subjective judgment and choice. It is too much to say that result is also a tendency to make everything more or less mechanical and automatic, with the outcome depending on the pigeon hole in which the case is placed, but intimations go in this direction.

What Might Be Better?

As noted above, the idea that some criteria for classification are suspect began not with a reference to race, as if the white race is as much entitled to protection as any other, but with a reference to "discrete and insular minorities." Owen Fiss is truer than the Court to this original reference. His suggestion, as noted before, is that instead of focusing on race as such, and on suspect criteria of classification, the courts should focus on any "state law or practice [that] aggravates (or perpetuates?) the subordinate position of a specially disadvantaged group" (Fiss 1976, 157).

Lawrence Tribe is attracted by this idea, speaking approvingly of "an antisubjugation principle, which aims to break down legally created or legally reenforced systems of subordination that treat some people as second-class citizens."

> The core value of this principle is that all people have equal worth. . . . The goal of the equal protection clause is . . . to guarantee a full measure of human dignity for all. The Constitution may be offended not only by individual acts of racial discrimination, but also by government rules, policies or practices that perennially reenforce the subordinate status of any group (Tribe 1988, 1515-16).

Catharine A. MacKinnon's stand with respect to the treatment of women is similar. Recall from Chapter 13 her position that the focus should be not so much on differentiation as to sex as on the subordination of women and the domination of men: the evil to be overcome is subordination (MacKinnon 1979, 106-27).

I would combine elements of current practice with the suggestions by Fiss, Tribe, and MacKinnon and add more. Like the courts, I would start out with the presumption, accepted by the equal protection clause, that people should get the same treatment. And, like the courts, I would say that the presumption is rebuttable through appeal to other values. Further, I would say that the other values include due respect for both the interests of the individual and the good of society, and I would balance the different values off about as the courts do, though not necessarily reaching the same conclusions.

Here, however, I would shift away from current judicial practice toward the Fiss/Tribe/MacKinnon prescription. Instead of saying that differentiation based on race is suspect, I would say that the well-being of specially disadvantaged or subordinated groups is an important value. At the very least their disadvantages or subordination should not be accentuated, and if reasonably possible they should be reduced.

I would not, however, limit myself to a concern for the well-being of specially disadvantaged or subordinated groups. I could easily adopt the idea of "a good society," and say that differentiating measures are to be judged in terms of their relationship to its achievement. But it probably would be better to follow the lead of other countries, as reflected in the international convention on racial discrimination, to which I have already referred at the end of chapters 2, 15, and 17. The convention fixes the equal enjoyment of human rights by everyone as the goal, and goes on to say that special measures taken to promote the advancement of certain racial or ethnic groups or persons toward the equal enjoyment of human rights shall not be considered discriminatory. This seems to me to be a desirable stance.

I am not suggesting that this revised framework for judgment would resolve all problems, only that it would put the focus more explicitly on the problem of choosing among conflicting values, which is the basic problem; and it would permit affirmative action of a forward-looking sort.

References

Books and Articles

Abernathy, M. Glenn. 1977. *Civil Liberties Under the Constitution*. 3rd ed. New York: Harper & Row.

Abrams, Morris B. 1986. Affirmative Action: Fair Shakers and Social Engineers. *Harvard Law Review* 99:1312-26.

Avner, Judith. 1984. Some Observations on State Equal Rights Amendments. *Yale Law & Policy Review* 3:144-67.

Babcock, Barbara Allen, Ann E. Freedman, Eleanor Holmes Norton, and Susan C. Ross. 1975. *Sex Discrimination and the Law*. Boston: Little, Brown.

Baldus, David C., Charles A. Pulaski, Jr., and George Woodworth. 1986. Arbitrariness and Discrimination in the Administration of the Death Penalty: A Challenge to State Supreme Courts. *Stetson Law Review* 15:133-261.

Bastian, Ann, et al. 1986. *Choosing Equality. The Case for Democratic Schooling*. Philadelphia: Temple University Press.

Becker, Mary E. 1987. Prince Charming: Abstract Equality. *Supreme Court Review* 201-47.

Bell, Derrick. 1987. *And We Are Not Saved. The Elusive Quest for Racial Justice*. New York: Basic.

Bell, Derrick A., Jr. 1979. Black Colleges and the Desegregation Dilemma. *Emory Law Journal* 28:949-84.

Bell, Derrick A., Jr., ed. 1980. *Shades of Brown. New Perspectives on School Desegregation*. New York: Teachers College Press, Columbia University.

Benign Steering and Benign Quotas: The Validity of Race-Conscious Government Policies to Promote Residential Integration. 1980. *Harvard Law Review* 93:938-65.

Benn, S. I., and R. S. Peters. 1959. *The Principles of Political Thought*. New York: Free Press.

Berger, Alison S. 1986. Equal Protection I: Sex Discrimination in Employment. *Annual Survey of American Law* 419-40.

Berlin, Isaiah. 1956. Equality. *Proceedings of the Aristotelian Society* 56:301-26.

Binion, Gayle. 1983. "Intent" and Equal Protection: A Reconsideration. *The Supreme Court Review* 397-457.

Binkin, Martin, and Shirley J. Bach. 1977. *Women and the Military*. Washington, D.C.: Brookings.

Blakey, William A. 1983. Black Colleges and Universities: Desegregation, Disintegration or Equity? *ISEP Monitor* 7:11-30.

Brandt, Richard B., ed. 1962. *Social Justice*. Englewood Cliffs: Prentice-Hall.

Brown, Barbara A., Thomas I. Emerson, Gail Falk, and Ann E. Freedman. 1971. The Equal Rights Amendment: A Constitutional Basis for Equal Rights for Women. *Yale Law Journal* 80:871-985.

Brudner, Alan. 1986. What Are Reasonable Limits to Equality Rights? *Canadian Bar Review* 64:469-506.

Calabresi, Guido. 1985. *Ideals, Beliefs, Attitudes, and the Law*. Syracuse: Syracuse University Press.

Califano, Joseph A. 1986. *America's Health Care Revolution. Who Lives? Who Dies? Who Pays?* New York: Random House.

Callahan, Daniel. 1987. *Setting Limits. Medical Goals in an Aging Society*. New York: Simon and Schuster.

Caplan, Arthur L. 1981. Kidneys, Ethics, and Politics: Policy Lessons of the SRD Expoerience." *Journal of Health Politics, Policy, and Law* 6:488- 503.

Chapkis, W. 1981. *Loaded Questions. Women in the Military*. Washington, D.C.: Transnational Institute.

Choper, Jesse H. 1987. Continued Uncertainty as to the Constitutionality of Remedial Racial Classifications: Identifying the Pieces of the Puzzle. *Iowa Law Review* 72:255-74.

Cohen, Carl. 1971. *Democracy*. Athens: University of Georgia Press.

Cohen, Carl. 1979. Why Racial Preference is Illegal and Immoral. *Commentary* 67:40-52.

Combs, Michael W., and John Gruhl, eds. 1986. *Affirmative Action. Theory, Analysis, and Prospects*. Jefferson, NC: McFarland.

Corbin, Robert E. 1989. Letter of January 24 to the President of the Arizona Senate, Robert B. Usdane, Interpreting the State Constitutional Amendment on English as the Official Language.

Daniels, Norman. 1985. *Just Health Care*. New York: Cambridge University Press.

Davidson, Chandler, ed. 1984. *Minority Vote Dilution*. Washington, D.C.: Howard University Press.

Davis, Jacquelyn K. 1987. Memorandum to General Anthony Lukeman, USMC. 1987 WestPac Visit of the Defense Advisory Committee on Women in the Services. August 26. Unpublished.

Department of Defense. 1986. *Military Women in the Department of Defense,* Vol. IV. April.

Department of Defense. 1988. Task Force on Women in the Military. David J. Armor, Chairman. *Report.* January.

Derfner, Armand. 1984. Vote Dilution and the Voting Rights Act Amendments of 1982. In *Minority Vote Dilution,* ed. Chandler Davidson. Washington, D.C.: Howard University Press.

Desegregation and Education Concerns of the Hispanic Community. 1977. Conference Report. Washington, D.C.: Department of Health, Education, and Welfare. October.

Diamond, Harley David. 1985. Homosexuals in the Military: They Would Rather Fight Than Switch. *John Marshall Law Review* 18:937-68.

Dimond, Paul R. 1978. *A Dilemma of Local Government. Discrimination in the Provision of Public Services.* Lexington: Lexington Books.

Dworkin, Ronald. 1977. *Taking Rights Seriously.* Cambridge: Harvard University Press.

Eisenstein, Louis. 1961. *The Ideologies of Taxation.* New York: Ronald Press.

Elias, Sherman, and George J. Annas. 1987. *Reproductive Genetics and the Law.* Chicago: Year Book Medical Publishers.

Ely, John Hart. 1980. *Democracy and Distrust. A Theory of Judicial Review.* Cambridge: Harvard University Press.

English, Jane. 1978. Sex Equality in Sports. *Philosophy & Public Affairs* 7:269-77.

Engstrom, Richard L., Delbert A. Taebel, and Richard L. Cole. 1989. Cumulative Voting as a Remedy for Minority Vote Dilution: The Case of Alamagordo, New Mexico. *Journal of Law & Politics* 5:469-97.

Estreicher, Samuel. 1974. Federal Power to Regulate Private Discrimination: The Revival of the Enforcement Clauses of the Reconstruction Era Amendments. *Columbia Law Review* 74:449-527.

Fallon, Richard H., Jr., and Paul C. Weiler. 1984. Firefighters v. Stotts: Conflicting Models of Racial Justice. *The Supreme Court Review* 1-68.

Farrell, Robert C. 1985. Integrating by Discriminating: Affirmative Action that Disadvantages Minorities. *University of Detroit Law Review* 62:553-94.

Fishkin, James S. 1983. *Justice, Equal Opportunity, and the Family.* New Haven: Yale University Press.

Fiss, Owen M. 1976. Groups and the Equal Protection Clause. *Philosophy & Public Affairs* 5:107-77.

Ford Foundation. 1989. Project on Social Welfare and the American Future. Executive Panel. *The Common Good.*

Foster, Lorn S., ed. 1985. *The Voting Rights Act. Consequences and Implications.* New York: Praeger.

Freedman, Ann E. 1983. Sex Equality, Sex Differences, and the Supreme Court. *Yale Law Journal* 92:913-68.

Friedelbaum, Stanley H., ed. 1988. *Human Rights in the States. New Directions in Constitutional Policymaking.* Westport, CT: Greenwood.

Friedman, Alissa. 1987-88. The Necessity for State Recognition of Same-Sex Marriage: Constitutional Requirements and Evolving Notions of Family. *Berkeley Women's Law Journal* 3:134-70.

Fuchs, Victor R. 1988. *Women's Quest for Economic Equality.* Cambridge: Harvard University Press.

Getman, Julius G. 1972. The Emerging Constitutional Principle of Sexual Equality. *Supreme Court Review* 157-80.

Gilligan, Carol. 1982. *In a Different Voice. Psychological Theory and Women's Development.* Cambridge: Harvard University Press.

Ginsberg, Morris. 1965. *On Justice in Society.* Ithaca: Cornell University Press.

Goldman, Alan H. 1979. *Justice and Reverse Discrimination.* Princeton: Princeton University Press.

Goldman, Nancy Loring, ed. 1982. *Female Soldiers: Combatants or Noncombatants? Historical and Contemporary Perspectives.* Westport, CT: Greenwood.

Goldstein, Anne B. 1988. History, Homosexuality, and Political Values: Searching for the Hidden Determinants of *Bowers v. Hardwick. Yale Law Journal* 97:1073-1102.

Goodman, Jill Laurie. 1979. Women, War, and Equality: An Examination of Sex Discrimination in the Military. *Women's Rights Law Reporter* 5:243-69.

Gordon, Diana R. 1984. Equal Protection, Unequal Justice. In *Minority Report. What Has Happened to Blacks, Hispanics, American Indians, and Other Minorities in the Eighties,* ed. Leslie W. Dunbar. New York: Pantheon Books.

Grofman, Bernard, and Arend Lijphart. 1986. *Electoral Laws and Their Political Consequences.* New York: Agathon Press.

Gross, Samuel R., and Robert Mauro. 1984. Patterns of Death: An Analysis of Racial Disparities in Capital Sentencing and Homicide Victimization. *Stanford Law Review* 37:27-126.

Grossman, Joel B. and Richard S. Wells. 1988. *Constitutional Law and Judicial Policy Making.* 3rd ed. New York: Longman.

Guerra, Sandra. 1988. Voting Rights and the Constitution: The Disenfranchisement of Non-English Speaking Citizens. *Yale Law Journal* 97:1419-37

Gutmann, Amy. 1980. *Liberal Equality.* New York: Cambridge University Press.

Gutmann, Amy. 1981. For and Against Equal Access to Health Care. Milbank Memorial Fund Quarterly/*Health and Society* 59:542-60.

Hansen, W. Lee, and Burton A. Weisbrod. 1974. Inequalities in Higher Education. In *Social Problems and Public Policy. Inequality and Justice,* ed. Lee Rainwater. Chicago: Aldine.

Haar, Charles M., and Daniel William Fessler. 1986. *The Wrong Side of the Tracks. A Revolutionary Rediscovery of the Common Law Tradition of Fairness in the Struggle Against Inequality.* New York: Simon and Schuster.

Harper, Michael E., and Ira C. Lupu. 1985. Fair Representation as Equal Protection. *Harvard Law Review* 98:1211-83.

Hartman, Paul J. 1981. *Federal Limitations on State and Local Taxation*. Rochester: Lawyers Cooperative Publishing Co.

Hester, Kathryn Healy. 1982. Mississippi and the Voting Rights Act: 1965-1982. *Mississippi Law Journal* 52:803-76.

Hetzel, James V. 1987. Gender-Based Discrimination in High School Athletics. *Seton Hall Legislative Journal* 10:275-97.

Hochschild, Jennifer L. 1984. *The New American Dilemma. Liberal Democracy and School Desegregation*. New Haven: Yale University Press.

Hochschild, Jennifer L. 1986. Overview: Reconsidering Social Welfare Policy—Part II. Approaching Racial Equality Through Indirection: The Problem of Race, Class, and Power. *Yale Law & Policy Review* 4:307-30.

Holm, Maj. Gen. Jeanne. USAF (Ret.) 1982. *Women in the Military. An Unfinished Revolution*. Novato, CA: Presidio.

Horan, Dennis J., Edward R. Grant, and Paige C. Cunningham, eds. 1987. *Abortion and the Constitution. Reversing Roe v. Wade Through the Courts*. Washington, D.C.: Georgetown University Press.

House Hearings, 1983. U. S. Congress. House of Representatives. Committee on Armed Services. Subcommittee on Military Personnel and Compensation. *Hearings. An Overview of U. S. Commitments and the Forces Available to Meet Them*. 98th Cong., 1st Sess. October-November.

Hutner, Frances C. 1986. *Equal Pay For Comparative Worth. The Working Woman's Issue of the Eighties*. New York: Praeger.

Inter-American Commission on Human Rights. *Annual Report 1986-87*. OEA/Ser.L/V/II.71.Doc.9/rev.1.

Jackson, Brooks. 1988. *Honest Graft. Big Money and the American Political Process*. New York: Knopf.

Jencks, Christopher. 1972. *Inequality. A Reassessment of the Effect of Family and Schooling in America*. New York: Basic.

Karlan, Pamela S. 1989. Maps and Misreadings: The Role of Geographic Compactness in Racial Vote Dilution Litigation. *Harvard Civil Rights-Civil Liberties Law Review* 24:173-248.

Kirby, Michael D. 1986. Bioethical Decisions and Opportunity Costs. *Journal of Contemporary Health Law and Policy* 2:7-21.

Kirp, David L., Mark G. Yudof, and Marlene Strong Franks. 1986. *Gender Justice*. Chicago: University of Chicago Press.

Kornblum, Lori S. 1984. Women Warriors in a Men's World: The Combat Exclusion. *Law and Equality* 2:351-445.

Lakeman, Enid. 1974. *How Democracies Vote. A Study of Electoral Systems*. London: Farrar and Faber.

Lehne, Richard. 1978. *The Quest for Justice. The Politics of School Finance Reform*. New York: Longman.

Leibowitz, Arnold H. 1982. *Federal Recognition of the Rights of Minority Language Groups.* Rosslyn, VA: National Clearinghouse for Bilingual Education.

Lind, Kermit J. 1982. Maintaining Residential Integration: Municipal Practices and Law. *Cleveland State Law Rev.* 31:603-47.

Lineberry, Robert L. 1977. *Equality and Urban Policy. The Distribution of Municipal Public Services.* Beverly Hills: Sage.

McDonald, Laughlin. 1989. The Quiet Revolution in Minority Voting Rights. *Vanderbilt Law Review* 42:1249-97.

McGuiddy, Kirk D. 1982. Taxing Out-of-State Corporations After Western & Southern: An Equal Protection Analysis. *Stanford Law Review* 34:877-99.

MacKinnon, Catharine A. 1979. *Sexual Harassment of Working Women. A Case of Sex Discrimination.* New Haven: Yale University Press.

MacKinnon, Catharine A. 1987. *Feminism Unmodified.* Cambridge: Harvard University Press.

Mansbridge, Jane J. 1986. *Why We Lost the ERA.* Chicago: University of Chicago Press.

Mead, Lawrence M. 1986. *Beyond Entitlement. The Social Obligations of Citizenship.* New York: Free Press.

Merrikin, Karen J. and Thomas D. Overcast. 1985. Patient Selection for Heart Transplantation: When Is a Discriminating Choice Discrimination? *Journal of Health Politics, Policy and Law* 10:7-32.

Metcalf, George R. 1988. *Fair Housing Comes of Age.* New York: Greenwood.

Mohr, Richard D. 1988. *Gays/Justice. A Study of Ethics, Society, and Law.* New York: Columbia University Press.

Moynihan, Daniel. 1972. Equalizing Education: In Whose Benefit? *The Public Interest* No. 29.

National Goal of Equal Opportunity and the Historically Black Colleges. 1975. A Partnership for Leadership. Washington, D.C.: National Association for Equal Opportunity in Higher Education.

Newburger, Harriet. 1984. *Recent Evidence on Discrimination in Housing.* HUD, Office of Policy Development and Research, Division of Community Development and Fair Housing Analysis.

Notes. 1985. The Constitutional Status of Sexual Orientation: Homosexuality as a Suspect Classification. *Harvard Law Review* 98:1285-1309.

Nozick, Robert. 1974. *Anarchy, State, and Utopia.* New York: Basic.

Official English. 1987. Federal Limits on Efforts to Curtail Bilingual Services in the States. *Harvard Law Review* 100:1345-62.

Okun, Arthur M. 1975. *Equality and Efficiency. The Big Tradeoff.* Washington: Brookings.

Parker, Frank R. 1984. Racial Gerrymandering and Legislative Reapportionment. In *Minority Vote Dilution,* ed. Chandler Davidson. Washington, D.C.: Howard University Press.

Parker, Frank R. 1987. Protest, Politics, and Litigation: Political and Social Change in Mississippi, 1965 to Present. *Mississippi Law Journal* 57:677-737.

Passerin d'Entreves, Alessandro. 1951. *Natural Law, An Introduction to Legal Philosophy*. London: Hutchinson.

Pechman, Joseph A. 1986. *The Rich, the Poor, and the Taxes They Pay*. Boulder, CO: Westview Press.

Player, Mack A. 1988. *Employment Discrimination Law*. St. Paul: West.

Prestage, Jewel L. 1982. A Political Taxonomy of Desegregation. *In Race & Equity in Higher Education*. Proceedings and Papers of the ACE-Aspen Institute Seminar on Desegregation in Higher Education, ed. Reginald Wilson. Washington, D. C.: American Council on Higher Education.

Prestage, James J., and Jewel L. Prestage. 1986/87. Special Report. The Consent Decree as an Instrument for Desegregation in Higher Education. *Urban League Review* 10:113-30.

Rawls, John. 1971. *A Theory of Justice*. Cambridge: Belknap Press of Harvard University Press.

Rawls, John. 1980. Kantian Constructivism in Moral Theory. *Journal of Philosophy* 77:515-72.

Rawls, John. 1982. The Basic Liberties and Their Priority. In *The Tanner Lectures on Human Values*, III, 1982, ed. Sterling M. McMurrin. Salt Lake City: University of Utah Press.

Revised Criteria (1978) Specifying the Ingredients of Acceptable Plans to Desegregate State Systems of Public Higher Education. *Federal Register* 43 (February 15), 6658-64.

Reynolds, William Bradford. 1983. The Justice Department's Enforcement of Title VII. *Labor Law Journal* 34:259-65.

Reynolds, William Bradford. 1984. Individualism vs. Group Rights: The Legacy of *Brown*. *Yale Law Journal* 93:995-1005.

Reynolds, William Bradford. 1987. Securing Equal Liberty in an Egalitarian Age. *Missouri Law Review* 52:585-606.

Rivera, Rhonda R. 1979. Our Straight-Laced Judges: The Legal Position of Homosexual Persons in the United States. *Hastings Law Journal* 30:799-949.

Robertson, John A. 1986. Involuntary Euthanasia of Defective Newborns: A Legal Analysis. *Stanford Law Review* 27:213-69.

Rockwell, Paul. 1989. Fighting the Fires of Racism. *Nation* 249 (December 11), 714-18.

Rosberg, Gerald M. 1978. The Protection of Aliens from Discriminatory Treatment by the National Government. In *The Supreme Court Review 1978*, eds. Philip B. Kurland and Gerhard Caspter. Chicago: University of Chicago Press.

Rossell, Christine H., and J. Michael Ross. 1986. The Social Science Evidence on Bilingual Education. *Journal of Law & Education* 15:385-420.

Sabato, Larry. 1987. Real and Imagined Corruption in Campaign Financing. In *Elections American Style,* ed. A. James Reichley. Washington: Brookings.

Salomone, Rosemary C. 1986. *Equal Education Under Law. Legal Rights and Federal Policy in the Post- Brown Era.* New York: St. Martin's.

Scales, Ann C. 1986. The Emergence of Feminist Jurisprudence: An Essay. *Yale Law Journal* 95:1373-1403.

Schmidt, Ronald J. 1989. Language Policy and Equality: A 'Value-Critical' Analysis." Prepared for delivery at the 1989 Meeting of the American Political Science Association.

Schwartz, Herman. 1987. The 1986 and 1987 Affirmative Action Cases: It's All Over But the Shouting. *Michigan Law Review* 86:524-76

Segal, Mady Wechsler. 1982. The Argument for Female Combatants. In *Female Soldiers: Combatants or Noncombatants? Historical and Contemporary Perspectives,* ed. Nancy Loring Goldman. Westport, CT: Greenwood.

Siegel, Reva B. 1985. Employment Equality Under the Pregnancy Discrimination Act of 1978. *Yale Law Journal* 94:929-56.

Singer, Peter. 1979. *Practical Ethics.* New York: Cambridge University Press.

Smith II, George P. 1984. Quality of Life, Sanctity of Creation: Palliative or Apotheosis? *Nebraska Law Review* 63:709-40.

Smolla, Rodney A. 1985. In Pursuit of Racial Utopias: Fair Housing, Quotas, and Goals in the 1980's. *Southern California Law Review* 58:947-1016.

Sorauf, Frank J. 1988. *Money in American Elections.* Glenview, IL: Scott, Foresman.

Stern, Philip M. 1988. *The Best Congress Money Can Buy.* New York: Pantheon.

Sullivan, Andrew. 1989. Here Comes the Groom. *New Republic* 201 (August 28), 20.

Sullivan, Kathleen M. 1986. Sins of Discrimination: Last Term's Affirmative Action Cases. *Harvard Law Review* 100:78-98.

Sunstein, Cass R. 1982. Public Values, Private Interests, and the Equal Protection Clause. *The Supreme Court Review* 127-166.

Sunstein, Cass R. 1987. Review of Catharine A. MacKinnon's *Feminism Unmodified. Harvard Law Review* 101:826-48.

Sunstein, Cass R. 1988. Sexual Orientation and the Constitution: A Note on the Relationship Between Due Process and Equal Protection. *University of Chicago Law Review* 55:1161-79.

Tollett, Kenneth S. 1981. Black Institutions of Higher Learning: Inadvertent Victims or Necessary Sacrifices. *ISEP Reprint No. 1.* Institute for the Study of Educational Policy, Howard University.

Tribe, Laurence H. 1988. *American Constitutional Law.* 2nd ed. Mineola, NY: Foundation Press.

Tussman, Joseph and Jacobus tenBroek. 1949. The Equal Protection of the Laws. *California Law Review* 37: 341-81.

Tuten, Jeff M. 1982. The Argument Against Female Combatants. In *Female Soldiers: Combatants or Noncombatants? Historical and Contemporary Perspectives*, ed. Nancy Loring Goldman. Westport, CT: Greenwood.

U. S. Congress. Senate. Committee on Labor and Human Resources. Subcommittee on Education, Arts, and Humanities. 1985. *Reauthorization of the Higher Education Act, 1985*. 99th Cong., 1st sess. Part 4.

U. S. Department of Education. 1984. *The Condition of Bilingual Education in the Nation.*

U. S. Department of Education. 1986. *The Condition of Bilingual Education in the Nation.*

Van Dyke, Jon M. 1977. *Jury Selection Procedures. Our Uncertain Commitment to Representative Panels.* Cambridge: Ballinger.

Van Dyke, Vernon. 1985. *Human Rights, Ethnicity, and Discrimination.* Westport, CT: Greenwood.

Veatch, Robert M. 1986. *The Foundations of Justice: Why the Retarded and the Rest of Us Have Claims to Equality.* New York: Oxford University Press.

Vetterling-Braggin, Mary, Frederick A. Elliston, and Jane English, eds. 1977. *Feminism and Philosophy.* Totowa, N.J.: Rowman and Littlefield.

Wade, Steven C., and Robert D. Hay. 1988. *Sports Law for Educational Institutions.* New York: Quorum Books.

Walzer, Michael. 1973. In Defense of Equality. *Dissent* 20:399-408.

Walzer, Michael. 1983. *Spheres of Justice. A Defense of Pluralism and Equality.* New York: Basic.

Weaver, W. Timothy. 1982. *The Contest for Educational Resources: Equity and Reform in a Meritocratic Society.* Lexington, MA: Lexington Books.

Weiler, Paul. 1986. The Wages of Sex: The Uses and Limits of Comparable Worth. *Harvard Law Review* 99:1728-1807.

Weitzman, Lenore J. 1985. *The Divorce Revolution. The Unexpected Social and Economic Consequences for Women and Children in America.* New York: Free Press.

Werwie, Doris M. 1987. *Sex and Pay in the Federal Government. Using Job Evaluation Systems to Implement Comparable Worth.* Westport, CT: Greenwood.

Williams, Wendy. 1982. The Equality Crisis: Some Reflections on Culture, Courts, and Feminism. *Women's Rights Law Reporter* 7:175-200.

Williams, Wendy. 1984-85. Equality's Riddle: Pregnancy and the Equal Treatment/Special Treatment Debate. *NYU Review of Law & Social Change* 13:325-80.

Wong, Glenn M. 1988. *Essentials of Amateur Sports Law.* Dover, MA: Auburn House.

Table of Cases

Abbott v. Burke. 1985. 497 A.2d 376 (N.J.).
Adams v. Richardson. 1972. 351 F.Supp. 636.
Alexander v. Choate. 1985. 469 U.S. 287.
Allegheny Pittsburgh Coal Co. v. County Commission of Webster County.
    1989. 109 S.Ct. 633.
Allied Stores of Ohio v. Bowers. 1959. 358 U.S. 522.
Am. Fed. of S., C., & Mun. Emp. v. State of Wash. 1985. 770 F.2d 1401.
Anderson v. Martin. 1964. 375 U.S. 399.
Argersinger v. Hamlin. 1972. 407 U.S. 25.
Arlington Heights v. Metropolitan Housing Corp. 1977. 429 U.S. 252.
Ayers v. Allain. 1987. 674 F.Supp. 1523.

Bachur v. Democratic Nat'l Party. 1987. 666 F.Supp. 763.
Beal v. Lindsay. 1972. 468 F.2d 287.
Beller v. Middendorf. 1980. 632 F.2d 788.
BenShalom v. Marsh. 1989. 703 F.Supp. 1372.
Board of Dirs. of Rotary Intern. v. Rotary Club. 1987. 481 U.S. 537.
Board of Estimate of City of New York v. Morris. 1989. 109 S.Ct. 1433.
Bob Jones University v. United States. 1982. 461 U.S. 574.
Boddie v. Connecticut. 1971. 401 U.S. 371.
Bolden v. City of Mobile. 1982. 542 F.Supp 1050.
Bowen v. American Hospital Ass'n 1986. 476 U.S. 610.
Bowers v. Hardwick. 1986. 478 U.S. 186.
Bradwell v. The State [Illinois]. 1872. 16 Wall 130.
Braschi v. Stahl Associates. 1989. 74 NY 2d 201.
Broderick v. Ruder. 1988. 685 F.Supp. 1269.
Brown v. Board of Education of Topeka. 1954. 347 U.S. 483.
Brown v. Board of Education of Topeka. 1955. 348 U.S. 294.
Buchanan v. Warley. 1971. 245 U.S. 60.
Buckley v. Valeo. 1976. 424 U.S. 1.

California Federal S. and L. Ass'n v. Guerra. 1987. 479 U.S. 272.
California State Employees Ass'n v. State of California. 1989 U.S. Dist. LEXIS
    13210.
Cardona v. Power. 1966. 384 U.S. 672.
Castro v. State. 1970. 466 P.2d 244.
Childers v. Dallas Police Department. 1981. 513 F. Supp. 134. Affirmed
    without opinion. 1982. 669 F.2d 732.
Chisom v. Edwards. 1988a. 839 F.2d 1056.
Chisom v. Edwards. 1988b. 690 F.Supp. 1524.
City of Richmond v. J. A. Croson. 1989. 109 S.Ct. 706.
Clark, Etc. v. Arizona Interscholastic Ass'n 1982. 695 F.2d 1126.
Clark v. Edwards. 1988 WL 168299.
Cleburne v. Cleburne Living Center, Inc. 1985. 473 U.S. 432.
Committee to Defend Reprod. Rights v. Myers. 1981. Cal. 625 P.2d 779.

Common Cause v. Federal Election Comm'n 1987. 692 F.Supp. 1391.

Commonwealth, Packel v. Pennsylvania Intersch. A.A., 1975. Pa. Comnw, 334 A.2d 839.

Craig v. Boren. 1976. 429 U.S. 190.

Dandridge v. Williams. 1970. 397 U.S. 471.

Davis v. Bandemer. 1986. 478 U.S. 109.

Diaz v. Pan Am. World Airways. 1971. 442 F.2d 385.

Edgewood Independent School District v. Kirby. 1989. Texas Sup. Ct., No. C-8353. 58 LW 2223.

EEOC v. Massachusetts. 1988. 858 F.2d 52.

Eisenstadt v. Baird. 1972. 405 U.S. 438.

Firefighters Local Union No. 1784 v. Stotts. 1984. 467 U.S. 561.

Fisher v. Dillard University. 1980. 499 F.Supp. 525.

Frontiero v. Richardson. 1973. 411 U.S. 677.

Fullilove v. Klutznick. 1980. 402 U.S. 1.

Furman v. Georgia. 1972. 408 U.S. 238.

Gay Law Students Ass'n v. Pacific Tel. & Tel. 1979. Sup. 156 Cal. Rptr. 14.

Gay Rights Coalition of Georgetown University Law Center v. Georgetown University. 1987. 536 A.2d 1.

Geduldig v. Aiello. 1974. 417 U.S. 484.

Geier v. Alexander. 1986. 801 F.2d 799.

Geier v. University of Tennessee. 1979. 597 F.2d 1056.

Gideon v. Wainwright. 1963. 372 U.S. 335.

Gilbert v. General Electric. 1976. 429 U.S. 125.

Goldberg v. Kelly. 1970. 397 U.S. 254.

Gomillion v. Lightfoot. 1960. 364 U.S. 339.

Graham v. Richardson. 1971. 403 U.S. 365.

Graves v. Barnes. 1972. 343 F.Supp 704.

Green v. School Board of New Kent County. 1968. 391 U.S. 430.

Gregg v. Georgia. 1976. 428 U.S. 153.

Griffin v. Breckenridge. 1971. 403 U.S. 88.

Griggs v. Duke Power Co. 1971. 401 U.S. 424.

Grove City College et al. v. Bell. 1984. 465 U.S. 555.

Guardians Ass'n v. Civil Service Comm'n, N.Y.C. 1983. 463 U.S. 582.

Harris v. McRae. 1980. 448 U.S. 297.

Hatheway v. Secretary of Army. 1981. 641 F.2d 1376.

Hawkins v. Town of Shaw, Mississippi. 1971. 437 F.2d 1286.

Heart of Atlanta Motel v. United States. 1964. 379 U.S. 241.

Hendrick Hudson Dist. Bd. of Ed. v. Rowley. 1982. 458 U.S. 176.

High Tech Gays v. Defense Indus. Sec. Clear. Off. 1987. 668 F. Supp. 1361.

Hooper v. Bernalillo County Assessor. 1985. 472 U.S. 612.

Hopkins v. Price Waterhouse. 1987. 825 F.2d 458.

J. A. Croson Co. v. Richmond. 1985. 779 F.2d 181.
J. A. Croson Co. v. City of Richmond. 1987. 822 F.2d 1335.
James v. Valtierra. 1971. 402 U.S. 137.
Jones v. Mayer. 1968. 392 U.S. 409.

Kahn v. Shevin. 1974. 416 U.S. 351.
Katzenbach v. Morgan. 1966. 384 U.S. 641.
Ketchum v. Bryne. 1984. 740 F.2d 1398.
Kirstein v. Rector and Visitors of University of Virginia. 1970. 309 F.Supp. 184.

Lantz by Lantz v. Ambach. 1985. 620 F.Supp. 663.
Lau v. Nichols. 1973. 483 F.2d 791.
Lau v. Nichols. 1974. 414 U. S. 563.
Lee v. Macon County Board of Education. 1970. 317 F.Supp. 102.
Local 28, Sheet Metal Workers v. EEOC. 1986. 478 U.S. 421.
Lodge v. Buxton. 1981. 639 F.2d 1358.
Los Angeles Dept. of Water & Power v. Manhart. 1978. 435 U.S. 702.
Loving v. Virginia. 1967. 388 U.S. 1.
Lynch v. United States. 1951. 189 F.2d 476.

Martin v. Mabus. 1988. 700 F.Supp. 327.
Martin v. Wilks. 1989. 109 S.Ct. 2180.
Mayer v. Roe. 1977. 432 U.S. 464.
McLaughlin v. Florida. 1964. 379 U.S. 184.
McCleskey v. Kemp. 1987. 481 U.S. 279.
McCray v. Adams. 1984. 750 F.2d 1113.
Memorial Hospital v. Maricopa County. 1974. 415 U.S. 250.
Meritor Savings Bank v. Vinson. 1986. 477 U.S. 57.
Metropolitan Life Ins. Co. v. Ward. 1985. 470 U.S. 869.
Mills v. Board of Education of District of Columbia. 1972. 348 F.Supp. 866.
Mississippi University for Women v. Hogan. 1981. 458 U.S. 718.
Missouri ex rel. Gaines v. Canada. 1938. 305 U.S. 337.
Mobile v. Bolden. 1980. 446 U.S. 55.
Moose Lodge No. 107 v. Irvis. 1972. 407 U.S. 163.
Morey v. Doud. 1957. 354 U.S. 457.
Munn v. Illinois. 1876. 94 U.S. 113.

NAACP v. Allen. 1972. 340 F.Supp. 703.
N.L.R.B. v. Intern. Longshoremen's Etc. 1977. 549 F.2d 1346.
Nebbia v. New York. 1934. 291 U.S. 502.
New Orleans v. Dukes. 1976. 427 U.S. 297.
Newberg et al. v. Bd. of Pub. Ed. et al. 1983. 9 Phila. 556.
N.Y.S. Club Ass'n v. City of New York. 1987. 513 N.Y.S.2d 349 (Ct. App.).

N.Y.S. Club Ass'n v. City of New York. 1988. 108 S.Ct. 2225.

Officers for Justice v. Civil S. Comm'n & C. San Francisco. 1973. 371 F.Supp. 1328.

Padula v. Webster. 1987. 822 F.2d 97.
Palmer v. Shultz. 1987a. 662 F.Supp. 1551.
Palmer v. Shultz. 1987b. 815 F.2d 84.
Patterson v. McLean Credit Union. 1989. 109 S.Ct. 2363.
Perez v. F.B.I. 1988. 707 F.Supp. 891.
Personnel Administrator v. Feeney. 1979. 442 U.S. 256.
Phillips v. Martin Marietta Corp. 1971. 400 U.S. 542.
Plessy v. Ferguson. 1896. 163 U.S. 537.
Plyler v. Doe. 1982. 457 U.S. 202.
Price Waterhouse v. Hopkins. 1989. 109 S.Ct. 1775.

Reagan v. Farmers' Loan & Trust Co. 1894. 154 U.S. 362.
Reed v. Reed. 1971. 404 U.S. 71.
Reproductive Health Service v. Webster. 1988. 851 F.2d 1071.
Republican Nat'l Committee v. Fed. Elec. Comm'n. 1980. 487 F. Supp. 280
Resident Advisory Bd. v. Rizzo. 1977. 564 F.2d 126.
Reynolds v. Sims. 1964. 377 U.S. 533.
Roberts v. United States Jaycees. 1984. 468 U.S. 609.
Roe v. Wade. 1973. 410 U.S. 113.
Rogers v. Lodge. 1982. 458 U.S. 613.
Rostker v. Goldberg. 1981. 453 U.S. 57.
Runyon v. McCrary. 1976. 427 U.S.160.

San Antonio School District v. Rodriguez. 1973. 411 U.S. 1.
Sanders v. Ellington. 1968. 288 F.Supp. 937.
Serrano v. Priest. 1977. 557 P.2d 929.
Shapiro v. Thompson. 1969. 394 U.S. 618.
Sharif by Salahuddin v. New York State Educ. Dept. 1989. 709 F.Supp. 345.
Sheet Metal Workers v. EEOC. 1986. 478 U.S. 421.
Shelley v. Kraemer. 1948. 334 U.S. 1.
Sims v. Baggett. 1965. 247 F.Supp. 96.
Stamps v. Detroit Edison. 1973. 365 F.Supp. 87.
Stanton v. Stanton. 1975. 429 U.S. 7.
Starns v. Malkerson. 1970. 326 F.Supp. 234.
State v. Frontier Acres Commun. Develop. 1985. Fla. 472 So.2d 455.
State v. Hall. 1966. 187 So.2d 861.
Steelworkers of America v. Weber. 1979. 443 U.S. 193.
Swain v. Alabama. 1965. 380 U.S. 202.
Swann v. Board of Education. 1971. 402 U.S. 1.
Sweatt v. Painter. 1950. 339 U.S. 629.

Taylor v. Louisiana. 1975. 419 U.S. 522.

Thornburg v. Gingles. 1986. 471 U.S. 1064.
Thurman v. Torrington. 1984. 595 F.Supp. 1521.

United States v. Carolene Products Co. 1938. 304 U.S. 144.
United States v. Dallas County Comm'n 1988. 850 F.2d 1433.
United States v. Guest. 1966. 383 U.S. 745.
United States v. Kras. 1973. 409 U.S. 434.
United States v. Paradise. 1987. 480 U.S. 149.
United States v. Price. 1966. 383 U.S. 787.
United States v. Starrett City Associates. 1987. 660 F.Supp. 668.
United States v. Starrett City Associates. 1988. 840 F.2d 1096.
United States v. State of La. 1988. 692 F.Supp. 642.
United States v. State of La. 1989. U.S. Dist. LEXIS 8319. Civil Action No.
    80-3300.
United States v. Yonkers Bd. of Educ. 1985. 624 F. Supp. 1276.
U.S. Railroad Retirement Bd. v. Fritz. 1980. 449 U.S. 166.
University of California Regents v. Bakke. 1978. 438 U.S. 265.
Uzzell v. Friday. 1977. 547 F.2d 801.
Uzzell v. Friday. 1979. 591 F.2d 997.

Vlandis v. Kline. 1973. 412 U.S. 441.
Vorcheimer v. School Dist. of Philadelphia. 1976. 532 F.2d 880.

Wards Cove Packing Co. v. Antonio. 1989. 57 LW 4584.
Washington v. Davis. 1976. 426 U.S. 229.
Watkins v. U. S. Army. 1988. 837 F.2d 1428.
Watkins v. U.S. Army. 1989. 875 F.2d 699.
Weber v. Aetna Casualty & Surety Co. 1972. 406 U.S. 164.
Webster v. Reproductive Health Services. 1989. 109 S.Ct. 3040.
Weinberger v. Wiesenfeld. 1975. 420 U.S. 636.
Wesberry v. Sanders. 1964. 376 U.S. 1.
Western Air Lines, Inc. v. Criswell. 1985. 472 U.S. 400.
Western & Southern L. I. Co. v. Bd. of Equalization. 1981. 451 U.S. 648.
Whitfield v. Oliver. 1975. 399 F.Supp. 348.
Whiting v. Jackson State University. 1980. 616 F.2d 116.
Wimberly v. Labor and Indus. Relations Comm'n 1987. 479 U.S. 511.
Windy Boy v. County of Big Horn. 1986. 647 F.Supp. 1002.
Woerner v. Brzeczek. 1981. 519 F.Supp. 517.
Wygant v. Jackson Board of Education. 1986. 476 U. S. 267.

Yick Wo v. Hopkins. 1886. 118 U.S. 356.

Zobel v. Williams. 1982. 457 U.S. 55.

Index